MODERN MARRIAGE REALITIES

MODERN MARRIAGE REALITIES

WOMEN'S WORK, MONEY, AND LOVE IN AMERICA

C. Soledad Espinoza, Ph.D.

Copyright © 2016 by C. Soledad Espinoza, Ph.D.
All Rights Reserved

For information on reproduction or to book an event with the author, visit website at www.tidespublications.com.

Manufactured in the United States of America. No part of this book may be reprinted or reproduced or utilized in any form or by any electronic, mechanical, or other means, now known or hereafter invented, including photocopying and recording, or in any information storage or retrieval system, without written permission prior to reproduction.

Product or corporate names, which may be trademarks or registered trademarks, are used only for identification and explanation without intent to infringe.

ISBN: 0692707468
ISBN 13: 9780692707463

Library of Congress Control Number: 2016902648
Tides Publications, New York, NY

DEDICATION

This book is dedicated to my husband, Daimon, and our son—your arrivals into my life with such support and patience allowed me to finish my work and love you at the same time. I am also indebted to the unwavering support of Dr. Katrina Bell McDonald—my advisor, mentor, and friend.

Preface

The current state and uncertain future of marriage has captured the nation's attention: Americans question the very purpose of marriage and feel a sense of urgency to better understand the modern basis of marrying. Headlines such as "In the Season of Marriage, a Question. Why Bother?" (The New York Times 2013), "The End of Men" (The Atlantic 2010), "Why Women Still Can't Have it All" (The Atlantic 2012), and "Princeton Mom to Female Students: 'Find a Husband on Campus'" (USA Today 2013) prod the popular notion that men, women, and our families are facing a crisis in the US. As a sociologist, I began to engage myself in these provocative conversations in the media as well as the controversial debates in scholarship about marriage and work when I personally faced these issues. As is the case with much scholarly research, my own interests and experiences motivated the research questions I began to explore.

After transitioning from a career in public service and the non-profit sector, I was just starting out as a researcher. Due to my later age, I was settling into the idea of possibly never marrying and never having children. All of my doctors had told me thirty-five is the age when women start to have declining fertility. As I passed that benchmark, I considered my own chances of motherhood to be slim. Further, I thought entering a new career would mean long work hours which would make starting a family difficult. Yet there were lingering personal doubts in my mind and new themes emerging from my research that motivated me to delve deeper into questions about marriage and the balance of work and family in the US. I set about to question our core cultural concepts about gender, work, and family. The conclusions of my research ultimately present a re-thinking about the economic basis of modern marriage.

At this moment, the American family is at a critical juncture. How do we define it anew in order to reconcile the persistence of traditional ideals with the modern realities of marriage? Is the present context of marriage a more positive foundation for family formation despite the classical perspective that changing social dynamics threaten gender relations and the primary incentives to marrying? Will marriage degenerate into an archaic institution—possibly an unobtainable ideal? Or will conservative activism and protest evolve into a nation-wide backlash and a return to more traditional family forms? Amid transformative changes in the political sphere (e.g., the first black president and, possibly, soon the first female president) and social policy (e.g., the end of welfare as we know it and new calls for paid family leave and other more family-supportive policies), what does the future hold for families across race and class?

I began my study into marriage by initially looking at how men's increasing job insecurity in the labor market and the declining role of government in protecting men's economic status and regulating men's work conditions had undermined the viability of the male breadwinner role. However, I ultimately concluded that change in men's earning power is an important but insufficient explanation for the major transformation in the economic basis of modern marriage. I find two other factors to be more critical. My research suggests that changing marrying patterns are primarily driven by women's changing economic status and much higher expectations of what it means to be ready to marry—both men and women now face much higher expectations.

Indeed, in the context of men's increasing economic uncertainty, the advantages of the mutual sharing of two incomes are even more apparent and more critical to sustaining a family household. Thus, women's increasing earning power makes the advantages of the dual-earner arrangement not only more attractive to women but also to men. Further, the greater financial benefits of sharing incomes across spouses compared to the sharing of just the husband's income can more successfully compete with the increasing conveniences of staying single, which have emerged since the mid-twentieth century. In the modern era where marriage is socially less compulsory, there is no longer the normative imperative to marry in order to pursue sexual relationships, mark the transition to adulthood, or, even, to have children. Today, marriage is more so driven by financial considerations and women's earning power is now a fundamental part of the centrally important financial incentives to marry.

In line with sociological tradition, this book unmasks for a broad audience—and calls for women and men themselves to unmask in their own individual lives—the realities of modern marriage, gender, and work. Individuals tend to face questions, uncertainties, and challenges about family issues privately. The cautionary tales of financial woes, infidelity, sexism, domestic abuse, abandonment, and dissatisfaction in our own homes are often hidden themes not generally shared in public discourse. Yet they are shared in this book as important lessons and illustrative examples of why it is the dual-earner marriage that has emerged as the typical American household structure. Despite the staying power of the traditional ideal of the male breadwinner model and still rosy picture of the sexual division of labor to some, my research suggests that having two wage-earning spouses in the household and more gender-equal earning power produces what is likely one of the most efficient (and, possibly, most harmonious) models of family and gender relations in human history.

In this book, I examine how and why women with higher earning power (i.e., higher levels of education, employment, and earnings) are now more likely to marry compared to women with lower earning power. I find that the dual-earner household model and greater gender equality is at the cornerstone of more satisfying family relations and self-actualization for the modern American man and modern American woman. The scope of this book does not include the study of marital duration or divorce rates, but other research shows that college-educated women now have lower rates of divorce compared to women with less formal education (Wang 2015).

Based on rich narratives and compelling cases, the data from this book unveils why American families across race and class have shifted away from the unrealistic and unobtainable ideal of the male breadwinner model—a critical but yet undocumented process of sweeping social change in the US. This book provides a race-gender-class analysis across the two generations that ushered in modern marriage, baby boomers and generation X. As such, it provides a multi-dimensional analysis by taking into account pragmatic micro-level behavior within the socio-historical context.

This book targets a diverse audience from scholars to the general public. However, the rigorous methodology (described in detail in the appendix) and rich, raw data are provided for researchers, students, and others to take into consideration the methods and evidence underlying my conclusions. This is one of the first books by a sociologist that rewrites the thinking on the new economics of marrying from an intersectional perspective. I illustrate how women's earning power became a positive force for family formation, gender relations, and household economics across gender, race, and class. There are many books on the sociology of marriage, gender relations, and work. However, most sociological analysis on marriage and family ignores the array of experiences across different social statuses within different historical contexts.

Books such as The Feminine Mystique by Betty Friedman (1964) and The Second Shift by Arlie Hochschild (1999) provide important introductions to the problems of the male breadwinner model and the emergence of the dual-earner marriage (of two wage-earning spouses). While these books are based on data from several decades ago, they are still popular because the challenges of modern marriage realities continue to be relevant. As a more recent example, Lean In: Women, Work, and the Will to Lead by Sheryl Sandberg (2013) has been widely influential because it calls for women, and men, to recognize women's increasing power in the workplace and to support a better work and family balance. Yet these works focus on middle- to upper-class white women.

Bringing in the guys' side, Guyland by Michael Kimmel (2009) focuses on the delay of mostly white college educated men in finding career stability and entering into marriage as they experience what is now considered a stalled transition to adulthood. In Promises I Can Keep: Why Poor Women Put Motherhood before Marriage by Kathryn Edin and Maria Kefalas (2011), sociologists discuss the challenges that poor women face in marrying given the uncertainty and insecurity of men's work among those at the lower end of the income distribution. Yet these examples of existing literature about changes in marriage, work, and gender relations in the US fail to fully address the intersectionality of race, gender, and class within changing social contexts.

This book discusses modern marriage realities across race, gender, and class in the contemporary era of women's mass entry into the labor market. My research spanning two US generations advances our understanding of the emergent positive effect of women's earning power on marrying across race. With women's higher earning power, marriage continues to be as important as ever to most Americans. However, there is a higher financial threshold for men and women to feel economically ready to plunge into what we now all perceive to be a riskier (but a potentially more rewarding) venture. For those concerned about the state of marriage in America, the higher marriage bar and the barriers to financial readiness that men and women both now face are the biggest threats to the viability of marriage as a social and economic institution. By better understanding modern marriage realities, we may be able to better adjust to the widespread rearrangements in work, family, and gender relations that represent both modern challenges but also new opportunities for the American family.

Key Words: Family, marriage, gender, race, ethnicity, class, generation, socialization, baby boomer, generation X, earning power, education, employment, wages, household economics, specialization, sexual division of labor, dual-earner household, traditional gender ideology

Table of Contents

	Preface	vii
Chapter 1	Introduction: Modern Marriage Realities and the Dual-Earner Household	1
Chapter 2	Degendering Wage Work and Still Gendered Household Economics	22
Chapter 3	Marrying for Money and Honey Now—It Takes Two	55
Chapter 4	Black Family Formation and the Deracialization of Working Family Women	92
Chapter 5	Stalled Latinas, Lagged Patriarchy, and Dreams Deferred	132
Chapter 6	Economic Restructuring and Marrying across the Business Cycle	181
Chapter 7	Discussion and Conclusion	220
Appendix	Methodology	243
	Works Cited	279
	Index	313

1

Introduction: Modern Marriage Realities and the Dual-Earner Household

Amid mass social, economic, and technological change, women's financial contributions have become central to the modern American family. In the late twentieth century, wives and mothers took on paid employment en masse (Oppenheimer 1982). As family women went from mostly doing nonpaid work within the home to entering the labor market, the United States experienced an unprecedented transformation of family roles, gender relations, and marriage patterns. The family responsibilities of wives and mothers now generally include the economic role of financially providing for their families. Women are the primary earner for two-in-five households with children, and they contribute to the earnings in most married households (US Census Bureau 2011). Overall, women now near parity to men in terms of earning power and labor force participation (US Bureau of Labor Statistics 2008, 2009).

Women's contemporary role as a wage earner in most married households motivated this study's sociohistorical analysis of the relation between women's earning power[1] and marrying. Given the unexpectedness of the emergence of the modern dual-earner model and its profound implications on the gains to marrying, I theorize that the modern arrangement of family women going to work resulted in a new economic basis of marrying in the United States. Among those that study household economics, early researchers argued that women's economic advances would undermine the incentives of marrying, while later scholars theorized that women's earning power bolsters the gains to marrying. Given this intriguing and still-standing debate, the focus of this investigation is on the shifting economics of marrying across the two US generations that ushered in the now typical dual-earner household model (Fry and D'Vera 2011 and US Census Bureau 2011).

I provide a gender-race-class analysis of the relation between earning power and marrying across a pivotal shift in the historical context of marrying from the baby boomer generation (born 1945–1964) to generation X (born 1965–1980). Using multiple qualitative and quantitative methods, I analyze how the mass entry of family women in the labor market, which occurred among baby boomers, resulted in a shift in the economic basis of marrying a generation later, among generation Xers. I find that across these two generations, the basis of marrying shifted from being a social imperative to being fundamentally an economic decision—a decision

---

1 In this study, earning power is a concept I use to refer to actual and potential earnings. Earning power can be measured by the proxies of education, employment, and/or earnings.

based on a new set of financial gains derived from women's and men's earning power. My research shows though that not until generation X were most Americans—both men and women—socialized to postpone marrying until they were economically ready to take on a provider role in the household.

Going further, I theorize that the emergence of a much higher economic threshold to marry is central to explaining the observed changes in US marrying patterns (the delay and decline). The shift in the typical married household—from being based on a sole male breadwinner model to now being based on two wage workers—has created a much higher financial standard for marrying. While fewer persons can meet this inflated economic marriage bar, marrying is more advantageous under this model for those who can meet the higher standard. As I will show evidence of in later chapters of this book, the gains to marrying have not vanished. Rather, the gains have been restructured.

Based on the findings that emerge from this study, I offer a plausible explanation for what I refer to as a macro-micro paradox in the relation between women's earning power and marrying. Due to an inflated marriage bar, there is an overall decline in marrying at the macro-level with women's overall economic advances. That is, at the national level, the rate of marrying decreased as the average earnings of women increased. Yet, at the individual level, women's own earning power has an increasingly positive relation to marrying. I argue that this micro-level relation is due to the increased gains to marrying based on the modern dual-earner model. These two countervailing forces explain the overall delay in marrying among persons with higher earning power and the apparent decline in marrying among persons with lower earning power.

As I will show, specific social forces—through a process I call transformative socialization—ultimately facilitated the emergence of a new degendered economic basis of marrying among generation Xers. This is despite that the major shift in women's labor force participation and earning power transpired among baby boomers. In this study, I analyze the historical break from the traditionally gendered economic basis of marrying (based on the economic gains of the traditional male breadwinner model) to the degendered economic basis of marrying (based on the economic gains of the modern dual-earner model). Under the traditional household structure, the economic gains of marrying are derived from household specialization based on a sexual division of labor. Here, the male assumes the provider role. He serves as the wage earner in the labor market. The female takes on the housewife role. She provides nonpaid domestic services such as housekeeping, childcare, cooking, and providing emotional support within the home. In contrast, under the modern household structure, the economic gains of marrying are based on the degendered sharing of wage labor. Here, the male and female both serve as wage earners to financially contribute to the household.[2]

Generation X was the first US generation to experience primary socialization (family of origin effects) and secondary socialization (peer effects) in the distinct modern

---

[2] The female may still take on the responsibilities of domestic services, often called the second shift (Hoschild 1989). In this study, however, the focus of the research is on the sharing of wage work (not on the sharing or still-unequal division of nonpaid household duties by gender).

context of marrying, which allowed and encouraged women to work irrespective of family or marital status. However, the change in the historical context of marrying from 1964 (typically the last baby boomer birth cohort) to 1965 (typically the first generation X birth cohort) is not necessarily an exact point-in-time transition. The underlying shape of the historical changes and the distinction between the two generations is more gradual than that. Thus, I focus the data analysis on birth cohort groups from each generation that represent less ambiguous distinctions that are theoretically meaningful: 1948–1958 (early baby boomers) and 1968–1978 (core birth years of generation Xers).

By 1978, most married women and women with children were working in the labor market (Hayghe 1981). Most Americans had adopted gender-egalitarian attitudes that supported family women working (Cherlin 1980 and Rindfuss, Brewster, and Kavee 1996). Baby boomers adjusted to economic and social change with both family men and family women participating in the labor market. Yet this was after most early baby boomers had already made their choices about marrying and spouse selection based on socialization and social norms that promoted the ideal and structure of the traditional male breadwinner model.

In other words, at the time of the degenderization of wage work and the shift to tolerant attitudes about wives and mothers working, most early baby boomers had already made critical decisions regarding educational attainment, work, and marriage.[3] By the pivotal marker year of 1978, the latest

---

3 In 1978, the median age at first marriage was 24.2 for men and 21.8 for women (US Census Bureau 2012).

early baby boomer birth cohort (1958) was twenty years old and the earliest early baby boomer birth cohort (1948) was age thirty. Due to the dissonance between the social norms of their early socialization and the gender and household arrangements of their adult lives, the baby boomer generation is a transitional generation in terms of family roles, gender relations, and household structure.

In contrast, in 1978, the earliest generation X birth cohort I analyze (1968) was just ten years old, and the latest core generation X birth cohort (1978) was born in that same year. Generation Xers experienced primary and secondary socialization during a new historical context in which the typical American married couple was coheading a dual-earner household. Generation Xers also grew up as children and experienced adolescence at a time when—for the first time in US history—structural arrangements throughout society provided broad support to both men and women to serve as wage laborers, irrespective of family status. Further, as I will show in subsequent chapters, generation Xers were raised in households in which the limitations and failings of the male breadwinner model and traditional gender relations were increasingly apparent.

Thus, there is an appropriate causal order and a reasonable logic that the shift in historical context influenced the early socialization and, thereby, the attitudes and critical choices of generation Xers regarding earning power, spouse selection, and family formation. The aforementioned changes in the historical context were experienced by generation Xers at the life-course stages most sensitive to the experiences of socialization (childhood and adolescence) and prior to making their own education, work, and family decisions. As I will show in this study, many generation Xers were effectively socialized to deviate from the gendered norms of their parents' generation.

Given this context, this study is designed to examine whether generation Xers came to consider women's earning power to be a positive determinant of marrying, as this would provide evidence that for this generation there was a shift in the economic basis of marrying. I theorize how and why this generation decided to marry based on women's (in addition to men's) economic readiness. The overarching proposition of this study is that the economic gains derived from the dual-earner household structure emerged as the fundamental incentives to marrying in generation X due to a transformative socialization process.

BACKGROUND

At the turn of the nineteenth century, a sizeable proportion of single women (43.5 percent) but few married women (5.6 percent) participated in the labor force (US Census Bureau 1970). Yet by the end of the 1970s, more than half of wives worked—along with their husbands—to provide income for their families (Hayghe 1981). As one of the most radical shifts in American household structure, married women entered the labor market en masse—a trend first observed among American baby boomers. Yet boomers grew up during the post–World War II era of economic growth, mass suburbanization, and the popular ideal of the male breadwinner nuclear family. Though never an empirical reality for most, this traditional model of family—a dad who goes to work to provide the sole income for the family and a dutiful wife who takes full care of the chores and children in the home—was the normative ideal for the white middle class in urban and (the emerging) suburban America at the mid-twentieth century (Coontz 1992).

The major increase in women's aggregate labor force participation primarily reflected new family and work patterns among whites. The concept of having a sole male provider for the family was a viable ideal for this racial group due to the higher and more secure socioeconomic position of white males (along with rigid patterns of marrying within race at the time).[4] Before the US civil rights movement of the mid-twentieth century, the political and union pressures on industry to uphold a family wage for workers were largely centered on white male workers (Zieger and Gall 2002). Yet the percentage of single white women who reported that they expected to be housewives reached less than 50 percent in the 1970s, and this percent declined sharply thereafter (Cherlin 1980). By 1980, more than half of all married women and more than half of all women with children were in the labor force across white, Latina, and black women (Hayghe 1981; Bureau of Labor Statistics 2008).[5] This marks the first observation of

---

4 As a legal and then economic imperative, black and many nonwhite women had to work outside their own home much earlier (than white women) in American history (Davis 2011).

5 Different researchers vary in how they explain the change in women's work attitudes and behaviors, but generally they are understood to be due to the inspirations of the feminist movement of the twentieth century, technological change in the areas of reproduction and household production, and/or structural changes in the US economy regarding higher demand and compensation for women's work in the labor market (Wootton 1997).

American family women taking on a provider role in the household across the major US ethnoracial groups.[6]

Contemporary patterns of gender-egalitarian family relations and the dual-earner household structure contradict the theory developed by many of the early influential scholars of the US family who argued that advances in American capitalism and women's emerging role as wage earners would result not in a transformation but in the fundamental erosion of the economic and social basis of marrying (Becker 1973, 1974, 1981; Parsons 1943, 1949; and Schumpeter 1942). Countering the predictions of such scholars, I find that women's more equal economic position and the modern dual-earner model of household structure provide important economic and social benefits to marrying.

The evidence I present in this study shows empirical support that women's increased participation in the labor market and higher earning power serve as important new bases for the economic incentives of marrying as well as for the foundation of companionate relations between spouses. Sharing in wage work across spouses helps to stabilize the total goods and services produced by a family's collective efforts (i.e., household production). It also fosters higher levels of gender egalitarianism in the family. Indeed, the results from this study suggest that women's earning power has become central to modern marriage, love, and family in America.

---

6 In some cases, family women in the labor force act as sole providers and in other cases as coproviders. This study focuses on married women who work in the labor market and the emergence of the dual-earner model as the typical American household structure.

This study relates to Oppenheimer's (1988, 1997) groundbreaking theory that women's mass entry into the labor market would increase the relative economic advantages of a married household compared to staying single and, thus, the incentives to marrying. Here, the benefits of sharing a woman's wages and her enhanced labor-market position add to the long-recognized economic benefits of a household sharing (traditionally, a man's) wages as a central incentive for family formation. This is because a dual-earner married family can share two salaries and not just subsist on one. As an extension of Oppenheimer's work, I explore the historical context of the degendering of wage work—which essentially took place among baby boomers—and how this change in economic conditions and labor-market patterns relate to the gendered structure of the economic basis of marrying in the same and next generation, generation Xers. Going beyond the rational choice approach taken in previous research on household economics, I analyze the pragmatics of the micro-level decision to marry more fully within the socio-historical context. I consider individual agency as well as the macro-level constraints of sociohistorical context and social location (e.g., gender, race, and class) to explain the micro-level decision to marry.

Women's fuller participation and increased parity in the labor market has been concurrent to emergent technology and privatization of household production, the decoupling of many of the traditional marriage benefits from marriage (e.g., initiating sexual activity or forming an independent adult household), and declining normative pressures to marry (e.g., the decline in the influence of traditional social institutions, such as the church and multi-generational household). Perhaps more significant at this time, however, is the increasingly apparent instabilities and contradictions of the normative male breadwinner model, which reached its peak empirically and in the popular US media during the 1950s (Hernandez 1993 and Halberstam 1994).

In the context of the degendering of the labor market and during a period when it is much easier to be single and much harder to uphold the male breadwinner model, I argue that women's increasing economic status is a critical yet often unrecognized factor that bolsters the economic gains to marrying. Going further, I consider whether there is a generational lag in the adjustment I expect (that women's earning power becomes a positive determinant of marrying) given the degendering of wage labor. This study shows that the degendering of the economic basis of marrying is not observed in the same generation as the degendering of the labor market (baby boomers), but rather in the next generation (generation X).

An underlying logic of birth cohort analysis is the understanding that each new cohort (people born in the same year) represents an opportunity for social change (Ryder 1956). I consider generation turnover to be analogous to an opportunity for a fresh start for the development of new norms and practices related to gender relations and the economic basis of family formation. In contrast to the prior cohorts who personally experienced past social conditions, subsequent birth cohorts can react to the distinct conditions ushered in by social change without the salient memories and internalized cultural meanings of the way things used to be (i.e., past things that they never directly experienced). Each subsequent generation shares the experience of historical change differently because they experience new conditions with a metaphorical blank slate. Further, a new generation inevitably experiences social change at an earlier, more formative stage in their life course. I apply these concepts in my study of the effect of the degendering of wage work on the gendered structure of the economic basis of marrying.

By conducting a generational analysis, I examine the processes of social and economic change as it relates to household structure across a pivotal break to generation X. This is the first US generation composed of individuals who experienced the contemporary set of gender-egalitarian patterns in the family and labor market without having directly experienced the traditional US gender regime of household specialization regarding wage work. For early baby boomers, I am studying a fundamental change in the gender context that was experienced at a later life stage, adulthood. Boomers were socialized as children and adolescents within the context of the traditional gender regime. Then, they and everything around them regarding gender and family roles started to rapidly change.

The baby boomer generation observed the modern transition to the degendering of wage work as a departure to the gender context of their childhood. Baby boomers were raised in a traditional and highly differentiated gender context: amid the popular images of the male breadwinner ideal and the widespread pattern of adult women taking on the roles of caretakers and homemakers. Yet with much more gender-egalitarian opportunities emerging due to economic structural change, baby boomers became the heads of the families that represented the pioneering waves of wives and mothers entering the labor market en masse. For baby boomers, wage work across gender and family status was a profound contradiction to many of the gender ideals and norms that were part of their early socialization.

In contrast, generation X was raised in a socially inherited context of modern gender egalitarianism and in the post–civil rights era. Generation X is a notable generation to study because these birth cohorts were the first raised in the modern gender context: family women working, women increasingly managing the family as head of the household, increasing rates of divorce and single motherhood, and mothers commonly using the much more broadly available option of childcare outside the home. Moreover, since birth for generation Xers, the ideal of gender equality was institutionalized via layers of protective federal legislation, such as the Equal Pay Act of 1963 and the Civil Rights Act of 1964.

Compared to the deep changes (and contradictions) in the gender context experienced by the baby boomer generation, there was much more legal, economic, and social agreement regarding the modern gender-egalitarian framework for generation X. For generation Xers, modern gender arrangements were personally experienced and widely observed during the formative years of primary socialization, and gender-egalitarian arrangements continued into their adulthood. Indeed, generation Xers who experienced the vestiges of the male breadwinner model commonly did so amid conflict, tension, and/or, ultimately, marital dissolution. Thus, rather than being experienced as radical change, modern gender egalitarian norms were embedded in the social context essentially endowed to this generation.

Yet each new generation does not experience the historical setting of collective socialization or individually experienced events in a social vacuum. Not only is a new generation raised by parents and exposed to social or professional networks of prior generations, but ideas, images, and events from the past may continue to influence successive generations. For example, across generations, religious fundamentalists and conservative political leaders—inspired by traditional ideals—launch vigorous attacks against modern reconfigurations of gender, work, and family.[7] Thus, I conduct my research under a theoretical framework that allows me to analyze the importance of the relation between earning power and marrying for each generation, baby boomers and generation X, while also taking into consideration the mechanism of intergenerational socialization and influences.

Though I am not aware of research that focuses on the generational analysis I conduct, historians of gender and marriage have long highlighted qualitative shifts in the gender context of marrying in the United States and globally (Gilman 1898;

---

7 The cadre of conservative baby boomers, such as radio host Rush Limbaugh (born in 1951), Congresswoman Michele Bachmann (born in 1956), and political commentator Ann Coulter (born in 1961), continue to try to challenge modern gender structures and family matters. Interestingly, conservative pundits Sarah Palin and Glen Beck were both born in 1964, the last birth cohort of baby boomers, just before the start of generation X. Upcoming conservative leaders Paul Ryan (born in 1970), Ted Cruz (born in 1970), and Marco Rubio (born in 1971), are generation Xers.

Goode 1963; Coontz 2006; Ryan 2006). Prior studies show how economic shifts across US generations have changed the gendered structure of the labor market and household production. As an extension of this body of research, I specifically am interested in the reformulation of the economic basis of marrying subsequent to the dramatic restructuring of gender in the US labor market during the mid- to late twentieth century. Central to this analysis is investigation into the internalization of new concepts about the gendered structure of work and family, and how it relates to the traditionally gendered economic basis of marrying.

Though there is emerging theory and growing empirical evidence of a (now) positive relation between women's earning power and marrying in the United States (Goldstein and Kenney 2001; Sweeney 2002; and Torr 2011), alternative theory that focuses on the decline in marrying at the macro-level being contemporaneous (and due) to woman's rising earning power is still influential. Considering these two conflicting perspectives, I argue that it is not an irreconcilable paradox that there is an overall decline in marrying at the macro-level as women's earning power (and even men's earning power) has an increasingly positive relation to marrying at the micro-level. While women with greater earning power have a higher probability of marrying, my research also finds that the normalization of the dual-earner model has resulted in a more important and an even higher financial threshold for marrying. The result is an elevated economic marriage bar that renders marriage unobtainable for more and more years of a person's life (the delay) and for more and more persons (the decline).

BOOK OUTLINE

As an overview of this study, I provide in chapter 2, "Degendering Wage Work and Still Gendered Household Economics," a historical analysis of earning power and marriage patterns by gender from the mid-twentieth century to the present in the United States. The entry of women into wage work and women's gains in educational attainment started prior to the mid-twentieth century. However, it was not until the post–World War II era that family women—wives and mothers—were pulled (by the war economy and labor market forces), pushed (by rising standards of household commodities), and inspired (by ideals of women's equality and women's right to family planning) into the labor market en masse.[8] Here, I review the existing theory about the relation between the 1950s mass entry of women into the labor market and subsequent shifts in gender relations and family structure in the household. This chapter is an introduction to both the empirical and theoretical study of the degendering of wage work and its relation to the traditionally gendered structure of the economic basis of family formation.

In chapter 3, "Marrying for Money and Honey Now—It Takes Two," I focus on how study respondents describe an increasingly higher marriage bar based on the modern standards of gender egalitarianism and the dual-earner household structure. This chapter considers an inflated US marriage bar as a plausible explanation of the macro-micro paradox in which advances in women's economic position is

---

8 World War II started in 1939 and lasted until 1945.

associated with a decline in marrying at the macro-level but also associated with an increase in the probability of marrying at the micro-level (based on women's own earning power). I observe that women's earning power is described as a criterion for marriage (and reason for postponing marriage) among generation X research participants. I discuss the financial as well as nonfinancial reasons for the establishment of a (higher) threshold for economic readiness prior to first marriage across gender.

In chapter 4, "Black Family Formation and the Deracialization of Working Women," I theorize about the effects of the normalization of gender-egalitarian relations and family women working across race. I argue that as black women were pioneers in family women entering the labor market, they were also pioneers in establishing more gender-equal relations in the family. Chapter 5, "Stalled Latinas, Lagged Patriarchy, and Dreams Deferred," offers a highlight on Latino family formation. I discuss complex changes in the economic and noneconomic basis of Mexican American family formation, which study respondents report as being profoundly affected not only by the broadly shifting gender relations at work and home in America but also by personal experiences (and critiques) of modern patriarchy and the lagged economic progress of Latinas.

Chapter 6, "Economic Restructuring and Marrying across the Business Cycle," provides a quantitative analysis of the historical relations between the business cycle and marriage patterns in the United States. I analyze patterns of marrying (entry into first marriage) across the recession and nonrecession years from 1978 to 2010, which covers the Great Recession (the recession immediately prior to the period in which I collected the qualitative data for this study) and the previous three US recession periods. Chapter 7 is a summary of the study's findings and conclusions. The methodology is discussed in more detail in the appendix.

OVERVIEW OF FINDINGS

As subsequent chapters will show, I find that the link between economic forces and marrying patterns are mediated by specific social forces of socialization. My results show that higher earning power for women is increasingly a positive determinant of marrying across the two sample generations. While low levels of earning power reduce the likelihood of marrying across the two generations, the relation is gender specific for baby boomers in contrast to being gender neutral for generation Xers. For baby boomers, the economic marriage bar is conceptualized as one that relates to the economic prospects of the male. For generation Xers, the economic marriage bar is conceptualized as one that relates to both members of the couple—male and female—as well as across the couple. Generation Xers generally believe that a couple must be able to achieve a minimum standard of living to make a marriage successful. However, they also believe that each person in the couple should be able to contribute their fair share financially and, further, that each person should be able to make it alone financially if the marriage dissolves.

Participants in this study report that there is a heavy burden on a marriage when the marriage bar (i.e., a minimum economic standard) is not met. Financially weak marriages are considered inherently unstable. Further, sample participants from generation X report concern for other negative effects on the marriage when either or both the man or the woman cannot financially contribute equally or at all to the household. Will the person who works or makes more money resent the one who stays home or makes less money? Will the woman or man feel insecure or unsatisfied with staying home or contributing less financially? How will they get along with their peers and coworkers from different social circles? Plus, for many, the very notion of companionship and romance is tied to having minimal levels of earning power and the financial capacity to afford what I refer to as conspicuous romance.

For generation Xers in this study, financial anxieties about marrying are commonly expressed. Underlying the doubts related to economic pressures is uncertainty about the potential durability of marriage and, more specifically, uncertainty about the viability and advantages of the male breadwinner model in case the marriage breaks apart. I find the risks of marital discord, unsatisfying spousal relations, marital dissolution, and economic insecurity to be central themes that motivate generation Xers across gender to establish, and seek in their prospective spouse, a minimal level of earning power before marrying. When considering the prospect of marrying, generation Xers in the research sample express the importance of the greater financial stability, more egalitarian (so more satisfying) spousal relations, and higher consumption conferred by the dual-earner model.

For many generation Xers raised in conflict-ridden and financially insecure households, marriage uncertainty is fostered by the process of early socialization. Male and female sample participants from this generation feel compelled to hedge their bets when it comes to marriage by pursuing economic readiness prior to marriage—a strategy, and expectation, shared across gender. For generation X, the degendering of the economic marriage bar and the dual-earner household reflect social and economic changes accompanied by new concerns. This includes a much more complex terrain of gender relations and the conscious managing of the apparent risks associated with marriage and labor market instability. Even when described as an ongoing negotiation of trade-offs, generation Xers express ideas and experiences related to gender egalitarianism and the dual-earner household structure that are more positive than the negative sentiments expressed by sample participants from the baby boomer generation. As I will show in subsequent chapters, this finding is observed among generation Xers in this study across race, class, and gender.

My research suggests that the gains of marrying have shifted to being based on the dual-earner model, and, further, that there is a much higher economic marriage bar. This can explain how an emergent positive effect of women's economic status on marrying at the micro-level coincided with an overall decline in marrying at the aggregate level in the United States. Here, the concept of a marriage bar refers to the likelihood of marrying being based on meeting a socially acceptable minimum standard of economic readiness (i.e., earning power). Yet under the modern dual-earner model, the marriage bar and expected norms for a family's standard of living and household structure are based on household-level and individual-level earning power derived from both a husband's and a wife's financial contributions.

Thus, I argue that while women's higher earning power increases the economic gains to marrying and probability of marrying, there are other factors that delay marriage and explain why Americans stay single longer (and why Americans with lower earning power appear to be facing an actual decline in marrying). In addition to various factors that make staying single comparatively more advantageous in the contemporary era, my research shows that a higher and harder economic marriage bar—marriage-bar inflation—makes marrying less viable for more and more people, especially those at the low end of the distribution of earning power and those with low education levels.

2

Degendering Wage Work and Still Gendered Household Economics

The labor force participation gap between men and women has narrowed from more than 50 percentage points in the early twentieth century to just above 10 percentage points (US Bureau of Labor Statistics 2011).[9] In the decades following World War II, dramatic changes in the household structure of American families unfolded. For the first time in American history, wives and women with young children left their homes and entered the formal labor force en masse (Oppenheimer 1982). Goldin (1981, 1993) argues that the shift in women's labor force participation unfolded based on the life cycle of women and around the needs of the family and the labor market. With the shift in the role of children from workers to dependents, only young, single women

---

9 While only 15.6 percent of married women reported being in the labor market in 1940 (US Census Bureau 1970), 61.0 percent of married women, 63.3 percent of never-married women, and 71.2 percent of all men were in the labor force in 2010 (US Bureau of Labor Statistics 2011).

entered the labor market during the early nineteen hundreds during industrialization and urbanization.

After the supply of young women was restricted due to the increase in college enrollment and the peak of family formation and fertility in the post–World War II era, then older married women entered the labor market. Amid the increase in the availability of contraception, professional childcare services, and higher wages for women, married women and women with young children entered the labor market en masse in the mid- to late twentieth century (see graphs 1 and 2). This chapter provides an overview of prior research and introduces new research on the attitudes and experiences of baby boomers as they relate to the traditionally gendered economic basis of family formation and the degendering of wage work in the United States.

In the study of the economics of marrying in the United States, the literature on household specialization theory and the gains to the traditional male breadwinner model is central. Household specialization theory offers a simple economic logic for marrying based on the sexual division of labor: efficiency. Later literature on women's mass career entry and the gains to the modern dual-earner household model critique this perspective. However, I first introduce household specialization theory in order to examine this classical economic rationale of the male breadwinner model and the traditionally gendered economics of marrying. In the next chapter, I introduce more recent theoretical research on the modern economic gains of the dual-earner household.

Pioneered by Gary S. Becker (1973, 1974, 1981), traditional household specialization theory claims, firstly, that the fundamental gains to marrying are economic and, secondly, that such gains are derived from complementary gender roles in household production. Per this model, the husband serves as the sole breadwinner (wage earner) in the household due to the male's initial comparative advantage in the labor market. Taking on the head of the household and provider role, the male spouse engages in wage work in order for the household to benefit from the increasing returns to his specialization in wage work. Per the economic concept of increasing returns to specialization, the more intensely he uses his specialized skills in wage work, the greater return he garners for such specialization. As an illustration, a worker with more tenure is generally more productive per hour, as he has accumulated more skill at the job (and likewise gets paid more) than a worker with less time on the job.

In contrast, the wife does the non-wage domestic work in the household due to the female's initial comparative advantage in household work. The wife specializes in caretaking and homemaking in order for the household to benefit from the increasing returns to her specialization in domestic work. As an illustration, an experienced wife and mother is generally more effective in household duties than the newlywed or new mother with little experience in domestic activities. For example, cooking a meal would take longer (and would be of lower quality) when one first starts out. As a housewife specializes her time in cooking and other nonpaid domestic activities (versus paid work), then she becomes increasingly more productive. Her investment in time results in increasingly greater skill, and so she garners increasingly greater returns to the time she spends in domestic specialization.

When the wife and husband trade, or share, in the higher returns they derive from specializing (e.g., her better-cooked meals and his higher salary), then each maximizes the return or benefits from their efforts. The upshot then is that they each could not do as well apart (i.e., being single) as they do together as a joint economic household (i.e., being married). Under this theoretical framework, the gains to marrying depend positively on levels of gender specialization—that is, gender differentiation in market (paid) labor and domestic (nonpaid) production (Becker 1973). Thus, when women have low earning power in the labor market compared to men having high earning power in the labor market, the fundamental (economic) gains to marrying are highest. Per this theory, a woman gains most from marrying based on the man's higher earning power and she gains least from marrying based on her own higher earning power.[10]

While Becker recognizes that multiple factors play a role in the decision to marry, his theory implies that among women there is a negative relation between earning power in the labor market and marrying. Conversely, among men there is a positive relation between earning power and marrying. I refer to this gender asymmetry as the traditionally gendered economic basis of marrying. Explaining how advances in the economic status of women would be linked to a decline in the gains to marrying, Becker wrote:

---

10 Conversely, a man gains most from marrying the higher the woman's productivity in the domestic sphere and the lower his own productivity in the domestic sphere.

A growth in the earning power of women raises the labor force participation of married women by raising the foregone value of time spent at nonmarket activities. It also raises the relative costs of children and thereby reduces the demand for children...The gain from marriage is reduced by a rise in the earnings and labor force participation of women and by a fall in fertility because a sexual division of labor becomes less advantageous. (1981, pp. 245–248)

Becker does not make central to his theory why men and women have different initial or endowed comparative advantages, be it due to innate sex differences, traditional gender norms, or contemporary gender discrimination. However, Becker essentially integrates economic analysis into the contour of social analysis because he connects a change in the traditional gender arrangement based on women's disparate earning power to a decline in the socially revered institution of marriage.

The traditionalist narrative that gender inequality and complementary roles between men and women provide important positive effects on the social order, family, and gender relations is an idea advanced by sociologists as well (Durkheim 1893; Parsons 1943, 1949). As a classical functionalist, Durkheim (1893) was an early proponent of the theory that gender asymmetry and complementary gender roles exist in society exactly because interdependence between the sexes has a central function in fostering the solidarity that bonds males and females and, thus, the family. From another but related perspective, Parsons (1943) argued that the core of male identity is based on gender asymmetry. He argues that the conjugal family is an economically independent household where "the primary basis of economic support and many other elements of social status lie typically in the husband's occupational status, his 'job'" (p. 27). Here, "to be the main 'breadwinner' of his family is a primary role of the normal adult man in [US] society" (p. 33–34).

From these traditional perspectives, a woman serving as a family wage earner conflicts with her normative social, economic, and family roles. Prior to the household and attitudinal shifts of the 1970s, working mothers were often perceived to be damaging the children and inappropriately straining the husband-wife relation (Parsons 1949 and Rindfuss, Brewster, Kavee 1996). Scholars thought that a woman working had a threatening effect on the male spouse and his role as the provider of the household (Zuo and Tang 2000; Miller and Ponnuru 2001; Brescoll and Uhlmann 2005). Not only was this a threat for competition in the labor market, but it threatened the husband's power dominance in spousal relations, threatening the man's masculine (dominant) identity (Hiller and Philliber 1986; Juster 1985; Microwsky 1987; Hunt and Hunt 1987).

Per Parsons (1949),

> The dominant mature feminine role is that of housewife or of wife and mother. Apart from the extremely important utilitarian problems of how adequate care of household and children are to be accomplished, the most important aspect of this fact is that it shields spouses from competition with

> each other in the occupational sphere, which along with attractiveness to women, is above all the most important single focus of feelings of self-respect on the part of American men. (p. 193)

Yet such classical theory on the sexual division of labor has been criticized as having a conservative orientation, ignoring historical power inequities in gender arrangements, and, for some, as validating sexist assumptions (Woolley 1996). Thompson and Walker (1989) argue that the gender power struggle results in women advocating gender equality based on their own vested interest, while men resist it (based on their own vested interest). Based on the General Social Survey, 1977 was the last year most women of childbearing age thought children suffer if the mother works. The same holds regarding support for the idea that it is better if the woman in the household takes care of the home and family. Further, over each year surveyed, mothers are less likely than the general population to agree with specific statements that reflect a traditional gender ideology about family women working (Rindfuss, Brewster, and Kavee 1996).

However, despite the controversy of the theory and evidence about attitudinal and behavioral changes related to traditional gender ideology, household specialization and gender complementary theory can help explain the macro-level association between the rise in women's labor force participation and an empirical decline in marrying since the 1950s. Empirically, we observe an apparent retreat from marriage as the comparative advantage of men over women in the labor market has narrowed. Comparing women born in the early 1940s to those born in the late 1960s, the percent of never-married women by age thirty-five has doubled to about 20 percent (Kreider and Ellis 2011). Overall, lifetime marriage rates for women have decreased by 5 percent (Goldsetin and Kenney 2001). The inverse association between women's economic advancements and the overall trend in marriage prevalence at the macro-level is congruent with the logic of household specialization theory. However, because the theory is based on individual-level behavior, it is important to examine it at the micro-level.

Using qualitative data from individual and focus group interviews from this study (see appendix for a more detailed discussion of the study's methodology), I analyze in the next sections of this chapter the complex experiences of baby boomers and their attitudes about the gains to the traditional model of marriage. This generation is an extremely important set of birth cohorts to study. Baby boomers were socialized as children and adolescents amid the normative expectations of traditional gender roles and the sexual division of labor in the household, yet they ushered in a revolutionary transformation in the gendered structure of the typical American household.

Baby boomers made the unexpected shift to adopting the modern dual-earner household model in their marriages despite that it conflicted with the social norms of their upbringing and, per many family scholars, the very motivation and function of marriage. I focus the analysis in this chapter on early baby boomers' views about the traditional household structure of the male breadwinner model. In the subsequent chapters, I examine the views of early baby boomers and generation Xers on the modern dual-earner model of marriage. Based on my theory that change in the gendered economic basis of marrying (due to the degendering of wage work) occurs only after a generational lag, my initial hypothesis is that the economic basis for marrying among the baby boomer generation is gendered. That is, I expect to find that only men's earning power (not earning power across gender) is a central determinant of marriage for the early baby boomers sampled in this study.

In addition to open-ended dialogue about the study participants' own experiences, I use research vignettes in this study to probe sample participants to discuss their attitudes about various types of romantic relationships and models of household structure. For the scenario of a couple based on the traditional male breadwinner model (a male with high earning power and a woman with low earning power), the hypothetical couple of Chris and Jessica are portrayed as high school sweethearts. Chris is a potential male spouse that finished college, works as a successful executive, and earns a high salary, while Jessica is described as a potential female spouse who did not finish high school and doesn't work much. I ask the sample participants, what would be some of the advantages and disadvantages for Chris and Jessica to marry? Based on the research vignette, should they marry? I then ask study participants about their own experiences and personal views about the gains to marrying and gendered (or degendered) provider roles in the household.

Among baby boomers, sample participants report positive attitudes about the traditional male breadwinner vignette couple and, in general, about men's economic prospects being important to his probability of marrying, the couple's readiness to marry, and the underlying gains to the couple marrying. Baby boomers do not uniformly share these same views about a woman's economic prospects. In the evidence, however, emerges a theme of cognitive dissonance among baby boomers due to the maintenance of attitudes that generally support the traditionally gendered economic basis of marriage. This is despite reporting seemingly negative experiences and negative observations of the traditional male breadwinner model. That is, positive attitudes about the traditional sexual division of labor are reported simultaneous to otherwise conflicting reports about the pitfalls of the traditional household specialization model and women's economic dependence on a male provider. Further, baby boomers express a weariness of the dual-earner model that seems to belie their own experiences of women's earning power having important positive effects for household consumption, financial stability, and more egalitarian spousal relations.

I attribute these findings to the effect of primary socialization in building a salient gender ideology among baby boomers that is based on abstract ideals about the traditional male breadwinner model. By primary socialization, I mean the learning of attitudes and norms of behavior that is driven by one's own childhood experiences in the family. Oppenheimer (1994) defines a social norm as a moral position or standard that is generally shared. Krebs and Miller (1985) distinguish between normative standards and normative behaviors as the difference between "how people should behave and [actual] patterns of conduct." Davis and Greenstein (2009) define gender ideology as the level of support for the belief in the traditionally gendered division of paid work in the labor market as the male or husband's role and domestic responsibilities in the home as the female or wife's role.

I conceptualize gender ideology to be a collective ideology about the normative standards and normative behaviors related to gender roles and the sexual division of labor that is shared at the aggregate level of each generation. This study focuses on how it is learned (and maintained or not maintained) by the subsequent generation. I emphasize generation turnover as it distinguishes a generation effect from a period effect. A period effect produces a normative effect among the individuals in society at a specific historical time. A generation effect occurs specifically because the effects of the period are experienced differentially by specific subgroups of birth cohorts (who inherently experience the historical context at different ages and through different experiences of socialization). Normative attitudes can be understood to have an effect at the micro-level if they are transmitted to and internalized by individuals of the social group (Coleman 1992). Based on primary socialization, the normative gender ideology of the parent generation can be reproduced when it is internalized by the child generation.

Some researchers find that there is a parent-to-child transmission effect regarding gender roles in the labor market, particularly from mother to daughter (Mason 1974; Waite and Stolzenberg 1976). Bulanda (2004) finds that fathers' attitudes about marital roles are significantly related to children's attitudes. Other studies find the mother's employment and education to be important in gender attitudes of their children (Harris and Firesone 1998; Fan and Marini 2000; Ciabattari 2001; and Bolzenbdahl and Myers 2004). Fathers are found to be more likely to socialize sons in terms of gender role attitudes and sex-typed experiences in the home (McHale et al. 2003, 2004; Bulanda 2004). Myers and Booth (2002) find that having both a mother and a father who are gender egalitarian is associated with the respective son being more gender egalitarian. Yet Davis and Greenstein (2009) conclude that beyond the still-significant gender effect where women hold more gender-egalitarian views than men, cohort replacement now largely defines gender ideology with later birth cohorts having more gender-egalitarian views than prior cohorts. These authors find the effect of a birth cohort to be more important than one's vested interests in gender equality or, even, exposure to egalitarianism. My study finds that that there is an intersection between one's pragmatic individual-level interests and the internalized views by birth cohort (or, more specifically, generation), which can be explained by the process of transformative socialization as I discuss further in the subsequent chapter.

BABY BOOMERS: EARLY SOCIALIZATION REPRODUCES TRADITIONAL GENDER IDEOLOGY

I find in this study that early baby boomers generally maintain a belief in the normative gendered economic basis of marrying and the abstract ideas of traditional gender ideology as still tenable and legitimate. This is despite that early baby boomers also report concrete experiences that relate to the disadvantages and risks of marriage and the sole male breadwinner model. Indeed, early baby boomers in the sample maintain both general beliefs about the normative standard of the gendered economic basis of marrying while having more specific gender-egalitarian beliefs about the emerging standard and (new) benefits of family women working. The evidence reveals a persistent disjuncture and cognitive dissonance between abstract beliefs in traditional gender ideology and concrete experiences that contradict the viability and legitimacy of such ideology.

Despite the de facto of family women from the baby boomer generation entering the labor market, I find that this generation's attitudes about the economic basis of marrying remained centered on gendered notions of the household provider being an expectation for males due to their primary socialization. Baby boomers' attitudes generally conform to the normative socialization of their childhood, where they learned that the male role in the household should be a financial provider and that the appropriate role for a woman should be a homemaker. As I will show, early baby boomers in this study report especially favorable attitudes about the economic benefits of a woman with low earning power marrying a man with high earning power (based on the research vignette of the traditional male breadwinner model). Yet the baby boomers expressed more positive attitudes about the sharing of the financial benefits of the male breadwinner model (based on the man's high earning power) than the sharing of domestic services (based on the presumed household specialization of the low-earning women).

Early baby boomers in the sample did not express having favorable views about the economic gains to a man with high earning power marrying a potential housewife with low earning power, but rather they discussed gains that I would characterize to be social in nature. They report that the benefit of a man with high earning power marrying a woman with low-earning women is that she will not compete with her husband's dominant status in the household. Another reported advantage is that her limited opportunities in the labor market will not compete with her taking on the household duties of homemaking and childcare. In this way, the family will experience less tension between the woman having to decide between opportunities for paid work and taking on family and household responsibilities. Though economists have understood these issues based on the economic concepts of opportunity costs and time constraints of productivity, sample participants generally do not.

According to Ruth Milkman (1976),

> The productive activity of women in the home is accorded lower social status than any other occupation: housework is a "labor of love" in a society whose universal standard of value is money… However, it does maintain and reproduce the ability of family members to work productively, their labor power, which they sell in the labor market for a wage. (p. 81)

Milkman argues that "women's production within the family, because it is not paid labor, is often not recognized as valuable… [Yet within the household] this work is necessary to the maintenance of the working ability, or labor power, of adult family members" (p. 73). Researchers of the wage premium long enjoyed by married men have theorized that a married man receives higher pay precisely because of the time he can invest at his job and in his career only given the respective wife's unpaid labor in the household (Berk and Berk 1983; Korenman and Neumark 1991; Gray 1997; Chun and Lee

2001). However, women themselves may also not be aware of the economic nature of their unpaid labor in the household because the cheapness of their labor obscures the economic role of women. Per Juliet Mitchell (1971), "Their exploitation is invisible behind an ideology that masks the fact that they work at all—their work appears inessential."

Thus, it is not surprising that the explanations reported by early baby boomers in this study regarding the gains to marrying and the sexual division of labor relate more so to Parson's (1949) theory of normative gender roles and the avoidance of spousal conflict. Baby boomers report that they married young because marriage was how a young woman and a young man were supposed to create an independent household. Marriage was the only sanctioned context of sexuality and procreation. Young men found jobs so they could embody their normative role as a provider, and women cleaned the house and had babies to fulfill the normative roles of housewife and mother. I find this normative basis of marrying underlies the early baby boomers' central attitudes about the gains to marrying.

Though socioeconomic conditions changed among baby boomers, traditional attitudes about gender ideology and the normative basis of marrying persisted. For baby boomers, the abstract ideas from their childhood about the sexual division of labor—that a man should be able to maintain the household as a sole earner or that a woman who works may threaten the husband's status—did not become defeated or discarded notions. They are considered still legitimate ideas. While the incongruence between the concrete experiences of the modern gender regime and traditional ideology creates a cognitive dissonance, it does not lead to an abandonment of the traditional notions about the gains and risks of marrying, as many baby boomers maintain romanticized notions of the household structure of their childhood.

Further, baby boomers do not report that the changes associated with women's entry into the labor force resulted in more favorable conditions for themselves or the family. They do not speak positively about the emergence of the centrality of women's economic role, or more specifically, the new financial role of women in the household (as a provider). On the contrary, baby boomers commonly report negative effects and tensions in their own households due to family women working. They maintain the belief that women's wages are secondary to men's wages, and so there is not a positive evaluation of the women's financial contribution to the household. I would argue, however, that this is partly due to the material conditions of sex-typed work at the time of their entry into the labor market.

Discussing the period of the mid- to late twentieth century, Milkman (1976) characterizes women's mass entry into a "female labor market" where

> the mere fact that a woman traditionally does a certain job is usually sufficient to stigmatize it as "women's work," to which members of the female sex are supposed to be "naturally" suited. Occupations in the "female labor market" are also characterized by low status and pay relative to men's jobs reflecting the sexual inequality rooted in the family and basic to the organization of American society…Sex-typing is an

> ideological mechanism which denies the existence of any conflict between women's family role and their role in paid labor, blithely labeling both "women's work." (p. 78)

Thus, for many early baby boomers, women's mass career entry into lower-paying, lower-status work (relative to "men's work") and traditional gender ideology did not necessarily conflict. Further, the benefits of women making the trade-off from the traditional family roles of mother and wife to entering the labor force for jobs that were still very much sex-typed were not clearly advantageous to them. Juliet Mitchell (1971) concludes that during the mid- to late twentieth century, even women who engaged in paid work nevertheless continued to view themselves primarily as wives and mothers, not as workers. I find that without apparent, compelling, and viable reasons to do so, the motivation to challenge and depart from deeply internalized yet rather general attitudes about the normative basis of marrying and sexual division of labor is lacking for many baby boomers—male and female.

As I will show later in this chapter, the in-depth statements of early baby boomers in this sample do agree with the more general beliefs that the male's appropriate role in the household is to be a provider and that the appropriate role for a female is to be a homemaker. However, they do not generally agree with specific statements of traditional gender ideology. For example, only a fraction of early baby boomers in this sample agree with the statement that a preschool child suffers if both parents work full time (33.3 percent). Most disagree that both spouses working full time hurts the spousal relationship (66.7 percent). About half disagree that a pregnant couple should marry for the sake of the child (53.3 percent). Further, most agree that it would be best if both spouses work to earn money for the household (86.7 percent).

Other studies have found that people can maintain the more general tenets of an ideology despite disagreeing with specific statements that are premised on the same normative ideas (Rytina et al. 1970). For example, a person may believe in the more general statement that in America there is equal opportunity for success among all individuals but disagree with a specific statement following the same logic. Rytina et al. (1970) find that a person who believes that the United States is a meritocracy may not agree with the counterpart statement that a poor child has the same opportunity for success as a wealthy child in America. I find this relation holds in regard to traditional gender ideology among early baby boomers. Many baby boomers have tolerant attitudes about family women working as specific, concrete statements of gender-egalitarian beliefs. Yet they maintain the general idea of traditional gender ideology in terms of the appropriateness and legitimacy of the sexual division of labor.

Following the theory advanced by Rytina et al. (1970), this may be because more specific ideological statements are testable and, indeed, tested by people's life experiences. The incongruence between ideology and one's own experiences can motivate revised (specific) beliefs. However, general ideological statements are more difficult to test. Thus, the more abstract attitudes derived from normative gender ideology are more difficult to adjust despite that changes in daily lives and concrete conditions may contradict their legitimacy or the benefits of maintaining such beliefs.

In the following passages, I illustrate how sample participant Madison, a female baby boomer born in 1949, did not change her internalized notions about the gendered economic basis of marrying despite her own negative experiences with the male breadwinner model and her own positive (and, I will show, necessary) experiences of working once married. As a typical case of a baby boomer study participant, Madison is a white woman who grew up in a small town in a traditional household of five siblings. Though she considers herself Catholic and conservative, Madison's responses are illustrative examples of the responses by baby boomers in the study. Like other baby boomers, her responses are marked by tension between the economic and social rearrangements of her generation amid the maintenance of traditional attitudes.

Madison grew up in an idyllic male breadwinner family. Her father was an architect, and her mother—though a college graduate—was a homemaker. She described traditional gender expectations as typical of her generation. She reported, "My generation, the main reason you went to college is to get a husband, and as successful a husband as you could get." Yet she was also aware of the alternatives for women that were emerging at the time, specifically in her own case. She continued, "I was an anomaly in that I really loved school. I wanted a career. I knew I'd get married, but I wanted to wait until I was at least thirty."

From an early age, Madison's family influenced her gender perspective and life trajectory. She said, "My mother was very, very, very beautiful, and that's hard to live up to, and she told me when I was about twelve that I wasn't pretty, but I had a very fine mind and that I should emphasize it…so I did." Madison explained that because she was not as beautiful as her mother, she did not feel that she would be able to find a successful husband to take care of her as her mother had. As an alternative, Madison had an important example of a career woman in her family. She described her aunt, who was a career woman, in the following way:

> She worked…sending telegrams, but I thought that was a hugely successful career…and she had a roommate, and I thought she had the exciting life, you know…She had beautiful clothes, and what it turns out was she was a lesbian in a time when you couldn't talk about that, and so it wasn't a roommate, it was her lover. But anyway, I admired her lifestyle, and from the time I was six, all I talked about was having a career.

Despite Madison's intrigue with women having a career, the centrality of the male provider role remained salient to her, and she described this as ever important to her friends. Her explanation about why the man should be the provider is based on a normative reference—the conventional gender roles that she and her peers grew up with. Madison said,

> I was brought up that the man is the provider, but even though supposedly we're all so much better educated and we're not chauvinists anymore, I still think women expect men to be the provider.

> I don't know anybody well who is the financial…a woman that is the financial provider. I don't know anyone that has made that work…The advantages [to the traditional model] is that [the man] will not feel threatened by [the women] because she is not anywhere as close as successful as he is, and I think a lot of men would be threatened if it was the other way around…She won't feel conflicted by a job if they want to have children…She gets to marry up because she, you know, with [a low] educational background and [low] job background…she gets to enter a successful relationship and be supported… Some women want that.

Baby boomers, even among those who had themselves experienced a household where the women worked, generally demonstrated the persistence of the traditional gender ideology about the sexual division of labor of their childhood. Indeed, when asked about whether a couple that involved a nontraditional sole female breadwinner model—with a low-earning male and a high-earning female—should marry, none of the early baby boomers supported that the couple should marry. Laughter often accompanied the question when asked. This is despite that early baby boomers generally supported that the hypothetical couple based on the traditional sole male breadwinner model—with a low-earning female and a high-earning male—should get married.

Lily, a female baby boomer born in 1958, explained the reasoning: "Most of the time, females want a guy that is more dominant than she is." Another female baby boomer, Rachel (born in 1955) reported that

> a woman, most women—no matter what—we still want a man to really know that they are kind of taking care of them to a certain degree. Even if she's a go-getter and really out there making money, and she's okay with that. There is a time where a woman wants to relax and know that a man is around taking care of her…Even a man wants to feel that he can take care of that woman. I don't care what anybody says. In general, we can say all these roles are out here now, but at the end of the day, we are all pretty much the same. A man really wants to take care of the woman, and the woman wants to be taken care of… And then if that man feels like he cannot do it, then normally there are going to be issues because men are sensitive…he might feel insecure. He may never even verbalize it, but it will affect their relationship one way or the other. I've seen it. I think as a society, it's an easier role to be in for a female to be at home with the children. That's normal—what we've always, you know, what is more acceptable, tradition.

For early baby boomers, persistent traditional attitudes about the sexual division of labor are more so related to their beliefs that they conform to the norms of society rather than based on the economic returns to specialization. However, some respondents did discuss the advantages of the male breadwinner model in terms of there being less difficulty in managing time and tasks between work and household responsibilities across spouses.[11] One baby boomer, Lela, a female born in 1955, explained that

> the traditional sort of home where the…one spouse stays home and the other one works, it makes it a little easier in terms of division of labor, if you will, because you know there's someone to drive the kids around, and there's someone to make the meals, and if somebody's sick, you don't have to [decide], okay, whose turn is it to stay home?—all that kind of stuff.

Yet it is the belief in the normative ideas about traditional gender roles that legitimizes assigning specialized tasks by sex. For baby boomers, I find it is accepted that it is appropriate for women, but not men, to forgo wage work in the market in order to be available for household responsibilities.

Despite the advantages and positive attitudes that they maintain about the male breadwinner model, Madison and other sample participants from the baby boomer generation were unable to describe their own experiences or those of couples they knew who made the male breadwinner model a truly harmonious or secure arrangement. The few (positive) concrete examples are based on their parents' generation. Most positive examples are drawn from abstract ideas about gender norms or fabricated media images from popular television sitcoms. In Madison's own relationship, the man she married dropped out of the labor market. She shared her own example:

---

11 Becker (2011) lectured on coordination costs as a benefit to specialization in his later years
(www.youtube.com/watch?v=Wq6CJzY1neY).

> I married a lawyer…He had credentials, but he preferred the [beach] life, and so without even asking me, he quit his good job, would not work…And I had to do everything, take care of the cars, take care of the housekeeping.

Ultimately, Madison became the primary provider for the household, and she divorced her husband. Though she continues to believe in the gendered economic basis of marrying and the traditional sexual division of labor, she has deep feelings about the inadequacies of the model. Madison reflected in response to a black male in the focus group who talked about frustration he sees among black women about relationships. Madison responded,

> I think what you kind of are alluding to is the so-called angry black woman. There are a lot of angry white women too. I think women feel very insecure…Who do you have backing you up, you know? Everybody wants somebody who's there in the bad times, and…I think white and black women in particular are very insecure about their futures. What's going to happen with this world, and will my marriage survive it, or will the person I'm living with want to continue living with me…[There's] great feeling of insecurity across races, across sexes, across ethnic background.

Though it was not expressed generally in their views about the basis of marrying, others also reported the benefits of women being financially independent before marrying due to the risk of losing the male provider. For example, Lily, a female born in 1958, reported,

> [My daughter] just graduated two weeks ago from college, and I haven't seen her happier. She didn't have any kids. She just got into her studies, and she is doing very well for herself now…She is twenty-five, and she is able to go out there and marry whoever she wants to marry without me having to worry about her supporting herself in case it doesn't work out, or, like she says, he may pass away. I know she is good.

Among baby boomers in this study, underlying the maintained internalization of traditional gender norms is a contradictory awareness of the insecurity of the male breadwinner model. The reported responses reveal that they are aware of the risks for a woman to rely on a male provider for financial security. Other study participants also shared stories of observing men unable to fulfill the role of primary household provider due to not only voluntarily opting out of the labor market but also due to involuntary reasons, such as job loss, illness, and even death. For some, deaths that transpired in World War II taught the lesson that a household must be ready in case the male breadwinner dies.

Cameron, a male baby boomer born in 1952, recounted that his parents "married when they were twenty-one. I was born when they were twenty-two. My father was dead by then. He had gotten killed in an airplane crash. He was in the air force." Thereafter, his mother worked to financially take care of the family. Interestingly, though, Cameron's mother then taught him to do the housework—another specific case of the discontent with the sexual division of labor. He reported that

> everybody did [housework]. I'll never forget. One day, my mom told me—um, I was talking about something having to do with chores—and she said, "Well, listen. Uh, when you get your wife, you're not gonna marry your wife because you need her to do things. You're gonna be able to do all these [household] things."

Even among early baby boomers, study participants generally report that the sexual division of labor leaves couples without a basis for long-term compatibility or gender-egalitarian spousal relations. Another study participant, Emma, a female born in 1954, shared, "My dad was the breadwinner most of [my parents'] married life." She continued, "My father was very authoritarian. My mother was very submissive. It was a very traditional kind of marriage."

Another sample person, Jeff, a male born in 1957, reported,

> My mom was a stay at home mom 'cause my dad was a twenty-year air force [serviceman] and had other skills, like a professional printer. He provided for the house and paid the rent, put the food on the table, and he ran around on my mom, kind of having his cake and eating it too…He treated my mom like "hey, here is the money for the rent and the food on the table. I got my money, and I'm over

> here playing the lottery. I'm drinking, and I got my girlfriend on the side and all."

Baby boomers in the sample often characterized spousal relations as generally incompatible under gender complementarity. They shared example after example of how traditional marriages result in unequal, incompatible, and unsatisfying spousal relations. Such tension in the traditional marriage contradicts Durkheim's theory that specialization fosters bonds across sexes and the commonly accepted notion that marriages based on gender specialization in the industrial era resulted in spousal relations based on compatibility and romantic love.

In fact, Madison is unique only in that she is the only one who reported that her parents represented a happy traditional marriage. She characterized her two parents as highly compatible. She described them:

> They would sit after dinner and talk for hours because she [her mother] could talk on his [her father's] level…and she was fascinated by all the things that he was doing during the day. They were meant for each other, and there's [sic] very few marriages like that where everything is so ideal.

Despite her own parents' case, Madison too perceived that basic spousal compatibility is generally undermined in the traditional model of household specialization. She said,

> Conversations…become boring because he's got a job that he can talk about, he's got an education, and

pretty soon the conversations aren't going to be all that scintillating if she doesn't have anything to…to hold her end of it.

Yet as we will see in the next chapter, the effect of structural change in the economy and revamped gender expectations fundamentally change the likelihood of there being many women like Madison's mother or many families like Madison's household in the contemporary era. The college-educated woman that is intellectually compatible to her college-educated husband is generally no longer content to stay at home while the husband is not likely to be content as the sole provider. Indeed, Madison later reported that her parents' atypical example set her up to being unable to adequately adjust to the actual pitfalls she later observed in her own marriage and in the marriages of her friends. Previous studies have documented that being a housewife and the traditional male breadwinner model can be very challenging and unfulfilling, even for households with higher incomes (Freidman 1963; Milkman 1976).

Further, with women's economic advances, the opportunity costs for women to stay at home have substantially increased. Opportunity costs are the costs of an alternative option that must be forgone in order to pursue a specific action. When a woman chooses domestic production over labor market work, the benefits she could have received by taking paid work—what she is forgoing—is higher the more she would be compensated in the labor market. The higher her earning power, the higher the opportunity costs. Following Becker's research on opportunity costs and household specialization, studies find that real wage growth, lessening discrimination against women in the labor market, and changes in the demand for high-skilled labor in sectors that favored women have resulted in an increase in women's labor supply (Smith and Ward 1985; Goldin 1984, 1988; Black and Juhn 2000; Welch 2000). The evidence illustrates that many households no longer decide to forgo the wife's increasingly higher earning power (in absolute and gender relative terms).

As a transitional generation between the traditional lucky few generation and the modern generation X, early baby boomers report nostalgia about the economics of the household structure they observed among their parents. The male breadwinner model and the gendered economic basis of marrying essentially remain as cognitive defaults. I find that baby boomers believe in the traditional gender arrangement of household specialization because they believe their parents' generation provided tenable and legitimate social standards. Yet early baby boomers in this study do not tend to contextualize how or why these standards were constructed. For the lucky few generation, there were no viable alternatives. For the generation before the baby boomers (their parents), women did not have jobs available that would substantially contribute to the financial status of the household. Further, reliable birth control and formal childcare were not widely available to facilitate mothers working en masse, and there were laws banning married women from working (Goode 1963; Cookingham 1984; Goldin 1988).

Far from ideal, the male breadwinner model that baby boomers observed as children is salient to them despite the negative experiences and pitfalls in the actual gender and work rearrangements they observed. As they personally experienced or observed conflict in both the traditional and modern models of marriage, the normative reference to their childhood prevails. The concrete experiences they share do not serve to discredit the abstract basis of the normative basis of marrying and traditional sexual division of labor. This is because to them it is not a defeated notion of household structure—they saw it as a viable ideal with their parents (and the influential television sitcom families of their childhood). They maintain the traditionally gendered economic basis of marrying because their general conceptualizations about the appropriateness and gains of the sexual division of labor continue to be deeply internalized.

This chapter illustrates the durability of social norms constructed during primary socialization and, thus, an underlying mechanism of the delay we observe in society's adjustment to changes in socioeconomic conditions (and even sociopolitical institutions) as they relate to mental concepts and, thus, social relations. Thus, though many family women went to work to financially supplement the household, the early baby boomers in the sample continue to perceive the value in the benefits of the male breadwinner model and complementary gender roles in terms of avoiding spousal competition. The gendered ideas and traditional attitudes that baby boomers report in this study represent a lagged adjustment in that they fail to internalize new concepts about gender relations and the economics of marrying, despite the legal and economic transformations of their generation.

I conclude that the reason that these social norms and ideals are persistent is that, firstly, they were deeply internalized among early baby boomers as part of their early socialization process. Secondly, among early baby boomers, the normative basis of marrying and traditional gender ideology was internalized as very abstract ideals and rather general notions. This makes them difficult to test and, thus, to verify or challenge based on concrete observations. Thirdly, and related to the first and second considerations, early baby boomers were able to more or less reconcile the incongruence between traditional gender ideology and their own contradictory life experiences by adjusting only a narrower and more specific set of gender beliefs about the apparently less harmful and more positive aspects of family women working (rather than abandoning the broader, more general, and more abstract notions of traditional gender ideology).

Graph 1. Increase in Proportion of Married Women in the Labor Force

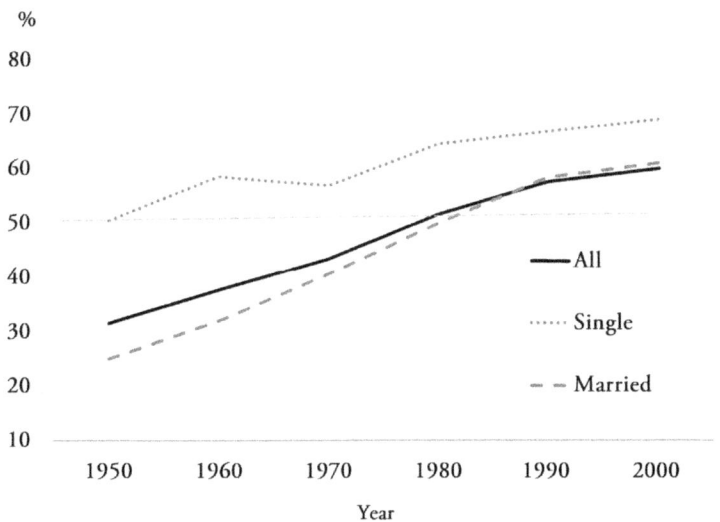

Women in the Civilian Labor Force by Marital Status
1950 to 2000

Source: Author's display of Current Population Survey (CPS) data. Persons 16 years old and over.

Graph 2. Increase in Proportion of Mothers in the Labor Force

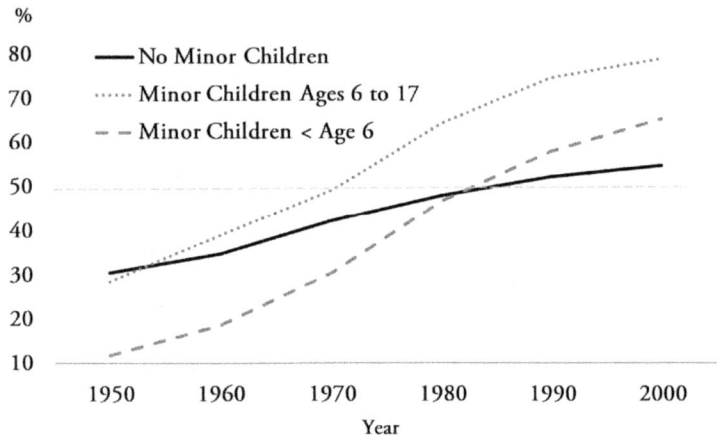

Source: Author's display of Current Population Survey (CPS) data. Persons 16 years old and over. Data for 1950, 1960, and 1970 based on married women in the labor force.

3

Marrying for Money and Honey Now—It Takes Two

This chapter focuses on the generational shift to the new central basis of marrying in the modern era, degendered earning power (i.e., financial status across gender). It discusses the consequences of this transition on marrying patterns, gender ideology, and spousal relations. Baby boomers and generation Xers both experienced women's mass entry into the labor market and a transformed social context of more gender-egalitarian law, custom, and economic forces. Yet the adjustment to these changes in terms of the internalization of the new financial basis of marrying is lagged by a generation due to the social forces of socialization. My research demonstrates how generation Xers became the first US generation to change from the traditional normative basis of marriage to the new economic basis of marrying. This new financial marriage bar, which is essentially gender neutral, explains the widespread delay and, for some, the decline in marrying. Despite continued desires to marry and persistent romantic notions of marriage across class and race, the new marriage bar is one that many Americans fail to meet for a longer portion of their lives, and for some, they essentially never meet it.

According to some scholars, with the rise of the nuclear family in the sixteenth and seventeenth centuries, marrying increasingly became a more personal choice based on romantic notions of love and companionship (Stone 1977; Shanley 1979). Referred to as "affective individualism," an emotional basis of mutual sexual attraction, romantic love, and personal fulfillment drives the companionate form of marriage (Stone 1977, p. 3). Studies show that sexual and emotional compatibility become more central to intimate relationships and marriage as the marrying decision increasingly becomes more voluntary (Gillis 1985; Giddens 1991, 1992). A common premise of this research is that the social forces and formal institutions that previously had constrained the individual choice to marry are now less salient or no longer relevant in the United States.

The romantic and companionate component of the basis of marrying has long been important in the United States, and it is still important now. In this research, the responses to my closed-ended questions show the romantic basis of marrying is slightly more central among generation Xers than among the earlier baby boomer generation. When asked to choose from a specific list of economic or romantic responses for "what is the most important thing for *you* to have set before marrying," 46.7 percent of early baby boomers and 63.6 percent of generation Xers report the response of being "in love with the potential spouse."

Furthermore, when asked to choose from a list of economic or romantic responses to "what is the most important thing for a *potential spouse* to have set before you would marry him or her?," 42.9 percent of early baby boomers and 61.9 percent of core generation Xers report the response that "the potential spouse is in love with me."[12] None selected as a response being able to take good care of housework, and less than 10 percent of each generation thought physical attractiveness was most important for either themselves or a potential spouse to have set before marrying. The remaining answers were about evenly split among the responses that referred to economic readiness (i.e., "stable full-time work;" "good salary/wages;" or "completed schooling/education goals").

However, the more in-depth responses I capture in this research add important nuance to the prior results. They reveal that the shift in the financial basis of marrying is fundamentally important even among those generation Xers who initially report romantic love to be the central basis of marrying to them. Indeed, as I will show later in this chapter, generation Xers express that the basis of love itself is financial. Generation Xers engage in what I call conspicuous romance, where the experience and indictors of love are rather costly (e.g., doing costly beauty/body modification projects in addition to expensive dinners, vacations, and gifts). Compatibility includes being at the same level in terms of financial status and financially contributing equally to the relationship across gender.

---

12 The closed set of responses available for the two separate questions (asked for self and then for a potential spouse) include the following: "I (or a potential spouse)...(a) have/has stable full-time work, (b) earn(s) a good salary/wages, (c) know(s) how to take good care of housework (e.g., cooking, cleaning, parenting), (d) have/has completed schooling/education goals, (e) am/is physically attractive/physically compatible to me, or (f) am/is in love with me.

In contrast, among the early baby boomers that report love as the most important thing to have set before marrying, they express doubt in the practical meaning of the standard financial indicators of employment, wages, or educational attainment. They do not have confidence that such indicators of earning power are really long-term markers of a more durable marriage. For example, Ava, a female baby boomer born in 1954, responded that the most important thing for a spouse to have set before marrying is being in love. However, she described this in the following way:

> I would have wanted the person to love me. That would have been more important than earning power, schooling, education, or stable work. One can always find work, so I don't believe that a minimum amount of yearly earnings is a reliable factor in determining readiness for marriage or the success of the marriage.

For Ray, a male baby boomer born in 1949, romantic love is what makes marriage a stable arrangement. He replied about what is most important to have set before marrying: "Love. I grew up in an unstable family situation. I was seeking stability and love." Cameron, a male baby boomer born in 1952, also reported his perspective that love is the primary foundation for a lasting marriage, while economic indicators are not. He explained in response to the same question: "I would choose 'am in love with the potential spouse' because all of the other criteria [such as earning power] can and will change. The only thing that I can affect truly is [if I] 'am in love with the potential spouse.'" Sam, a male baby boomer born in 1955, also expressed how he responded based on a belief that love is the enduring basis of a relationship: "Love someone and being loved in return make life's little problems like child's play."

Further, as shown in chapter 2, early baby boomers describe how normative pressures encouraged them to believe that the appropriate context to experience opposite-sex love and sexuality is within marriage. Thus, for early baby boomers, the companionate and romantic basis of marrying is embedded in the overriding social pressures to marry as part of the normative life transition to independent adulthood, opposite-sex adult friendships, sanctioned sexuality, and the legitimate path to procreation.

For generation Xers, the companionate and romantic basis of marrying is embedded in the overriding economic pressures to marry only once each individual—both the male and the female—as well as the couple together is financially ready to marry. Based on this logic, romantic courtship itself may have to wait until one is financially ready, since it alone is a costly stage. The alternative is staying single and/or "hooking up"—what many sociologists now study as a recent phenomenon (Kimmel 2012 and Allison and Risman 2014).

For generation Xers who report love as the most important factor to have set before marrying, they subsequently report more in-depth answers that reflect a shared belief that love is not enough to make a marriage last and that the financial basis of marrying is more central to them. For example, Ben, a male generation Xer born in 1975, responded, "I would say that the most important thing for me will have to be [being] in love with my potential spouse.

The reason I say that is because I have to be in tune and in love with my partner to consider marriage. I think that's very important." Yet when asked whether a man with high earning power should marry a woman with low earning power—the hypothetical research vignette couple of Chris and Jessica—Ben was against it. He explained, "I say no… [The] disadvantage will be if Chris happens to lose his job while Jessica is not working—it can become a financial burden…It can become stressful for the relationship if only one spouse is working, and he may feel pressure, especially if they have children."

Chloe, a female generation Xer born in 1972, also reported that love is the primary basis for marrying. Yet this initial response conflicts with her later responses that detail how important the financial basis of marrying is to her. For example, initially Chloe responded, "Love provides the foundation of a great marriage. This means you have the ability to conquer all the challenges that come with marriage." Yet then she responded to the hypothetical vignette couple with low earning power in the following way: "I would suggest that they hold off [marrying] until they're able to take care of themselves financially. So if they both want to finish school and they're just not there yet, I would encourage them to be financially stable first [before marrying]."

Chloe reported negative attitudes about the low financial status of both the male and the female: "I just don't believe in someone—in supporting someone who doesn't want more for themselves…if they want someone to take care of them." She explained further,

I think, once they're married, that means if they're both not financially set, they're going to be looking for others to help both of them, not just one of them. So it's not one person you have to take care of—it's two. And if in fact they have children, then you're talking more. So you want to be able to take care of yourself and your family, I think, before [marrying] and not put that burden on other people. So I think, you know, being financially stable to do that—and I'm not saying you have to have a lot of money—I'm just saying that you need to be able to take care of yourself and your family [before marrying].

Likewise, for Jacob, a male generation Xer born in 1974, he first responded that "I believe the emotion of 'love' is at the heart of any marriage." Yet he then continues, "I believe there is no minimum amount [of money] that has to be established in terms of actual numbers. However, enough money needs to be made for both individuals in a relationship to support themselves." Subsequently, Jacob suggests for the hypothetical vignette couple to postpone marrying until each are financially set. He ultimately responded, "I would advise against [marrying] until both establish strong careers for the kids that come later." So even for the generation Xers that report prioritizing romantic love as the primary basis of marrying, more in-depth explanations fundamentally rest on the requisite to marrying being based on financial readiness across gender.

It has long been theorized that in the modern era—with American couples and the nuclear family model breaking away from the traditional multigenerational household—love is a more important basis of the cohesion that underlies romantic adult relations and the decision to marry in the United States (Goode 1970). However, among generation Xers and more recent birth cohorts in the United States, adults can pursue both opposite-sex companionship and romance outside of marriage given that deep opposite-sex friendships and sanctioned sexuality no longer require the context of marriage (Ryan 2006). Romance may be more central to the explicit rationale of the bond between adult couplings for many generation Xers. However, romantic love does not truly account for what is fundamentally a shift toward a more financial basis of the decision to marry (and romance itself) across US generations.

Among generation Xers I interviewed, the financial basis of marrying is important irrespective of whether they initially express sentiments that love should be the primary basis of marrying. For many generation Xers, being in love is a conscious rationale for marrying; however, the manifest explanation of romance as the primary basis of marrying conflicts with the more in-depth responses later provided. Indeed, for many generation Xers, the economic marriage bar based on earning power across gender is important because it helps to avoid the stress of financial, interpersonal, and social strain that can erode the romance of a marriage.

The modern ideals of companionate and romantic marriage generally presume equal levels of a husband's and a wife's financial (and nonfinancial) contributions that higher earning power confers. As an example of nonfinancial contributions, many sample respondents report that maintaining positive gender-egalitarian spousal relations depends on spouses being at the "same level" in terms of earning power (be it based on education, employment, and/or earnings). Per the sample respondents, couples should have similar things to talk about, work colleagues should be compatible, and each member of the couple should be able to contribute a "fair share." As previously mentioned, modern romance itself requires a higher level of earning power to afford the gender-mutual standards of conspicuous romance and the expensive courtship stage that is financed now by each individual in the couple (i.e., across gender).

These findings help explain why even in an era where marriage is conceptualized as a social institution based on romance and companionship, the likelihood of marrying has nevertheless become increasingly based on earning power. Prior studies show that marriage is more and more out of reach for Americans with low earnings or earning power (e.g., education), and those with high earnings or earning power increasingly marry others with high earnings or earning power (Smith et al. 2014; Hiroshi et al. 2014; Espinoza 2013). My focus in this research is to understand how this new financial basis of marrying pattern emerged, and, more specifically, why the degendering of the financial basis of marrying emerged among generation Xers (but not among early baby boomers).

Generation X was raised under a set of shifting gender arrangements that conflicted with the traditional gender norms and household arrangements of prior generations. During the 1970s, there was a shift in American social attitudes away from the presumption that women take on the traditional housewife role. Public support for women taking on a provider role in the household became widespread (Cherlin 1980). Prior to the attitudinal shift, working family women were often perceived to be hurting the children and/or inappropriately straining the husband-wife relation (Parsons 1949; Rindfuss, Brewster, Kavee 1996). Public approval for women to work as an earner in the household did not converge between men and women until the mid-1970s. Then, both began highly supporting the concept (Mason, Czajka, and Arber 1976; Cherlin and Walters 1981).

By the late twentieth century, survey data show that social attitudes adjusted to accept and expect that women serve as wageworkers irrespective of family status as a wife and/or a mother (Spitze and Huber 1980). With attitudes newly adjusting to the mass entry of all women in the labor market, working wives and working mothers were no longer considered as aberrations or stigmatized cases in the late twentieth century—they became an accepted, and increasingly welcomed, norm.[13]

However, given that most married women were already working by this time, this shows that behavioral shift preceded attitudinal change. In other words, married women

---

13 This gradual but somewhat delayed change may be considered consistent with Ogburn's concept of the cultural lag. Per Ogburn (1922), there is a period of social maladjustment during the delay in the adjustment by society in responding to rapid change in material conditions. This concept has previously been applied to the delayed change in gender ideology about traditional household roles in response to the economic change of women's increased participation in the labor force (Brinkman and Brinkman 1997). However, central to my study is the distinct concept of a generational lag, which speaks to the literature regarding the importance of cohort and generational turnover as it relates to historical events, life course effects, and social change (Ryder 1965).

had begun working when most of the public still maintained negative attitudes or disapproval of such behavior. Attitudinal change followed the behavioral change that involved different segments of women being pushed and pulled into the labor market. Women entered wage work en masse between 1940 and 1960 (Oppenheimer 1982). However, it was only in the mid- to late twentieth century that married women (and women with young children) started to engage in the trend on a broad scale.

In the late 1970s, the typical household structure reflected a crossover from the male breadwinner model to the dual-earner model (Hernandez 1993). The proportion of married women working was about 17 percent in 1940 (US Census Bureau 1970). By 1968, the proportion of dual-earner to male breadwinner families was equal, each at about 45 percent of married couples. Thereafter, there was a continuous increase in wives' labor force participation. By 1978, only 33.7 percent of married whites, 25.2 percent of married blacks, and 39.7 percent of married Hispanics were in a male breadwinner family. Most married couples (51 percent) were in a dual-earner arrangement (Hayghe 1981). [14,15]

A woman serving as a wageworker has become less and less in conflict (and I would argue increasingly congruent) with family considerations due to various other sources of historical change. With advances in household technologies and the mass production of many household goods and services,

---

14 The remaining marriages included cases where the husband was not an earner at all or where the wife and the husband were not earners.
15 Most women with children (51 percent) were in the labor market by 1977 (Bureau of Labor Statistics 2008).

a family woman has more available time and can contribute to the labor market without it competing as much with domestic responsibilities (Greenwood, Seshadri, and Yorukoglu 2005). Further, a woman's wage is more and more critical to the household as the household attempts to make the market purchases necessary to keep up with the fashions and costs of mass-produced domestic products and rising standards of increasingly machine-based housework. Additionally, childcare outside the home is increasingly normalized and accessible across income levels (Coelen et al., 1977; Hofferth and Phillips 1987). This means that a woman pursuing the benefits of working in the labor market can find wage work to facilitate the responsibilities of having children, taking care of the household, and supporting a spouse (emotionally and financially).

After the 1960s, there is also a weaker basis for male economic dominance in the United States (Gerson 1993; Hunt and Hunt 1997). Subsequent to the abandoning in the 1950s of labor market policies against married women working (Goldin 1988), gender equity in the labor market is legally protected further with the Equal Pay Act of 1963 and other policies against gender discrimination and sexual harassment in the workplace. Further, men face greater precariousness in the labor market due to higher rates of unemployment, more underemployment, less earning mobility, harsher business cycle effects, and generally unfavorable effects on men's labor status due to globalization, economic restructuring, weaker unions, and deregulation (Gerson 1993; Kimmer 1998).

As women have more to contribute to the household financially and men face greater economic insecurity in the labor market, a woman's wage work is increasingly perceived to be less in conflict with having a good husband-wife relation. Micro-level evidence shows that men who are more reliant on women's earnings perceive a wife's employment to be a benefit to maintaining the household rather than as a threat (Zuo and Tang 2000; Zuo 2004). In this way, a man's financial precariousness is a condition that can lead to an increase in his incentives to marry (in order to enter a more financially secure dual-earner household). Further, a man's declining economic status can facilitate more gender-egalitarian attitudes, as it results in a man appreciating the value of a woman contributing income to the household.

This apparent relation contradicts the claim by many that a narrowing gender gap in earnings or men's stagnating or declining economic status necessarily erodes the (economic) gains to marrying and undermines spousal relations (Sawhill 2013). Rather, with women's mass entry into the labor market and women's increasing earning power, we observe a new set of economic gains to marrying that is based on the dual-earner household structure and a degendered financial basis of marrying. However, these gains are largely available only to men and women who can meet the inevitably higher and harder marriage bar (now generally based on two incomes). This explains why marrying patterns are now delayed but still maintained among those with high earning power and financial status while marrying has declined among those with low earning power (Espinoza 2012).

NEW HOUSEHOLD ECONOMICS AND THE MODERN GAINS TO MARRIAGE

Valerie Oppenheimer (1988, 1997) advanced an alternative theory to Gary Becker's classical theory of specialization. Oppenheimer's theory considers the effect of women's mass career entry on marrying patterns to be positive (though Oppenheimer also thought women's higher earning power would involve a delay in the timing of marriage). Here, women's improving earning power and their transition from specializing in homemaking to contributing as an earner in the household makes the marital union more appealing for both women and men. Per this model, both spouses engaging in wage work garner the most benefits to household production and marrying. The central advantage to marrying is achieved via the economies of scale from joining the previously separate single households of the man and the woman and the increased consumption, saving, and investment made possible for each spouse via resource pooling.

Furthermore, there are also gains in terms of enhanced economic security as two wage earners present less risk to the financial foundation of household production and market-based consumption than one earner. For example, if one spouse is unemployed, injured, disabled, or leaves the marital union through divorce or death, then the other spouse can continue to financially provide for the household. Indeed, for the children of baby boomers who experienced the stark rise in divorce and single parenthood in the United States, I find that degendered notions of individual self-sufficiency and the importance of financial readiness to marry emerge as internalized beliefs—a logical conclusion for the "latchkey kids" who learned the importance of self-reliance at an early age. This generation does not perceive marrying to be a decision based on normative pressures to marry or based on the economic gains to the sexual division of labor. Rather, in line with Oppenheimer's theory, they perceive marriage to be a risky endeavor that is to be undertaken only when a person—male or female—is financially ready to take on the risks and responsibility of the marital union (whether it lasts or dissolves).

The strength of Oppenheimer's theory that the dual-earner household structure maximizes the gains to marrying is empirically bolstered by the growth and now predominance of the dual-earner family structure. Recent data from 2010 show that most married-couple households report earnings from both the husband and the wife (54.1 percent) or the wife alone (8.0 percent). Only 18.7 percent have earnings from the husband alone (US Census Bureau 2011). According to the Pew Research Center, 59 percent of married adults without a college degree and 67 percent of married adults with a college degree were in a dual-earner household in 2009 (Fry and D'Vera 2011). Oppenheimer had theorized that the advantages of resource pooling would not only make the dual-earner family structure more beneficial than remaining single, but that it would also disadvantage the one-earner model of specialization:

> When the income contribution of each spouse is equal, given economies of scale, neither partner could live as well on his/her own or save and invest as much…The mutual dependence of the two-earner

family may not only contribute to their own gain to marriage but may also reduce the relative gain to being single and to marriages characterized by a specialized division of labor. (Oppenheimer 1997, pp. 445 and 446)

Yet Oppenheimer's so-called career entry literature has been critiqued in that it does not fully account for the array of marriage patterns or for the observed decline in marriage rates at the macro-level (Moffitt 2000). Further, Oppenheimer's theory holds that the positive effect of women's earning power on the incentive to marry is driven by an economic mechanism. Thus, an inevitable and full transition to the dual-earner model would be expected after the degenderization of wage work and women's mass entry into the labor market.[16] Yet such a deterministic effect has not materialized: most but not nearly all marriages are in a dual-earner household structure. Additionally, some adults increasingly prefer to stay single (an alternative that includes the choices to live alone and/or cohabitate).

Thus, further thinking is necessary to sufficiently explain the link between the degendering of wage work (i.e., women's mass entry into the labor market), changing household economics, and the gendered or degendered financial basis of marrying. Oppenheimer's theory holds that women's

---

16 Here, I refer to the degenderization of wage work only as the shift to where both men and women explicitly work for pay in the labor market. Given the persistence of gender disparities within the market (such as occupational segregation), this statement is not intended to imply a degenderization of *how* women and men work for pay.

increasing earning power should have a positive relation to marriage formation based on a new structure of household economics. Going further, I find that sample participants report positive attitudes about women's (and men's) earning power as a gain (and basis) of marrying due to their childhood socialization in which they learned about the inadequacies of the male breadwinner model. That is, they internalized new attitudes in line with Oppenheimer's theory but due to specific social forces of intergenerational and early childhood experiences (not just economic forces). Early baby boomers generally did not have such childhood experiences, and I find that they maintain traditional gender attitudes about the appropriateness of the sexual division of labor and gendered economic basis of marrying.

BABY BOOMERS: NORMATIVE MARRIAGE AND THE SOFT MARRIAGE BAR

For many baby boomers I interviewed, the normative basis of marriage emerges as the most salient factor for marrying. Among early baby boomers, the specific reasons to marry include family pressures, social expectations, and the normative pattern of the life course. Baby boomers report that for their generation, getting married was a generally expected part of the life transition to adulthood.

For example, Ray, a male baby boomer born in 1949, said,

> The big deal in my high school was at the senior prom, and then on graduation day, women would show their engagement rings—the girls would show their

> engagement rings...It meant they were married or they were going to get married. They were engaged... They were going to have a family. They were, you know, they were joining the cycle of life.

When asked about the reason why so many young people wanted to get married, Ray replied, "Who cares if you were eighteen? Your parents probably got married when they were eighteen because that's the way that it was." Going further, Ray talks about how traditional attitudes engendered suspicion by others about any man who might delay marriage too long. Ray said, "The families of potential wives are going to look at you and say, 'What's wrong? Why isn't he married? Oh, he's a playboy, or maybe he just doesn't—he's lacking in other ways. Maybe he's a jerk.'"

For baby boomers, getting married followed the gender norms of the time because rigid gender roles, heterosexual activity, and procreation within marriage were part of the normative social expectations for men and women. In many cases, baby boomers talk about how the normative pressures to marry were at least in part enforced via the intact relationships between youth and their parents. For example, Emma, a female baby boomer born in 1954, reported,

> [My parents] probably would have wanted me married at eighteen...I don't know if it was marriage so much as the shame that would come to the family if there was a pregnancy outside of marriage...It was that, that horrible, horrible shame that would come

to them and the family if there was a pregnancy [outside of marriage].

However, underlying the reported ideals of family life and social expectations to marry were economic conditions that made marrying not only a social but also an economic imperative for the baby boomer generation. For example, then a wife could not solve the challenges of the balance between wage work and household responsibilities given that widespread household technology and accessible childcare outside the home had yet to emerge as alternative solutions. Likewise, a man could not work the long hours required by his occupation if there were not a person in the home dedicated to domestic work. Conversely, a breadwinner husband was an economic imperative for women, who at the time were excluded from wage work due to legislation that prohibited married women from working and a broader gender regime that restricted gainful employment to men. A woman could not obtain a home or purchase market products without a male who could finance the emerging American consumer lifestyle.

Yet these latent economic reasons to marry are generally concealed by the rhetoric of social norms reported by baby boomers—social norms that were reportedly imposed upon youth on the precipice of entering adulthood. Young men and women married to avoid the stigma of promiscuity, having children out of wedlock, or becoming shameful spinsters or suspicious bachelors. In this context, marriage is a compulsory institution, and it is one imposed without much prejudice or many barriers.

There is essentially what I call a soft marriage bar among baby boomers exactly because they nearly universally report being expected to marry. For this generation, most men and women could achieve the relatively low bar for economic readiness at the mid-twentieth century. For women, the economic marriage bar meant being ready to take on domestic responsibilities (domestic production) in the household. For men, the economic marriage bar just required that they were positioned to enter the labor market.

The early baby boomers I interviewed reported that the social fitness and moral character of a prospective spouse are the most important markers of marriageability—more so than education or other now-conventional indicators of earning power. However, this is due to economic and noneconomic reasons that are inextricably linked to the social and economic context in which baby boomers married. Firstly, for many baby boomers, the prospects for work were not directly tied to the typical (contemporary) indicator of education level. Many of their parents did not hold college degrees, and when baby boomers were growing up, they did not perceive education to be a requisite for building a successful career.

Generally, the reported perceptions among baby boomers are that it just takes the appropriate values or ethics to have a successful career and family: the ethics of hard work, perseverance, and being trustworthy. In regard to the study's research vignette of a low-earning couple, Ava, a female baby boomer born in 1954, said,

> They haven't finished school. So what? There are a lot of things that they could do…So you know, unless this

> guy was a drug addict, a drug dealer, a really shady character, I'd give them the benefit of the doubt. I'd want to know a little more, but I don't see that education is going to be necessarily the "be all, end all."

Ray further described the lack of a direct link between education, work, and family for the baby boomer generation thus:

> There were jobs available for people who had not finished a high school degree. Unions still had apprenticeship programs. I grew up in the port city of Los Angeles. One of the biggest employers there were the docks, and probably the most important thing for someone that graduated from high school or didn't graduate was to get a union card so they could work on the docks…The other big industry was commercial fishing, and you didn't need a high school diploma to be a commercial fisherman… There were no entry requirements. They were acquired skills and…it was sort of learning by doing…You typically begin at the lowest level and work your way up. A lot of my friends did that. A lot of them were successful…but you didn't need a high school diploma.

Ray talked about the low economic marriage bar of his generation and, more specifically, the low financial marriage bar that many of his male friends faced and achieved soon after leaving high school:

> I should mention that a lot of the guys who married high school girls at that time were already out of [high] school. These were guys who did have jobs. I mean, you had to pretty much either have a job or real expectations that you were going to get one if you were going to get married…Of course it was because they were in love, but in order to get—in a lot of the cases—the blessings of the family, you had to have a job. And I mean, women aren't stupid. I mean, why would you marry a guy who didn't have a job or didn't have reasonable prospects of getting a job?

So while early baby boomers I interviewed reported that the economic basis of a marriage is important, they presume that unless a man is morally flawed in some way, he can demonstrate economic readiness for marriage. Applied only to the man at that time, financial readiness is met then by just getting a job or being ready to get a job, basically any job—I refer to this as a soft economic marriage bar.

I conceptualize the soft marriage bar as a standard that most can meet, and it can be met at a relatively early age. Interestingly, for baby boomers, it was imposed often by the family of the potential spouses rather than by the two individuals of the (usually, young) couple. Other than those with deviant character or deep personal flaws, the marriage bar was a temporary barrier (if at all a barrier). Despite the expectation that marriage requires some level of earning power on the part of the male to establish and financially maintain an independent household, the markers for readiness were not based on durable indicators, such as education level (which is generally persistent after early adulthood). With having any job or prospects for a job being the threshold applied, the barrier was not durable in the sense that in the economic prosperity of the mid-twentieth century, any unemployment was likely short term for the typical male.

Further, that the financial dimension of the economic marriage bar was not generally applied across gender speaks to the persistent gendered economic basis of marriage among baby boomers. That is, baby boomers maintain traditional attitudes about the sexual division of labor as a normative model of gender relations. Per Ava, a female baby boomer born in 1954, when asked about the benefits of the traditional male breadwinner model, she provided no specific gains and instead replied, "It's just what [our] generation did."

I find the traditional attitudes among baby boomers to be retained as vestiges of socially inherited ideas that they have generally failed to give up or replace despite the pitfalls of their own experiences or their observations of the new realities of marriage and the modern household economics of the dual-earner model. While they lack specific explanations about the comparative economic gains (versus the social basis) of the traditional model of marriage, early baby boomers I interviewed can articulate the comparative risks and economic disadvantages of the model compared to the dual-earner model.

For example, Ava reported that she supports there being two earners in a marriage because the woman "is not dependent" so "she is able to survive on her own." For Ava, this is important because "she can survive quite well without him, should they divorce, should the marriage fall apart, should he die." Clearly then, Ava is aware of the risks of the male breadwinner model. Yet she still considers the dual-earner model to be problematic. She warned, "[But] there could be some doomsday ahead for the two" if the man "felt that [the woman's] trying to climb up the ladder was a problem for him." Further, she continued, "Children…could change things, particularly as [the woman] would probably be the one who will have to wind down her career." Ava's statements reflect that she still defines her expectations for spousal relations and household structure based on traditional attitudes about the sexual division of labor.

The normative ideals of conventional gender norms and the traditional male breadwinner model remain the cognitive defaults of many baby boomers I interviewed. While these are now abstract ideas that are essentially antiquated ideals to subsequent US generations, these abstractions are still relevant to many baby boomers because they still perceive that the male breadwinner model was a functional model for their parents. Further, while many baby boomers recognize the advantages of the dual-earner model, they fear the dual-earner household structure because they maintain the early thinking that the dual-earner model is an inherently doomed arrangement.

The results in this study suggest that early baby boomers do not negate the mythical normative ideal of the male breadwinner model because they generally experienced conflict-laden realities in response to the major social and economic transformations they personally experienced. For them, the dual-earner household is equated with a threatened husband and a conflicted wife and mother. In other words, it's an arrangement that they have not seen function without severe tensions and stress. My research suggests that for baby boomers, the normative (gendered) basis of marriage persists. I find that the financial and degendered economic basis of marriage emerges in generation X, not the baby boomer generation.

GENERATION X: FINANCIAL MARRIAGE AND THE HARD MARRIAGE BAR

For many generation Xers I interviewed, the financial basis of marriage emerges as the most salient factor for marrying. I find this is both because the traditional social basis for marrying is reported to be weaker as well as because the centrality of the economic pressures of marrying is much stronger. Generation Xers, across gender, report that becoming economically self-sufficient is the primary objective as one transitions from youthful dependence to adult independence. Further, this objective is independent and ordered prior to the objective of marrying. Among the generation Xers I interviewed, family influences and intergenerational relations facilitated rather than discouraged their departure from the traditional social basis of marrying toward the modern financial basis of marriage.

In a process I refer to as transformative socialization, the socialization of generation Xers by their parents appears to have induced social change rather than to reproduce social norms. Firstly, I find a lack of encouragement from the baby boomer parents of generation Xers in regard to getting married as an important life goal. The most often reported influences that parents had in socializing generation X about marriage was usually in a negative way, either by showing the pitfalls of marrying without being financially ready or by directly providing the children verbal warnings about such pitfalls. Generation Xers report that, as children, they observed or received warnings about the marital strains caused by unequal or unhappy spousal relations and about the risks of marital dissolution.

For example, Janet, a female generation Xer born in 1978, talked about her family experiences and the advice she received from her mother:

> My parents were the traditional family. My father was the breadwinner…He always had a job, and my mother stayed home…One thing that my mother once mentioned that she instilled in both her daughters was that…to be sure you have an education so that if you needed to…you could support yourself…She felt somewhat trapped…I think that she, um, probably felt that if she ever did want to leave [the marriage], she couldn't.

Jade, a female generation Xer born in 1967, reported the advice she received from her mother: "[The] advice was 'you'd better be able to take care of yourself. Don't trust no man'… I had a mother who always told me you need to take care of yourself because you know a person can go…Your goal is to take care of yourself…Take care of yourself and depend on nobody else." Though her parents were married and they stayed together, Jade explained, "It was just…you know, my parents, they had a lot of hostility."

Male generation Xers also shared the sentiment that women should not go into a marriage financially dependent on a man due to uncertainty about the durability of marriage.

Ron, a male generation Xer born in 1972, expressed his feelings about the hypothetical couple of a low-earning woman marrying a higher-earning man in the research vignette:

> If she was my daughter, I would say, "Look, don't trust the man. Get your education so if things change in this marriage within six months, one year, two years, you're prepared to provide as the sole person for your child and your family going forward. It's one thing to be romanticized with the one big happy family, the white picket fence, but things change quickly from marriage to children, and just being married for an amount of time...you know, things happen with fidelity, so you have to be prepared as an adult to carry on and move forward in case the relationship breaks down and you're emotionally broke down"...If the relationship doesn't work out and she feels like he was the provider [but] now he is gone...[she'll think], What do I do? Where do I go?

Generation Xers report that their fathers also gave advice to seemingly discourage them from replicating their marrying patterns, including warnings about the negative effects of the traditional sexual division of labor. For Janet, in addition to her mother, her father also encouraged her to be self-sufficient. She said, "My father...kind of encouraged us to get our education before we got married...My father was very adamant that just a high school education was not enough to get a job and support yourself."

Jacob, a male generation Xer born in 1974, reported, "Once [my dad] got out of the army, he was having a hard time getting a job...We struggled from the aspect that my mom didn't have [an] education." Jacob recalled that [his father would say], "She's home. She can't get a job." Jacob added, "That was a big stressor...So I think that's when he started giving me advice to make sure you have everything set [before you get married]." Jacob's father encouraged him to get an education and to seek a wife who had an education so that he might not struggle as much as his father did as the sole male breadwinner in the household.

For generation Xers, the centrality of the financial basis of marriage is shared across gender. Chloe, a female generation Xer born in 1972, talked about how she and her now husband together planned to be financially secure before getting married due to their personal objectives of being financially self-sufficient and achieving a high standard of living together:

> To get married, we definitely wanted to—I as well as my husband—definitely wanted to be financially stable...It was very important to be financially stable, for us, to be comfortable...We like things. We like expensive things. We like to travel. We like to do whatever we want to do and not have to worry about how we're going to pay for it and how we're going to do it. And we didn't want the burden of asking family for money...I think it was just, uh, the whole wanting of just being able to provide for ourselves, just not having to depend on people.

For Chloe (and she insisted for her husband too), her financial contributions to making sure the household is financially secure is equally as important as her husband's financial contributions. For them and many other generation Xers in the sample, financial readiness is an objective a couple is to achieve prior to getting married.

Kailey, another female generation Xer born in 1972, also talked about the financial basis of marriage across gender. She reported, "I need to be able to take care of myself and contribute to the household expenses and contribute to the marital entertainment budget…Love doesn't pay the bills." For Kailey, the ability to pay the bills is indicated by educational attainment, because otherwise she feels financial stability is hard to achieve. She said,

> College education would make [a couple] more marketable in case they lost the good job they currently have…make it easier for them to find another job if they had to…Then if they were to marry, then hopefully that would eliminate or minimize one of the stressors I think a lot of young couples have… when they get married is money and trying to manage a household and manage, um, manage bills.

Generation Xers report that they perceive marriage as too risky to consider if there is not a set basis for managing the household financially. For Kailey and others, this includes a rather high standard of living, including having a "marital entertainment budget."

Another generation Xer emphasized that, for her, being financially set is an important strategy in case anything goes wrong in the marriage. Graciela, a female generation Xer born in 1976, said, "I feel that having a decent salary/wages is something that I should have before marrying because coming into a partnership without it will or could be problematic in the future. I should be able to support myself before entering a marriage, and if it doesn't work out, I should be able to bounce back and not be dependent on my partner." Like Chloe, Graciela feels that this is the case across gender: "A partnership should be fifty-fifty…Of course I'd expect the same thing from him."

I find marriage-bar inflation to be very much linked to the new model of financial marriage based on the dual-earner household structure. Generation Xers not only define economic readiness based on earning power across gender (rather than only in relation to the man), but they set their standards based on a much higher standard of living. I argue the standard is now set by households pooling incomes across two spouses, which has resulted in an inflated marriage bar. Chloe specifically described that in order for her and her husband to afford the things they wanted for their lifestyle once married, they both must work at financially secure jobs.

Indeed, I would argue that the very notion of the American standard of living is now based on two incomes, with the wife's income central to achieving the standard. Firstly, most American households are married and have two earners. Thus, the average American household income is essentially driven by the pooled income of dual-earner households. Furthermore, the average married household without a wife working is much lower than the median or mean income for the average married household with a wife working or that for single households (see graphs 3 and 4).

Modern marriage-bar inflation results in a standard of living for married households that is higher and harder for couples to reach. The insecurity of achieving the expected standard of living causes generation Xers to delay marriage not only until the male has a job but until both the male and the female achieve an established trajectory of completed schooling, steady employment, and secure income. For many, this now implies that the person obtains the education level he or she aspires to as well as acquire sufficient experience in the labor market before getting married. This necessarily preempts the high school marriages (or marriages immediately after high school) of the early baby boomers since these standards generally cannot be met at such an early age. Indeed, the average age at marriage has increased by six years across gender since the 1950s era of the male breadwinner ideal (US Census Bureau 2011). This is congruent with the longer time period it takes for young adults to now meet what I refer to as the hard marriage bar, which requires more education credentials and work experience across gender.

It is important to note that the hard marriage bar that generation Xers describe is one that is not only higher, but it is also more durable. As mentioned, rather than general social fitness or moral character requirements, generation Xers fundamentally value earning power as the central marker of being ready for marriage. Yet instead of the temporary status of employment versus unemployment being the marker of whether one can meet the economic marriage bar, it is usually based on education level. An individual's educational attainment has to some extent replaced family socioeconomic status as the marker of one's class, with class being more so of an individual-level marker than a primarily family-level marker. To illustrate this point, sample participants did not speak about whether a potential spouse comes from a wealthy family or middle-class family, but rather they debated whether the individual has sufficiently achieved his or her own educational or career goals—this is the marker of potential earning power, and social class, that was reported as mattering most to those I interviewed.

If it takes a certain level of education to meet the modern marriage-bar threshold, then a person who is not likely to meet it early in life is not likely to ever meet it. Most people's educational attainment is set at an early age, and it is persistent throughout life. That is, for example, those who do not obtain a college degree or high school degree as part of the standard educational trajectory (based on age-standard milestones) are not likely to later acquire such degrees. I find in this study that part of the reason why education is an important marker for earning power among generation Xers is the uncertainty about lasting employment. Generation Xers report feeling that a job is insecure, and they perceive the higher earning power conferred by education to be more secure (than employment).

This may explain my findings in my earlier research that while for those who are college educated there appears just to be a *delay* in marrying, for those with lower education levels (high school degree or less) there appears to be a *decline* in marrying. I find that, among generation Xers as compared to baby boomers, the lower probability of marrying at younger ages does not rebound in later years for those with lower education levels as it does for college-educated generation Xers (Espinoza 2012). Given that the age at marrying has increased across education levels in generation X, this previous research shows a lower probability of ever marrying by the age of thirty-five for those with a high school degree or less but not necessarily those with a college degree (because we see those with higher education levels catching up, so to speak, by marrying at older ages).

Regarding the research vignettes of this study, generation Xers I interviewed reported a lack of support for the hypothetical low earning power couple to get married; however, for the higher-earning couple, they suggest delaying marriage. This generation of sample participants reported that the low-earning couples should not get married, because, as they explained, marriage requires a strong financial foundation. Without either person in the couple meeting a minimum economic threshold based on earning power, they did not consider love and compatibility to be sufficient bases for marriage. Generation Xers describe the marriage bar as requiring that one achieves education goals, establishes a career, be able to afford a home, and not only be able to pay the bills but also be able to afford conspicuous romance (e.g., entertainment, travel). For this generation, romance has a financial dimension because you have to be able to afford the leisure time and activities that support the underlying romantic bond that leads to, and sustains, a marriage.

Among early baby boomers and previous US generations, traditional institutions—such as the church—socially mandated marriage as the appropriate context of heterosexual sex, procreation, and the transition from youth dependence to independent adult living. Marrying among baby boomers at this time was based on broader social norms rather than being fundamentally driven by economics. Even the disparate economic status of women at the time was a reflection of broader social arrangements where rigid social hierarchies intersected with an explicit gender order at all levels of US society, from the national economy to the individual household (Ryan 2006). As baby boomers were encouraged by their parents to maintain traditional social norms and the traditional sexual division of labor, I refer to this process as normative socialization in contrast to what I describe to be a process of transformative socialization among generation Xers.

The drastic social and economic changes of the mid- to late twentieth century challenged and ultimately undermined the traditional social basis of marrying. American family women were pulled and pushed into the labor force as the limits and negative consequences of traditional family and gender arrangements—including the nuclear family model and the sexual division of labor—were becoming more evident. Though this was not fully apparent to baby boomers (the parents pioneering these shifts), it was more broadly apparent to their children—generation X. Generation X also came to face a much higher financial standard of living. This generation experiences an inflated economic marriage bar that now applies across gender. This creates a degendered financial basis for marrying—what I refer to as financial marriage.

The (mostly imagined) viability of the sexual division of labor within the baby boomers' parental household facilitates the male breadwinner model prevailing as a cognitive default among baby boomers. Despite an awareness of trade-offs between traditional and modern gender relations and household structure (which is shared across the baby boomers and generation Xers), I find that it required a new kind of primary socialization to make Americans turn away from the cognitive default of the male breadwinner model. That is, there is a generational lag. Among generation Xers, the male breadwinner model broke down in the context of primary socialization and only then were the modern concepts about the dual-earner household and the degendered financial basis of marrying internalized.

Graph 3. Dual Earner Couples Set Highest Standard for Household Income

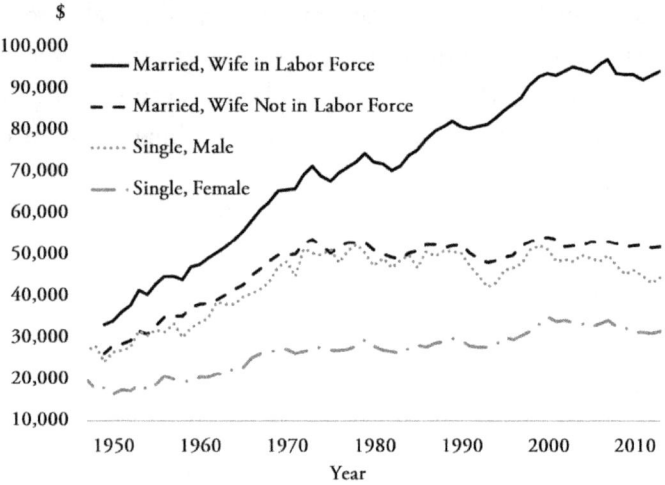

Source: Author's display of Current Population Survey (CPS) data. 2013 dollars.

Graph 4. Dual Earner Model Emerges as Most Typical American Household

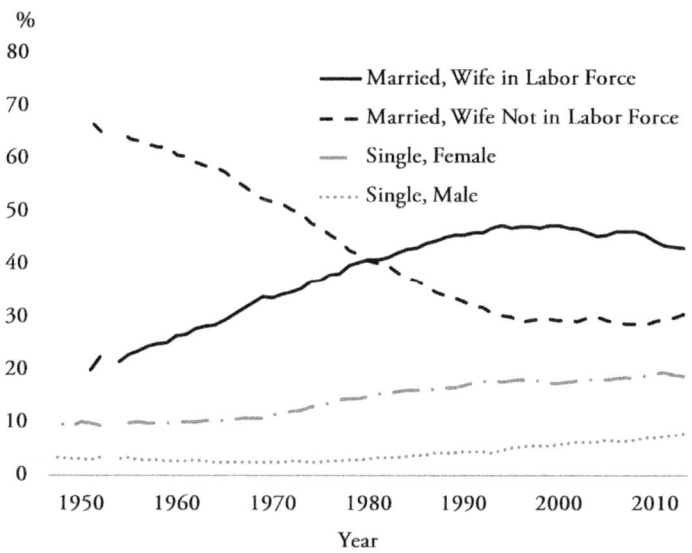

Type of Household Structure among US Families, 1950 - 2010

Source: Author's display of Current Population Survey (CPS) data.

4

Black Family Formation and the Deracialization of Working Family Women

In the United States, women of color have had different experiences compared to white women in terms of working in the labor market, gender relations, and family roles (Bowen and Finnegan 1969; Newman 1978; Browne 1999). Nonwhite women have been treated differently than white women under the racialized economic structures, normative values, and gender role expectations of dominant American (white) society. Historically, a nonwhite woman was more likely to be a domestic servant outside her own home than to be a housewife (Collins 1990; Coltrane 1996; Davis 2011). During slavery, virtually all black women worked. The "cult of domesticity" and venerable female housewife norm that lasted into the 1950s was generally an ideal constructed for and by whites. Historically, the ideal was financially viable among only whites because sustaining a household on one income required the relatively higher earning power available only to middle- to upper-class white males.

Even among those married, women of color have long had to enter the workforce due to the financial imperatives of sustaining the family. Data from multivariate analysis show that when in a husband and wife household, black and Mexican American women are more likely than white wives to be employed (Tienda and Glass 1985). Despite the historically shared lower socioeconomic position of blacks and Latinos compared to whites in the United States, there are two patterns that emerged in the literature to characterize how the distinct family and labor-market patterns of these groups unfolded. At one end, there are black gender roles and family structures that are considered to be comparatively more matriarchal than those among whites. At the other end are those among families of Latino descent who are often still portrayed in the sociological and family literature to be more patriarchal compared to whites.

Overall, the departure of nonwhites from the family and gender role patterns of whites has been theorized to be a source of negative socioeconomic outcomes. Yet it is important to note that empirically white women have now generally caught up to nonwhite women in regard to labor force participation rates. In 1954, 33.3 percent of white women worked and 46.1 percent of nonwhite women worked. By 2004, 73.6 percent of white women and 74.8 percent of black women worked (Juhn and Potter 1980). This reflects a marked shift toward a convergence in women's labor force participation rates by race.

Considering the changes in women's labor force participation and household structure amid consistent racial differences in marrying patterns, I study the relation of women's earning power on marrying among the two largest nonwhite US ethnoracial groups of blacks and Mexican Americans in contrast to whites. I first discuss in this chapter modern matriarchy and the relation between black women's earning power and family formation. In the subsequent chapter, I discuss modern patriarchy and the relation between women's earning power and family formation among Mexican Americans.

MODERN MATRIARCHY

The matriarchal departure from the white norms of gender roles and household structure has been argued to be an important determinant of disparate marriage outcomes as well as higher poverty rates among black Americans (Moynihan 1965; Spain and Bianchi 1996). Married black women have been more likely to enter the labor market and less likely to exit the labor market compared to married white women (Long and Jones 1980). By the start of the twenty-first century, lifetime marrying rates for black women had declined by 30 percent (Goldsetin and Kenney 2001). By the age of forty, current data show that black women are 25 percent less likely to marry compared to white women (Graefe and Lichter 2002).

Given a time when it was the male's normative role to be the breadwinner in the household, black matriarchy in the family allegedly reflected a harmful deviance from whites (Moynihan 1965). Moynihan wrote,

> In essence, the Negro community has been forced into a matriarchal structure which, because it is so

out of line with the rest of the American society, seriously retards the progress of the group as a whole, and imposes a crushing burden on the Negro male and, in consequence, on a great many Negro women as well…It is clearly a disadvantage for a minority group to be operating on one principle, while the great majority of the population, and the one with the most advantages to begin with, is operating on another. This is the present situation of the Negro. Ours is a society which presumes male leadership in private and public affairs. The arrangements of society facilitate such leadership and reward it. A subculture, such as that of the Negro American, in which this is not the pattern, is placed at a distinct disadvantage. (p. 29)

Interpreted as a formidable threat to black socioeconomic advancement, the deviance of black family patterns from white family patterns was understood by some to be rooted in, and determinative of, the cultural-historical difference between African Americans and European Americans. Subscribing to the conclusions of E. Franklin Frazier's (1939) research on the black family, Moynihan (1965) reported that the dominance of black women and the manifest deficiencies of black men were due to a long history of gender role and family breakdown since black enslavement. For Moynihan, at the core of the pathology of black families was the matriarchal household structure. Moynihan (1965) continued,

> Fifty-six percent of Negro women, age 25 to 64, are in the work force, against 42 percent of white women. This dependence on the mother's income undermines the position of the father and deprives the children of the kind of attention, particularly in school matters, which is now a standard feature of middle-class upbringing. (p. 25)

Additionally, Moynihan (1965) makes claims about the limits of the black maternal role to support the appropriate personal and academic development of the black son as compared to the black daughter. Particularly of concern was the effect of women's gender-equal status on male identity and his non-gender-dominant status. The anticipated adverse effects of black matriarchy included damage to the black male position as well as economic limits and social disadvantage of the female-headed household structure. As a family scholar who argued this position, Rainwater (1966) wrote, "Since men find the overt debasement of their status very threatening, the Negro family is much more vulnerable to disruption when men are temporarily unable to perform their provider roles."

Foretelling an independent negative effect of the matriarchal family structure on the future socioeconomic position of black men and blacks overall, Moynihan wrote that "the matriarchal pattern of so many Negro families reinforces itself over the generations" (pp. 30–31). From this perspective, the theorized negative outcomes of the matriarchal family structure are manifested via an intergenerational process. Rainwater (1966) also advances the intergenerational perspective that "[the black mother] often receives her training in how to run such a [matrifocal] household by observing her own mother manage without a husband" (p. 195). Further, Rainwater notes that the prevalence of nonmarried women of the prior generation serves to act as a lesson of "disillusionment" with marriage. They do not observe marriage as providing any more secure economic base than a black woman can achieve on her own. Rainwater interprets this intergenerational relation and its predicted negative consequences as a process by which the racial hierarchy (or, in the author's terms, the "caste system") is transmitted through the family.

It is important to note, however, that for many scholars of black family studies, the focus on the earlier and persistent entry of black family women in the labor market was not necessarily linked to primary socialization or a cultural continuity of matriarchal patterns developed either during the era of slavery or, alternatively, from deeper African cultural origins. Rather, this alternative perspective holds that the underlying cause of the pattern of black family women working was directly linked to the contemporary and actual lived conditions of black males having limited economic means to serve as a sole breadwinner to sustain a household.[17] That is, it is the present material conditions of the limited socioeconomic status of black men that drive the marrying behavior and household roles of both black women and black men.

---

17 Per Ralph Ellison (date unknown), "Even as life toughens the Negro, even as it brutalizes him, sensitizes him, dulls him, goads him to anger, moves him to irony, sometimes fracturing and sometimes affirming his hopes; even as it shapes his attitudes towards family, sex, love, religion; even as it modulates his humor, tempers his joy—it conditions him to deal with his life and with himself."

Per Rainwater (1966), in referring to the mid-twentieth century, even lower-class blacks know that the "normal American family" is supposed to be based on "a father-husband who functions as an adequate provider and interested member of the family, a hard working home-bound mother who is concerned about her children's welfare and her husband's need, and children who look up to their parents and perform well in school and other outside places to reflect credit on their families" (p. 182). Rainwater continued,

> Many [blacks] make efforts to establish such families but find it impossible to do so either because of the direct impact of economic disabilities or because they are not able to sustain in their day-to-day lives the ideals which they hold. While these ideals do serve as a meaningful guide to lower-class couples who are mobile out of the group, for a great many others the existence of such ideas about normal family life represents a recurrent source of stress within families as individuals become aware they are failing to measure up to the ideals or as others, within the family and outside it, use the ideals as an aggressive weapon for criticizing each other's performance. (p. 183)

Rainwater maintains that much that is distinctive about black family life stems from the fact that "many wives feel they owe the husband nothing once he fails to perform his provider role. If the husband is unemployed the wife increasingly refuses to perform her usual duties for him." For example, one woman, after mentioning that her husband had cooked four eggs for himself, commented, "'I cook for him when he's working but right now he's unemployed; he can cook for himself'" (p. 190). That is, when black family men fail in the traditional male breadwinner role due to unemployment, black family women are observed to adjust by doing less in terms of the traditional female homemaker role. Here, economic conditions are observed to affect the maintenance or discontinuation of the then-normative gender relations and traditional sexual division of labor in the household.

Going further, that a woman may observe or be taught that a man may not be able or willing to dutifully fulfill the provider role in the household may affect how she evaluates the prospect of marriage. Rainwater wrote (1966) that as "the girl has good reason to be suspicious of the likelihood that men will be able to perform stably in the role of provider; she is reluctant to be tied down by a man who will not prove worth it" (p. 188). This perspective may be understood as an argument that a woman may construct a single female-headed household not so much based on her financial capacity (as is typically explained) but rather due to the lack of financial security of her male counterpart. In order to financially sustain a family, it is simply not viable to depend on or expect a man to be the provider. Essentially, the traditional exchange of a woman's domestic services for a man's financial contribution to the household is in default; thus, the institution of marriage is devalued (from the woman's perspective).

In this study, I apply the nuanced concept of an *economic imperative* to stress that for some women it is an economic mandate to serve as a provider to sustain the household (rather than a voluntary arrangement induced by the relative advantages of working versus a viable alternative of not working in the labor market). The economic imperative argument is in contrast to the *economic incentive* argument (which I will discuss further in subsequent chapters). There is an economic incentive to work for those women who want to serve as a provider in the household as a willful choice based on the greater advantages of working that are conferred by women's increasing earning power. Thus, I conceptually distinguish between nonvoluntary arrangements of family women working due to economic deprivation versus voluntary arrangements of family women working due to the financial advantages of working.

A related distinction of women's voluntary versus nonvoluntary entry into the labor market in relation to women's own and men's earning power was made by Ruth Milkman in her 1976 study of family women working during the Great Depression. Though she uses other terms, Milkman finds the voluntary versus nonvoluntary distinction to have implications on the attitudes about family women working. Milkman (1976) wrote,

> For these women and their families, the experience of sex-role reversal—either a complete shifting of responsibility for earning money from husband to wife or simply an increased reliance on the wife's unpaid work and her strategies for survival—was a part of a painful period in the family's history. The

deviation from traditional sex roles was thus, to say the least, negatively reinforced by the accompanying experience of economic deprivation for most families. (p. 85)

Milkman explains that during the Great Depression of the 1930s, role reversals between husband and wife were common yet "precisely because of the negative reinforcement given to sex role reversal, which resulted from its origin in economic deprivation, traditional sex roles [not gender-egalitarian roles] were reinforced" (p. 85).

As we can see from Milkman's research, if gender relations and household structure are a function of material conditions and needs rather than the reproduction of traditional culture, then women of other ethnoracial groups may also manifest similar family patterns as blacks (i.e., family women working and adjustment in gender roles) as men from other groups face deteriorated economic status. In other words, the family patterns observed among blacks are not inherently specific to black culture, and so, based on social and economic conditions, they may be observed among nonblacks. Indeed, Furstenberg (2009) argues that the narrowing black-and-white racial divide in teenage and nonmarital childbearing reflects the economic basis of family formation patterns as economic precariousness becomes deracialized.

Conversely, family patterns and gender relations within the black community may also change as a consequence of exogenous economic shifts. Rainwater clearly makes this argument as follows:

> If we are right that present Negro family patterns have been created as adaptations to a particular socioeconomic situation, it would make more sense to change that socioeconomic situation and then depend upon the people involved to make new adaptations as time goes on. If Negro providers have steady jobs and decent incomes, if Negro children have some realistic expectation of moving toward such a goal, if slum Negroes come to feel that they have the chance to affect their own futures and to receive respect from those around them, then (and only then) the destructive patterns are likely to change. (p. 208)

Yet, alternatively, some black family scholars posit that black marrying patterns are determined by a distinct black marriage market (the forces of supply and demand). This school of research focuses on the effect of a gender ratio imbalance in the marriage market due to a combination of adverse demographic, social, and economic conditions of black men. The theory is that having more men than women in a marriage market decreases the relationship commitment on the part of marriageable black men (i.e., when men have a disproportionately greater number of women available to them, their motivation to marry is weaker).

Per Wilson (1987, 1996, 2009), the lower prevalence of marrying among blacks is attributable to a shortage of "marriageable" black men that are financially or otherwise secure. Essentially, Wilson refers to not just a demographic ratio but rather a gender imbalance that is socially constructed and socially defined. Here, the focus is not on black women's economic need to serve as a provider in the household or black women's lack of motivation to marry due to cultural or socialization effects. Rather the outcome of interest is whether black men are motivated to marry given the greater quantity of black women compared to (marriageable) black men.

Using qualitative data to support this argument, Wilson reported in *When Work Disappears* (1996) the perspective of a twenty-five-year-old unmarried black male: "Well, most black men feel now, why get married when you got six to seven womens [sic] to one guy, really" (p. 100). Though Wilson's focus is on the relation between family deterioration and black male joblessness, his position is that the outcome of black men's economic precariousness is "especially weak support for the institution of marriage" (Wilson 2009, p. 120). Implicitly, this would mean that the gains to the specialization model or the dual-earner model of marriage are not sufficient to motivate the choice to marry when men have disproportionately more women available in the marriage market.

Yet alternative studies find a high aspiration and expectation to marry among black men and black women alike. This research stresses that it is the economic standard for marriage that bar minority men from marrying (Edin and Kefalas 2005). Though a distinct perspective, this marriage-bar literature brings back the analysis to the economic basis of marrying. Indeed, some studies find that the prerequisite of male economic readiness for marriage is strongest among African Americans (Edin 2000; Tucker 2000; Edin and Nelson 2013).

In relation to black men but here also in relation to black women, it is the average black person's inability to meet economic expectations that is a primary barrier to black family formation (Gibson-Davis, Edin, and McLanahan 2005). An unobtainable marriage bar may be why some studies find that the nature of marriage markets cannot fully account for the racial differences or changes in the black-white marriage gap (Brien 1992; Oropesa, Lichter, and Anderson 1994).

On the other hand, Rainwater (1966) touches on joblessness as a factor that may possibly erode the propensity to marrying based on noneconomic reasons. However, his research may not necessarily imply a cultural continuity perspective but rather a structural perspective about the importance of actual, lived conditions. He wrote that there appears to be an increase in distrust or actually observed behaviors that are more likely to cause discord in a committed relationship when a man is not regularly employed (e.g., alcohol/drug consumption, sexual infidelity, or jealousy). A man (and the woman in relation to the man) may adopt a different relationship orientation based on the man's work status given a different structure of time constraints (i.e., much more leisure time) and/or the psychological effects of not working work (e.g., lower self-confidence).

Milkman (1976) also links the effects of joblessness during the Great Depression to poorer relationships and family life:

> [Unemployed men] hung around street corners and in groups. They gave each other solace. They were loath to go home because they were indicted, as if it were

their fault for being unemployed. A jobless man was a lazy good-for-nothing. The women punished men for not bringing home the bacon, by withholding themselves sexually...These men suffered from depression. They felt despised, they were ashamed of themselves. They cringed, they comforted one another. (p. 84)

The male economic decline and male joblessness arguments primarily focus on the effects that unemployment has on men's psyche and the then normative social position of masculine dominance in society. They are premised on the ideology that the male breadwinner model is inherently a functional arrangement (Parson 1964; Moynihan 1965). Such literature fails to consider, let alone examine, that family women working might have positive effects on the family (e.g., to survive temporary or persistent economic precariousness) and/or women (e.g., to achieve more gender-egalitarian status in the household). More specifically, this literature generally fails to incorporate the importance of how a woman's economic status may play an increasingly important positive role in the decision to marry with women's increasing earning power (as the dual-earner household would become more financially advantageous).

Black women started to reach parity with their male counterparts sooner and faster than white women to white men (Bureau of Labor Statistics 2009). With women's increasing earning power and labor force participation in gainful employment, it may be that the greater financial gains to the dual-earner marriage would have rendered the economic status of black women increasingly important to marrying. Further, as the trend of the dual-earner marriage emerged among white women (becoming deracialized), it may be that the dual-earner arrangement would also become destigmatized and perceived to be a more voluntary, and so a more ideal, arrangement.

It might be that the theorized negative effects of women working were due to the pioneers—black family women—having too early a jumpstart in the labor market. They worked en masse at a time when their employment conflicted with the white normative model of the male breadwinner, female homemaker. However, the pattern of white women's changing earning power and its effect on white marrying patterns and household structure may have an effect on the black family through a normative force. As some argued in the mid-twentieth century that the detrimental effects of black women heading the household was based on its social deviance from the white pattern, it may essentially be that just being different from the mainstream—and the subsequent stigma—caused the negative social outcomes.

For example, did black men not want to marry a working black woman when it was understood by mainstream society to be a signal of deviance or demasculinization? Did black women not want to marry into a household with a black man who might be dependent on two earners or a nontraditional female breadwinner model when it was understood by mainstream society to be a source of shame or negative family outcomes? If the early timing of the mass entry of black women in the labor force affected its ultimate effect on marrying, then how would the mass entry of white women in the labor force and the emergence of the modern dual-earner model as an accepted social norm change this relation?

From a normative perspective, it may be that the economic status of black women would become increasingly positive with the trend of white women entering the labor market en masse. As forming a dual-earner marriage becomes a norm for gender relations and household structure among whites and a model positively evaluated by dominant society, I examine how these trends among whites affect the black family and black marrying patterns in ways not yet fully explained. The first generations of pioneering married black women who worked did not have a social context that supported women working or the balancing of working with family responsibilities. It is quite logical that such a broad change in the historical context of marriage would induce a shift in the effect of black women's earning power on marriage to being positive or, if already positive, even more positive.

DERACIALIZATION OF WOMEN'S (PAID) WORK

As a reflection of the socioeconomic context in which black family women have long been part of the US workforce, black sample participants report undergoing a process of transformative socialization regarding the traditional sexual division of labor across the two sample generations. Black sample participants—both males and females—report being socialized by their parents in a manner that encourages a departure from the normative male breadwinner model and the traditionally gendered economics of marrying. Black sample participants report learning about, and internalizing, views that the male breadwinner model and the traditional sexual division of labor are inadequate and untenable arrangements. However, among sample participants in the latter generation, generation X, there is a shift in the basis of the positive perception about family woman working and the positive relation between women's earning power and marrying. Firstly, the perceptions are deracialized, and, secondly, they are more positive in terms of black sample participants perceiving the dual-earner arrangement to be both more voluntary and more advantageous.

Among black baby boomers in the sample, the inadequacies of the male breadwinner model are understood to be based on race-specific considerations and a disadvantaged socioeconomic position. Specifically, they are explained to be based on the lower earning power of black men both in absolute terms and in relative terms. Black baby boomers perceive that black men's earning power in the United States is generally below the minimum economic threshold to sustain a family. Further, they perceive that black men's earning power is generally not higher than black women's earning power. However, black women's earning power is also understood to be relatively low. Thus, black family women working is understood to be a forced alternative based on the motivation of meeting just basic household requirements. Thus, it is not perceived to be a more advantageous arrangement compared to the male breadwinner model.

To black baby boomers in the sample, the dual-earner arrangement is not ideal nor clearly superior to the normative model of the white male breadwinner model. That is, the benefits of black family women working are not reported as advantages of the black dual-earner model in comparison to the white male breadwinner. Indeed, prior to the late twentieth century, black dual-earner households did not earn more than white male breadwinner household at the aggregate level (see graph 6). Rather, the black dual-earner family is a survival strategy taught and adopted in order to establish a minimally economic viable household because blacks from the baby boomer generation perceive that the higher earning power necessary to maintain a male breadwinner household is generally not available to black men or black households.

At the aggregate level, single black women have not actually had a relatively higher level of earning power compared to single black men, single white women, or single white men (see graph 8). Thus, for baby boomers, the perception of the financial benefits of black family women working is not based on it being a means for upward socioeconomic mobility or relatively higher consumption levels compared to the normative (white) male breadwinner model. Only by supplementing the wages of black men could the financial benefits of black family women working help black households in the baby boomer generation catch up to the earnings of households headed by white male breadwinners.

Yet after 1970, we do start to see the median income of black and white dual-earner households diverging from the median income of male breadwinner households to result in a larger gap by household structure. Thereafter, the median income of white and black dual-earner households relative to the male breadwinner household model of each respective race has steadily increased. Among blacks, dual-earner households earned at least two times the median income of a male breadwinner household (wife not in the labor force) for the first time in 1981. However, black dual-earner households still earn only a fraction of white dual-earner households (see graph 6).

Thus, the dual-earner model, as a departure from the sole male breadwinner model, is understood based on a racialized framework in the baby boomer generation—that is, black family women must work because black family men cannot sustain their households on a sole income. Further, not only are the origins of black family couples working in the baby boomer generation based on economic deprivation but the outcome was often economic deprivation as well. As a result of the low earning power of black women, the financial status of black dual-earner households is not financially advantageous compared to the financial status of the normative white male breadwinner model.

This may explain why among black baby boomers in the sample I find that there is a maintained ideal about the male breadwinner model and traditional gender roles based on masculine dominance. For example, Andre, a black baby boomer born in 1954, talked about the experiences of growing up in a dual-earner model but from the perspective that it did not allow his family to even exit poverty:

> My parents, they worked in factories and they worked really hard. They worked hard to the bone to make sure I wouldn't be without. I didn't realize I was poor, because my parents always made sure I had everything I needed. But I was poor. My parents were poor.

For Andre, a family woman working is not associated with the advantage of achieving a high level of household consumption, and Andre maintains the traditional male breadwinner model as a normative ideal. However, he is also aware that it is difficult for a man to achieve a minimum economic threshold and that this may negatively affect the spousal relationships in a marriage. He said, "I think that the man should be the breadwinner. [But] I feel that if a couple can't start off monetarily good, it's a challenge for them to grow."

There is awareness among the black male participants of the baby boomer generation that they cannot likely sustain a household as a sole provider nor necessarily maintain economic dominance over their wives. However, they maintain the traditional masculine ideal that men should achieve male dominance in the household. The dissonance between their socioeconomic conditions and gendered ideals about household structure inspires alternative ideas about the contributions and position of the black male in the household. For example, Lee, a black baby boomer born in 1959, said,

> When it comes to a man being the dominant one in the family, people still seem to think, especially in black communities, that black woman make more than black men. Therefore society is shaped, it's molded, right, that the black man has been removed from being the dominant person in the relationship based on the reality of finances…But that doesn't say I'm less of a man…I'm very well secure within myself. I'm so secure that that doesn't or will not bother me…Because of the fact that you [are] making a little bit more, um, than I'm making currently, that's not

going to hold me back from me loving you or our relationship, or I'm going to be like oh, I can't be with her because she makes a dollar more an hour than I am. So what! Man up, be a man. Up your game—you know what I mean. But that won't keep me from marrying you. Please!

Essentially, Lee redefined the financial basis that it takes for a man to be dominant in the relationship as a way to preserve the dominant masculine role in a relationship despite having low economic prospects. He continued,

Now as long as [the man] is able to accept responsibility, and he is secure within himself, and he is accepting responsibility and taking care of the household, taking care of her, and taking care of the child, and still [is] the dominant factor in the relationship, you understand, then guess what? Then him working for McDonald's flipping burgers or working for the corporation in the office, you know what I mean, it's all the same. As long as he is the male doing the responsibilities and taking care of the responsibilities of a man within that relationship, it doesn't necessarily have to be, uh, whether he is working or not.

Likewise, another black baby boomer (born in 1952), Cameron, also redefined what it takes to be the provider in the household. He stressed that it is not based on financial contributions to the household:

> Um, okay, my wife made more money than I did, so technically somebody could call, could say she was the provider, but she wasn't. Because aside from money, I provided the things I was supposed to provide, okay…Uh, like I said, when my kids would have a question or something like that, they'd come and ask me, and most times than not, their mother said [to] go ask your daddy, you know, like that…It's definitely more than money.

I interpret these findings to reflect how black men from the baby boomer generation contested normative ideas about the basis of masculine dominance in a way that reconciles their own ideal of masculine dominance (based on traditional gender-normative expectations) with black men's limited earning power. By stressing that they could perform a masculine-dominant role in the household irrespective of their limited financial contributions, they are able to make claims about maintaining a gender-dominant position in the household and defend their masculine role in the relationship. Rachel, a female black baby boomer born in 1955, talked about this attitude being persistent even to this day:

> I think it's [traditional gender ideology] still the same. Women have the capability of making more money than they ever made before, but it's still…the psyche is still there…As a rule, in general, people, gentlemen still want to be able to say, "I'm the breadwinner." Even if you're not the breadwinner…he probably still says, "I'm the one that's taking care of the household."

> The psyche is still there…[Men] just feel funny about a woman making more money.

Other reports by black baby boomers in the sample reflect tension and, ultimately, instances of marital dissolution due to the contradiction between what I find to be retained traditional attitudes about gender roles and the inability of black men to actually maintain higher levels of earning power than their female counterparts. For example, Cameron reported,

> I started doing what God called on me—I started teaching—my salary was actually going down. [My wife's] salary started going up, okay…Something changed with her. Her mentality changed. It became a point of well, you know…economics, okay… That's what this was. Bottom line—this is my second marriage, okay? My first marriage ended like that.

As another example, Andre, stated,

> As my wife and I got older, we started growing apart from one another because we both had good educational skills, but she wanted her master's degree. I was done with school, and she wanted to get her master's. About a couple of years after her master's, she was shooting in a whole different direction than I wanted to go in…You know, you've got your goal you want to reach. I've got my goal that I'm satisfied with. And we wound up splitting from one another

because she had to go…she had these other objectives that she wanted.

Thus, among baby boomers, black men's claims to having achieved male dominance in the household without the establishment of achieving financial dominance in the household appears not to be supported by their experiences. Rather, the contradiction of maintaining traditional gender attitudes without the man having relatively higher earning power than his female partner appears to lead to marital tension and, in some cases, marital dissolution. Further, black participants of the baby boomer generation do not report the financial or nonfinancial advantages of family women working. For them, a woman's relatively higher earning power is reported to be a source of marital strife and/or dissolution. This is in contrast to the advantages I will show to be reported by black sample participants from generation X, which include higher household consumption and more gender-egalitarian relationships.

Like whites, black male and female generation Xers report positive attitudes about the dual-earner arrangement. While black men report having a racialized insecurity about not financially contributing as much or more than their females counterparts across the two generations, the benefits of the dual-earner household itself are appreciated from a race-neutral framework in generation X. That is, black men report insecurity about female economic dominance across the two generations; however, black male (and female) sample participants of generation X report positive attitudes about men and women being coproviders in the household in a race-neutral manner. Generation Xers perceive that black family women working now aligns with broader social arrangements of the typical American family woman, including white family women, working.

For example, David, a black male generation Xer born in 1974, reported that he wants a woman to be an equal partner to him due to race-neutral economic insecurities and race-neutral benefits to the dual-earner arrangement:

> If I do have a good job and just to say I lose it, then what do I do? You know, I can't depend on her. You know, she's not benefitting either, so...so in the long run, we both, like, help each other out. If one goes down, the other one can help pull the other one up. As the other goes down, the other will help pull the other one. So it's like a, in a way, an equal playing field. It's like, in a way, putting your own welfare benefits within each other...[I want] a sense of fairness because in my generation I'm also noticing the financial burdens are much more harder, and it's much more demanding, so...you know, what I'm trying to explain is...social security...I'm also looking at the bigger picture, how the economy is now, maybe if I...got married back in the 1970s, then I'd probably be more leaning towards [an] ideal [traditional] marriage, but seeing how the economy is now and it's getting much more of a dog-eat-dog world out there, I would prefer that we both are more like a team...[i.e., as in the dual-earner model].

Further, David perceives education to be the basis of him being economically set for marriage. He said, "I have to have an

education to back me up on that. Now everything is paper based. There's no such thing as experience…everyone must have a degree. There's no such thing as an apprentice."
However, David also revealed racialized insecurities about not being able to match the expectations (or earning power) of black women. He said,

> It's depowering. Yeah, as a male, you know, as a black male, it's depowering what one says about a black male because, uh, I live in DC, and most of your counterparts are successful women, so it's…very hard, you know, in relationships that, you know, our women demand that you should be on this level… Well, you have more black women…because our males have been put to jail, more women…had to step up to the plate.

But David does not think this means that black men are less likely to marry, even in the case of not earning as much as the woman in the relationship. David said that "black men feel *okay* about marriage if the women makes more…Independent black woman does not mean that you need to be by yourself."

I find that the benefits of the dual-earner model are evaluated positively based on a deracialized framework in generation X. Like their white counterparts, the dual-earner model is perceived to be based on a more voluntary and benefit-centered framework among black sample participants in generation X. That is, family women—black or white—*should* work because of the greater financial and nonfinancial advantages of a family woman working compared to the normative male breadwinner model. The financial advantages include greater consumption levels but also enhanced financial security. The man and woman in the couple can feel more confident that together they can meet the minimum threshold to feel economically ready for marriage.

Don, a black male generation Xer born in 1977, said, "Money is important in starting marriages. Although there isn't a minimum amount of money I see as a threshold…there has to be a certain amount of earning power. Earning power would allow them [the man and the woman] to get or keep a job." For him, "stable full-time work is the most important because marriage is a union, and bringing [financial] instability to the union is not a good way to start." Like David, Don argues that educational attainment is a secure financial basis, and he too refers to general economic instability from a deracialized perspective. In his interview, he applied this perspective to a woman's high earning power being able to help the household and marriage despite economic instability:

> Even if her job goes away and it's incredibly hard to keep the job and the company is sinking, she still has earning power. She still has earning potential. She can still kind of put her résumé out there and still get a job, hopefully. And so even if the stability in the marriage financially kind of goes away for a little while, hopefully, she will be able to get another job sometime soon and the marriage will be okay after that.

The central benefits of the dual-earner model are based on the risks that generation Xers perceive about marriage—across race. For example, Nancy, a black female generation Xer born in 1976, described how her parents' experiences affected the views she reported during the interview. She said,

> My parents got married—my mom was seventeen, and my dad was nineteen, and my mama was pregnant. I don't know if I would describe their relationship as deeply in love. I think they were just young and pregnant. I think they decided they were just going to get married. Fortunately, my dad went to the military and could provide for a good living for my family, until they got divorced. And my mom had a high school education and not a very good one at that, so you know when they divorced she was like, "Oh my god." We did not have a very good standard of living after they got divorced.

Nancy reported that the economics as well as love and respect (as the foundation for a gender-egalitarian relationship) are important to her: "I would only marry if we were willing to put our finances together and be a family. He has to be stable with work or schooling, and most importantly, we have to be in love and have respect for one another."

Caroline, another black female generation Xer (born in 1972), expressed that "the only [marital] advice I ever got was my mom, you know, would always tell us, never be totally dependent on a man. Always be able to take care of yourself." For Caroline, though, family women working was something related to intergenerational socialization and the economic imperative. She said,

> I just think it was something passed down from generation to generation, because as far as I know, everyone [all the woman] worked. Now, it may have been informal, like my great-grandmother was a... loan shark. But that's how she made money. And my grandmother was a hairdresser and a nurse.

Caroline went on to explain,

> Well, my grandmother, her first marriage broke up, so she always had to, you know, she had to take care of herself. And my great-grandma, um, I never knew my great-grandfather, so I think he died young, so she needed to be able to take care of herself, so [I learned] just always be able to, um, take care of yourself and have your, you know…have your own…your own money.

However, in her own case, Caroline observed her parents working such that it did facilitate a middle-class lifestyle and improved spousal relations. She said, "[Both parents working] just made them…more compatible because of that. We were always able to have two cars…We had a very financially stable household."

As part of her interview, Caroline identified the main advantages of a dual-earner relationship—whether married or not—as "sharing expenses and, um, pooling, you know… financial resources." Yet she, like others from her generation, stressed that the economic basis of marrying is to be considered only when they are present along with love: "It is important for a couple to be emotionally connected before marriage. [Economic] factors are important but don't matter much if there is not any love between the couple." She considers marrying important in making the relationship a more formal commitment across time. She said, "I think for marriage, to me… it's just…it's just more permanent. You know, it's more like, you know, that's the decision that we're going to, you know, build…build a life together. You know, that we're, you know, in it for the long haul."

Among sample participants in the X generation, the attitudes about the dual-earner model are comparable across race. Black sample participants were socialized by their parents to appreciate the enhanced financial security, if not the economic necessity, of having a family woman work for reasons that are now similar across race. That is, across race, sample participants from generation X report being aware that the realities of the risks of job loss, divorce, and death make women and their children at risk for financially relying on the male breadwinner model.

As the economic insecurities of the labor market and macroeconomy are perceived to be threats across race, the vulnerabilities and comparative shortcomings of the traditional normative male breadwinner model are apparent to Americans across race. Thus, the economic advantages of the dual-earner model compared to the male breadwinner model make the dual-earner model a race-neutral superior alternative whereas in the past it was considered a race-specific mandate among blacks.

Just as importantly, the higher incomes women can now draw from working in the paid labor market mean that they are contributing to the class mobility and higher consumption of the household to a degree women never have prior in US history. Women's higher earning power makes the advantages of the dual-earner model more apparent across gender. Whereas in the past a women working might not necessarily increase the household income by a substantial factor, women in generation X do so. Among generation Xers, for the first time in US history, men as well as women can enhance their class status by marrying. This is a departure to prior generations, where a woman's and a household's class status was driven by the male's occupation (Parsons 1943). Men and women with higher earning power (who tend to marry each other) have even more substantially increased earning power by entering a dual-earner marriage.

In contemporary times, a man may more than double his potential consumption of market-based goods and services by marrying (when taking into account women's higher earning power and the economies of scale of sharing a household). In the past and based on the sole male breadwinner model, only women garnered such steep financial gains from marrying. Historically, men only directly garnered nonfinancial gains to marrying. However, my findings and past research (Mitchell 1971 and Milkman 1976) suggest that the nonfinancial economic gains of marrying (i.e., nonpaid domestic production) as well as the indirect financial economic gains of marrying (i.e., the marriage premium) are not as highly valued as the financial economic gains from marrying (i.e., increased income from paid market production). Further, the nonfinancial economic gains of marrying may be comparably less valued in modern times because most domestic services have been commoditized such that they can be purchased rather cheaply (and possibly, at higher quality) in the market (Greenwood, Seshadri, and Yorukoglu 2005).

The increased incentives of the dual-earner arrangement render the model to be more positively evaluated because it is perceived to be a voluntary rather than an imposed arrangement that is more financially advantageous than the male breadwinner model. I find that when the dual-earner arrangement is understood to be based on economic imperatives (as it was among most blacks in past generations and low-income people even to this day), the dual-earner model is not more positively evaluated compared to the traditional male breadwinner model. Not only is the dual-earner model then not perceived to be more financially advantageous, but it also is not perceived to result in more gender-egalitarian or spouse-compatible relations. Generally, a dual-earner model that is driven or results in economic deprivation is an arrangement associated with a marital union of gender insecurities (rather than gender egalitarianism), strife, and instability. As Liam, a black male generation Xer (born in 1968), explained in quoting Rudy Ray Moore, "Romance without finance is a damn nuisance."

Overall, I find that deracialized views about the degendered economic basis of marrying emerge among black sample participants (and white sample participants) of the later research generation, generation X. Generation Xers express the benefits for family women working from a deracialized framework whereby the financial benefits and economic imperatives to family women working are generalized and understood to be based on the shared socioeconomic context of the modern American economy. However, these benefits are classed in the sense that generation Xers across race perceive the benefits of the dual-earner to be based on a minimal economic threshold.

The modern economic marriage bar is generally set by a minimal level of earning power that secures a financially secure start and a gender-egalitarian foundation of a marriage that can persist across time. For generation Xers, education level is an indicator that couples can meet what I have characterized to be a higher and harder marriage bar. For many generation Xers, a college education becomes the indicator of such earning power and gender-egalitarian spousal relations.

The pooling of incomes across spouses is most attractive to generation Xers when considering a couple where the male and female are both high earners. This adds a different class perspective to the analysis of the meaning and advantages of the dual-earner model. Most prior research focuses on the attitudes and strategies of nonwhites and low-income whites pertaining to family women working (Easterlin 1978; Goldstone 1986; Watkins 1984; Edin and Nelson 2013). This research argues that blacks and low-income whites delay marrying or marry less because women and men of low socioeconomic status cannot meet the economic marriage bar. Due to the economic imperatives of their class position, low-income family women feel pressure to work since their male counterparts cannot meet the economic marriage bar set by the normative male breadwinner model.

However, I find that the positive evaluations of the central benefits to the dual-earner model compared to the normative male breadwinner model are at the high end of the income distribution, not at the low end. This finding on the classed basis of the deracialized phenomenon of family women working may explain why the decline in marrying has been sharpest for those at low end of the earnings distribution, while the college advantage in marrying emerged across gender in generation X (Espinoza 2013). The benefits of the dual-earner arrangement are not evaluated more positively than the benefits of the male breadwinner model when they are based on imposed economic imperatives or result in economic deprivation.

Rather, I find that the benefits of the dual-earner model are perceived as comparatively more advantageous to the traditional male breadwinner model only when the dual-earner model is premised on (1) a clearly more financially advantageous arrangement across gender, (2) a foundation for more gender-egalitarian spousal relations, (3) being a voluntary (rather than an imposed) arrangement, and (4) each person in the couple being financially self-sufficient (at least potentially). These conditions are generally only met when a couple, including the woman, has a high level of earning power. The conditions generally are not met for couples of lower socioeconomic status or where either the woman or man is of low socioeconomic status.

Due to the multiplier of the modern economic marriage bar being set based on the dual-earner model, couples of low earning power are much more disadvantaged in meeting the marriage bar compared to when the standard was set by the traditional economic marriage bar (based on the sole male breadwinner model). The gap between the new modern marriage bar (based on the dual-earner standard) and the earning power of low-income couples is wider than ever before in American history. Further, the gap is more persistent when considering that earning power is now generally based on an indicator that is more durable—that is, education level. While in the past the economic marriage bar was softer (based on the less durable status of employment) and lower (based on the male's sole earning power), the modern economic marriage bar prohibits marrying for more people and for longer periods of their life. Yet I find that it renders women's earning power as more positively associated with marrying across race in generation X.

The emergence of the dual-earner model as the typical household structure in the United States, along with the increasingly voluntary decision to maintain a dual-income household, fundamentally reconfigures its meaning. From being perceived as a negative and imposed household arrangement (as it was characterized in the past from a racialized framework), it is now perceived to be a positive and esteemed household arrangement under a deracialized framework. As white women entered the labor market en masse, their integration into paid work outside the home essentially normalized, and I argue deracialized, the traditionally stigmatized depiction of working family woman.

From a critical perspective, some politicians, scholars, and the media characterized black family women working as reflecting a pathological matriarchy. The departure from the white norm implied negative social consequences on the status of black men, black spousal relations, and the well-being of black children (Moynihan 1965). Despite that the black family was adapting to economic conditions that afflicted not only poor whites but also would soon affect American families across race and class, early family scholars privileged the male breadwinner model as the appropriate American household structure and male economic (financial) dominance as the basis of appropriate gender relations in the family.

Due to this reaction to black family women working, the earning power of black women was understood to have a negative effect on the probability of marrying, and it was assumed to help explain the racial disparities in the marrying patterns of black women marrying at a lower rate than whites. However, I argue that women's earning power does not have an inherently negative relation to marrying. Rather, the perception of the negative relation is due to the historical conditions in which blacks could not meet (let alone exceed) the financial standard set by the traditional economic marriage bar (based on the white sole male breadwinner model).

While I do find that women's economic independence and a degendered financial basis of marrying results in a delay in marrying, I find that black women's earning power has a more positive relation to the likelihood of marrying in generation X. Further, sample participants across race report attitudes about the dual-earner arrangement that are deracialized, more voluntary, and more positive in generation X compared to the baby boomer generation. Among baby boomers, the attitudes about women's earning power and marrying are racialized and based on what are perceived to be race-specific and nonideal economic imperatives.

Rather than facilitating the role of black women in both financially and domestically caretaking for their family or facilitating the role of black men (and broader society) in supporting black family women working, influential policy makers, scholars, and the media of the mid- to late twentieth century directed attention to what may now be argued to be failed attempts to make viable the sole male breadwinner model among blacks. The irony is that this perspective, and the related policy interventions that were recommended, was sustained during an era in which the sole male breadwinner model was coming to be perceived as no longer viable among Americans across race due to its inherent risks (e.g., due to increasing male joblessness and divorce) and it being comparatively less advantageous compared to the modern dual-earner model (due to women's increasing earning power). I consider this paradox to be reflective of an initial, and often overlooked, step toward what many scholars now refer to as the stalled revolution. The stalled revolution refers to men in American society generally refusing to make the social and individual adjustments to women's entry into the public sphere and paid labor market (Hochschild 2012).

The inadequate individual-level and society-wide adjustment to black family women working had the twofold effect of, firstly, neglecting to organize the social supports that black women might have utilized to more successfully balance their family and work roles and, secondly, discouraging (or at least failing to encourage) black men from assuming a more constructive role as a coearner and codomestic caretaker in the black family. The inadequate adjustment by men and broader society in response to white family women working is now increasingly critiqued by contemporary feminist and family scholars (Hochschild 2012). However, it is important to point out that the stalled revolution started much earlier with the inadequate social adjustment to the first waves of black women entering the labor market en masse.

Graph 5. Dual Earner Advantage Increases Moderately among Black Households

Source: Author's display of Current Population Survey (CPS) data. 2013 dollars.

Graph 6. Racial Gap in Relative Advantage of Household Structure

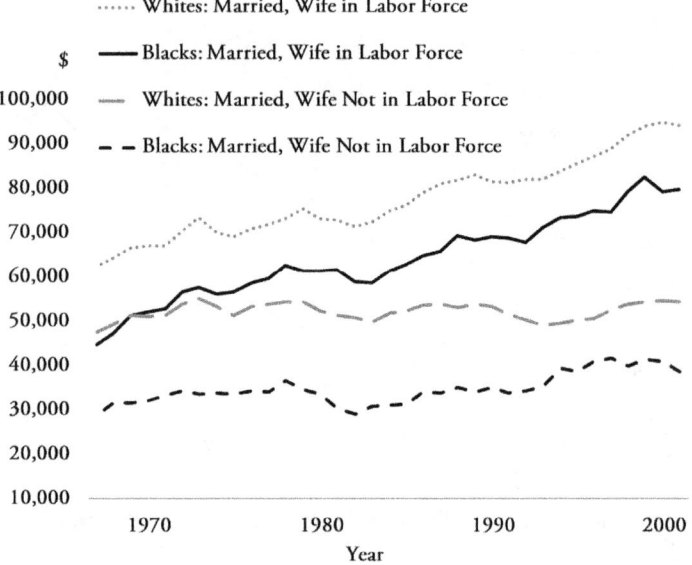

Source: Author's display of Current Population Survey (CPS) data.

Graph 7. Female Co-Providers Persist and Female Heads of Household Increase

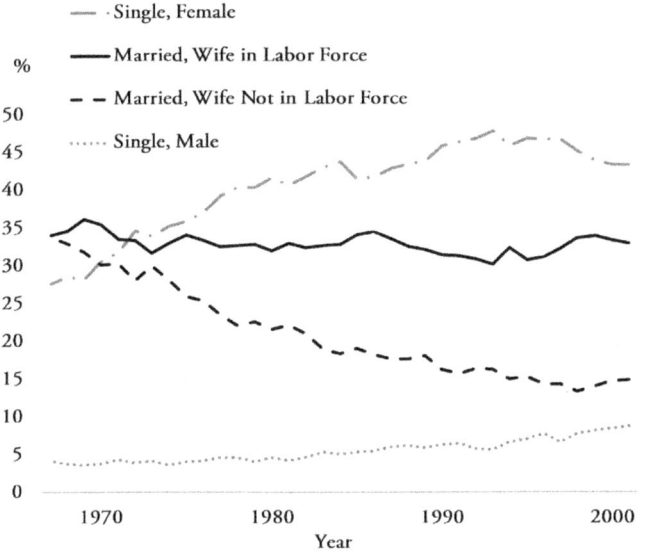

Type of Household Structure among Black Families
1970 - 2000

Source: Author's display of Current Population Survey (CPS) data.

5

Stalled Latinas, Lagged Patriarchy, and Dreams Deferred

Among Latinos of Mexican descent, the more traditional gender roles, higher rate of family formation, and patriarchal household structure have long been contrasted to the gender and family patterns of whites (Oropesa 1996; Vega 1990). While having a high level of family commitment has been lauded and held responsible for comparatively higher indicators of health and well-being among Mexican Americans (especially given their relatively low socioeconomic position), some scholars have criticized Latinos—as with blacks—for having family patterns deviant from white norms. Keefe (1984) wrote, "Mexican American extended families have been characterized as pathological and maladaptive in urban industrial society where the Anglo [nuclear family] norm is believed better suited" (p. 68). Per Oropesa (1996), this interpretation is generally due to a value-based explanation that collectivism and the culture of familism among Mexican Americans may limit individual achievement and/or stall the emergence of gender-equal relations in these families.

There is no consensus as to whether the cultural argument of familism is expected to be a temporary or permanent feature of the analysis of Mexican American families and marrying behavior. According to Landale and Oropesa (2004), the percent that remain never married by age twenty-five is lowest among native-born Mexican Americans (64.0) compared to blacks (83.6) and whites (67.7). The pattern by immigrant generation shows that Mexican Americans from the third immigrant generation and beyond have marrying patterns nearer to blacks and whites than to foreign-born or second-immigrant generation Mexicans (Oropesa and Landale 2004).

Some scholars argue that cultural effects weaken across immigrant generations due to greater exposure to the white social context and the process of assimilation to US mainstream norms (Sabogal et al. 1987; Valenzuela and Dornbusch 1994). During the mid-twentieth century, several studies found change among Mexican Americans toward more gender-egalitarian attitudes and a household structure more similar to the patterns of whites. Miller and Swanson (1958) found that the responses from Mexican Americans regarding gendered household roles were similar to "typical Americans." Further, Grebler et al. (1970) found that younger Mexican Americans and those of higher socioeconomic status show low levels of traditional patriarchal attitudes.

Yet others argue that the nearness of the United States to the Mexican border and the continual replenishing of Mexican immigrants to the United States may provide a persistent traditional cultural influence by Mexican-origin coethnics. Per this perspective, the "replenishing of ethnicity" preserves traditional marrying values and the traditional household structure among Mexican Americans (Mirandé 1977; Jiménez 2010). However, from a racialized assimilation viewpoint, it also may be that Mexican Americans continue distinct behavioral patterns if segregation and/or discrimination serve as structural barriers to Mexican Americans being exposed and influenced by dominant (i.e., white) society (Golash-Boza and Darity 2008).

It is important to note that part of the critique of the literature on Mexican-origin families is that some of the focus on patriarchy and familism is overly generalized and static. Studies show that major demographic shifts are occurring in Mexico and throughout Latin America (Landale and Oropesa 2007). This calls into question the determinedness of traditional Hispanic culture on gender roles, family formation, and household structure. Some studies question the very merit of the original characterization at all (Ybarra 1982 and Zavella 1984). They cite that among Mexican Americans, like other groups, economics conditions (not cultural forces) drive women's labor force participation and gender egalitarianism in the household.

For example, Oscar Lewis (1975) made the inference that a more gender-egalitarian spousal relation may be related to women's financial contribution to the household. Based on one of his five case studies of Mexican families (in Mexico), he noted that "the Gutierrez family comes closer to an equality of status and power between husband and wife than any of the other families, and significantly this is the only one in which the wife is a major economic support of the family" (p. 18). Others made this inference about Mexican-descent Latinos in the United States. Citing congruence with the findings of another study of Chicana women by Beatriz Pesquera (1985), Lamphere et al. (1993) found that "a wife's shift to mainstay provider—especially among Hispanos[18]—leads to a more equitable division of housework, with a few men performing even more household and child-care chores than their wives."

More recent studies document the dynamic nature and increasingly symbolic or weakening role of culturally prescribed male dominance in the Mexican American family. Pinto and Coltrane (2008) found that in regard to household structure, "Mexican immigrant and Mexican American families respond to practical concerns like time constraints and relative resources rather than automatically responding to normative [traditional] cultural pressures" (p. 493). Other studies have also found that the maintenance of the male patriarchal ideal is contested with the broadly experienced rise in the dual-earner household structure (Zinn 1982; Zavella 1987). Both decision-making and housework are more so shared in Mexican American dual-earner households than in Mexican American traditional male breadwinner families (Ybarra 1982; Zinn 1980; Zavella 1987).

Going further, I would argue that based on higher rates of male employment and lower levels of women's earning power, there may be weaker economic imperatives and weaker financial advantages of the dual-earner model among Latinos. As discussed in prior chapters, black and white family women

---

18 The term *Hispanos* is a New Mexico–specific concept that generally refers to nonimmigrant Latinos of Spanish and Mexican descent. Most of the *Hispanos* that participated in the study by Lamphere et al. (1993) are monolingual English speakers (p. 13, 21–23).

increasingly entered the labor market based on women's own growing earning power and due to the increasingly evident financial precariousness of the male as the financial provider in the household. Generally, Latinas have lower earning power than white women and black women (see graph 8). Thus, the financial gains of the dual-earner model compared to the traditional male breadwinner model are lower among Latinos than whites and blacks. Further, historically, Latino men have higher labor force participation rates than black men and white men (see graph 9). Latinos also have lower rates of divorce than blacks and whites (Kreider and Ellis 2011). Thus, the level of financial insecurity of the male breadwinner model due to male joblessness or divorce is lower among Latinos.

Latinos have a weaker exposure to the economic forces that facilitate the transition from a traditionally gendered to a degendered economic basis of marrying compared to whites and blacks. This may explain the lower prevalence of the dual-earner model among Latino married households compared to white or black married households (see graph 11). Furthermore, Latinos report less positive attitudes about the relation between women's earning power and marrying in generation X. Latinos have not yet faced the economic imperatives that pushed blacks, or the economic incentives that later pulled whites and more blacks, into a degendered economic basis of marrying (i.e., where earning power is positively evaluated in relation to marrying for both men and women).

Yet the dual-earner model and a degendered economic basis of marrying emerge albeit to a lesser degree among Latinos in generation X due to social imperatives. They still face a relatively higher and harder marriage bar as well as the social pressures of achieving more gender-egalitarian spousal relationships. It seems that the social forces and normative effects related to the widespread emergence of the dual-earner model in generation X explain why even Latinas' earning power is more positively evaluated in relation to marrying among Latinos. Like white women and black women, Latinas negatively evaluate the shortcomings of the male breadwinner model, but this is more so in relation to concerns about gender inequalities in the household. Further, the social imperative of keeping up with the higher and harder marriage bar set by the modern dual-earner standard also has an influence in terms of women's earning power becoming more important to Latino families in meeting inflated modern household standards.

As an overview, the types of forces I find to be underlying both the motivation of family women working and the (positive or negative) evaluation of women's earning power in relation to marrying are (1) economic imperatives (due to perception of the financial precariousness of men's earning power, family women *must* work), (2) economic incentives (due to perception of the financial advantages garnered by women's higher earning power, family women *should* work), (3) social imperatives (due to the perception of a relatively higher and harder marriage bar, family women *must* work), and (4) social incentives (due to new social norms of gender egalitarianism, family women *should* work). Conceptually, I distinguish these types of economic and social forces between imperatives and incentives. I consider imperatives to be generally negative forces that mandate family women to work as an involuntary and, thus, generally negatively evaluated arrangement. I consider incentives to be generally positive forces that make the arrangement of family women working to be perceived as a voluntary arrangement and, thus, generally evaluated positively.

This framework helps explain why Latinos report lower economic pressures and incentives for family women to work outside the home. Latino men have relatively higher rates of employment, and Latinas have relatively lower earning power. These underlying forces can explain why Mexican American households can be characterized as experiencing lagged patriarchy. They continue to value the male breadwinner model since the dual-earner model is not necessarily more financially advantageous than the traditional male breadwinner model. Latino families thus have experienced stalled change in terms of Latinos more slowly or more weakly transitioning to a degendered economic basis of marrying. Latinos more positively evaluate women's earning power in relation to marrying in generation X (as compared to baby boomers), but the transition is weaker when compared to the transition among whites and blacks of generation X. Essentially, the effect of social forces driving the shift to dual-earner households and more gender-equal relations in the family is weaker among Latinos compared to the combined package of social and economic forces that underlie the positive evaluation of women's earning power in the family among blacks and whites.

Recent literature and the interviews I analyze in this book suggest that the often still-highlighted forces of traditional Mexican culture are not so strong as to circumvent in perpetuity the broader societal-level forces that have transformed even the white patriarchal breadwinner household structure to a more gender-egalitarian household in the United States. In the subsequent sections of this chapter, I examine the effects of the emergence during generation X of the new package of economic and social forces that underlie the motivations and evaluations of family women working in the era of modern marriage in America.

As the dual-earner model has become widespread in the modern era, Mexican Americans also more positively evaluate the relation between women's earning power to marrying. However, the shift is more moderate than the shifts I find among whites, because the earning power of Latinas has not increased on par to the earning power of white (or black) women. It follows then that I find more gender conflict and economic disadvantage among Mexican American households.

With the stalled economic advances among Latinas and lagged patriarchy among Latino households, Mexican Americans are not yet situated to adequately adjust to the modern era of marriage. Latino men are not as well positioned to view favorably the modern degendered economic basis of marrying due to the lower financial advantages of Latina family women working (based on Latinas' relatively lower earning power). Further, Latinos are disproportionately burdened by the higher and harder marriage bar (based on the lower earning power of not only Latinas but also of Hispanic men).

BABY BOOMERS: THE SOCIAL BASIS OF MONEY AND HOUSEHOLD ECONOMICS

Among both baby boomers and generation Xers, Mexican Americans are especially critical of their experiences with authoritative patriarchy during childhood. Many Mexican Americans report observing a traditional gender ideology and a male-dominant sexual division of labor in their parental household. As with other baby boomers, Latinos in the baby boomer generation attribute the traditional gender ideas and practices of their parents to be based on broader American social imperatives. However, unlike whites, they do not perceive the traditional male breadwinner model to be one that results in a positively evaluated ideal for family life.

Across the two US generations, I find positive evaluations of women's earning power in relation to marrying to be formed based on negative experiences with gender inequality in the parental household. However, Mexican Americans do not express that there are inadequacies of the male breadwinner model, or that there are new advantages to the dual-earner model, primarily based on economic considerations, as other generation Xers in the sample do. That is, they do not reference a greater insecurity of men's earning power or the greater financial advantages of women's earning power as underlying their attitudes about traditional (or modern) gender ideology. I find a degendering in the economic basis of marrying with women's and men's earning power being positively evaluated in relation to marrying due to more social rather than economic considerations.

For example, Emma is a Mexican American female baby boomer born in 1954. Both her native-born Mexican American parents have low levels of education (less than a high school degree). She was raised Catholic in a small town in the Southwest. Emma married later in life at age fifty, and she has no children. She connects her decision to prioritize her education and delay marrying to wanting to avoid a gender unequal marital union. She explains this is in turn directly influenced by the gendered experiences she had in her parents' household. Further, despite her general preference to marry a Latino man, she married a man who is not Latino (her husband is white). She felt as though she could not find a compatible Latino man who appreciated her educational and career achievements. Emma and her husband both worked in paid employment in the first year of marriage, and now she contributes about half to the household income.

Emma's most negative perceptions about the traditional male breadwinner model stem from the unequal gender relations in the household she observed among her parents. She said,

> My father was very authoritarian. My mother was very submissive. It was a very traditional kind of marriage…My dad was the breadwinner most of their married life. My mother brought in minimal income even when she went to work. My father used the fact that he made so much more money than [my mom] did. I think he used it as a manipulative tool…I just remember…my dad turned to my mother, and he said, "Well, you make, you make three cents to every dollar I make." And I just thought that was so cruel and insensitive.

Like other baby boomers (and generation Xers), Emma saw the traditional sexual division of labor as conferring limited or no freedom to her mother. She continued,

> I don't think my mother had a choice with anything, even, you know, the paint in a room hardly...I don't think she had any choices with anything that she did with her life or anything around her, us, anything...I don't think she had any choices at all...I just remember one time...her saying something like, "I just want to know what is it that I do that's worth doing," or something like that. Like she had no, no idea that [she brought value]...Even to this day, I don't think that she has any idea of the value that she has.

Emma was not explicitly socialized by her parents to reject the male breadwinner model, but the negative experiences she had in a patriarchal household discouraged her from reproducing a traditional household structure or mimicking her mother's patterns regarding marriage and family. Emma said, "So I determined that I was not going to have a relationship like [my parents'] and I was not going to be under somebody's thumb...I wanted a voice and a choice in things that affected me."

Emma pursued higher education and achieved a successful career despite that she perceives her parents did not support her academic or professional accomplishments due to their own traditional gender ideology. She explained,

> For me, the expectation for myself was that I should complete an education and thereby a job would eventually present itself. I had no financial support and no expectation from my parents that I should

complete college. However, my brothers were expected to be the breadwinners and were expected to learn a skill. Why? My parents were traditional and conservative...They took [my brother] to different universities so that he could go check them out, whereas not with me. They didn't do any of that...and even just small things, not just in education. I mean, he learned to drive before I did...I was a year older; I should have been able to drive before him...I don't think they were even aware of...those preferences, those prejudices... what I think of as misogyny really...I don't think they thought about a woman working. I think it was just assumed, you know, I would be at home making babies, I guess.

Though Emma's parents encouraged only her brothers' educational ambitions (and not Emma's), her educational goals were inspired by historical changes in newly expanded opportunities for women in terms of education and enjoying life in the public sphere. Emma said,

I firmly believe that women need to have a skill and education before marrying. Without an education, women make themselves vulnerable to men and a society that already has misogynistic tendencies. Beyond vulnerability, being able to support oneself when [there is a] loss of a job, loss of a husband, or sickness is smart and wise. Additionally, an education opens up horizons, widens opportunities, and enhances one's life. I received an education primarily to support myself, but also to have an adventurous life, to travel, to attain some measure of wealth, to experience the arts...essentially to have a better life.

Emma also connects her value of education to her father not being able to go to school. She recounted,

[My father] wanted to finish school, but he was the eldest of his family, and he had to, um, leave school. Well, two things: there were no schools where they lived, beyond eighth grade...It wasn't required to go to school until...Actually, it was Kennedy in the '60s really, when it was, you know, you had to go to school till you were sixteen years old. Before then it wasn't required. And so he ended up having to leave school. Well, as I said, two things—there were no schools, but he could have gone to school [downtown] had there been money, but there was no money, and he had...to help support his brothers and sisters. He had to help his mom and dad. So for him education was really, really important for us. He pushed that throughout our schooling. But when it came to women and me in particular, you know, it wasn't expected.

Like other baby boomers, Emma also sees economic risks in the male breadwinner model, but she does not attribute this to widespread precariousness in the economy (as I show is reported among many generation Xers). Rather, Emma cited concerns about the risks of divorce and death. She said,

> [The male breadwinner model] has a lot of disadvantages. [A woman] I think exposes herself to a lot of vulnerabilities…I think [women] put themselves at a disadvantage if they, um, if they don't complete an education [before marrying]. Um…[the husband] could die. He could, you know, want a divorce…She could want a divorce, whatever, but you know if they have children, she's the one that's often left with the children to raise them. She would be at a disadvantage. Women in general lose substantial wealth at divorces and even at the death of their spouses if they don't have an education.

Lela, another Mexican American female baby boomer (born in 1955), also shared that she made choices in her own life in order to be different than her mother. Both her Mexican American parents are native born, and neither graduated high school. Lela and her family religiously identify as Protestant (Christian). Lela married at thirty-eight years old and has two children. Like Emma, she married someone who is not Latino (her husband is white), and Lela has worked outside the home throughout the marriage.

Lela described her mother's position in the household and the spousal relations between her parents in a very negative way, but she is not certain that the experiences in her parental home are related to her decision to marry later in life. She said,

> My mother sort of worked in between children and catering...[My parents'] whole social norms were different [than now]...They stayed together all their lives, but my mom didn't have much of a network outside the home. You know, she had family, but my father had lots of things he could do outside the home...My mother stayed home almost all the time, you know, because she had children. And my father was a little freer to be out doing things. So I think that created some...some friction with them and, um, just challenges in the relationship.

Lela continued,

> I don't know that I'd [have] consciously said that I'm not going to get married, but because I was focusing on my career—education and career—I just [hadn't] found somebody that I thought I could live with for the rest of my life. It's possible that in the back of my mind I was thinking I don't want to get anywhere near a relationship like my parents had...I thought my mother had a horrible life. You know...we had a large family, so she spent all her time raising kids...You know, she just wasn't ever able to do much of what she wanted to do

because of family. She sacrificed everything for the family.

Her responses indicate that Lela developed strong feelings about the importance of establishing her own earning power in terms of having an education and a career (before marrying) based on her deep concerns about having a more gender-egalitarian relationship than her parents'. She said, "It was important to me as a woman to have my own education and career. I wanted to be independent of a husband for my own support. This was both social and financial; I saw how hard it was for my mother to be dependent on a husband." Lela added, "I wanted an equal relationship."

Joseph, a male Mexican American baby boomer born in 1960, also spoke about his family and parental household as providing a model he wanted to avoid. Both his native-born Mexican American parents attended some college, but neither completed a college degree. Joseph identifies as Protestant (Christian), but his family religiously identifies as Catholic. Joseph married at twenty-eight years old and has two children. He is still married. Like Emma and Lela, Joseph married someone who is not Latino (his wife is white), and they formed a dual-earner household. In the first year of marriage, and now, Joseph contributes more than half to the household income, but his wife also works. Like many of the Mexican Americans I interviewed, Joseph also reported negative perceptions about the gender relations in his childhood household, and more specifically, he particularly regrets the position and treatment of his mother in the family. He said,

I think almost everything about my family is what I didn't want my family to be…is pretty much the bottom line. In terms of my immediate family… there are no good models there. Everything that I learned was I don't want to be like my immediate family, which is a good lesson too. Um, you know, I wanted to be a father that was going to be there in the home, that provided stability and hopefully treat my wife with respect…My mom…she did the best she could do, you know, and I'll always love her and respect her for that. So if there's a model, it's, you know, [my mother], somebody who gave her life for her family. She did the best that she could do, and [she] didn't become what she wanted to because of her family, her commitment to her children.

In contrast, Ava, a female Mexican American baby boomer born in 1954, did not recall a gender-unequal relationship in her parents' marriage, which is reflected in her continued idealized perceptions of the male breadwinner role and positive (or, at least, not negative) perceptions about gender asymmetry in the household. Ava is the only Latina who did not report negative memories about her parents' spousal relationships or how she felt treated in her household as a woman. Both her Mexican American parents were native born. Her mother studied some college, and her father completed a college degree. Ava has no religious identification, but her family religiously identifies as Catholic. Ava married and divorced at age twenty-eight and does not have any children. Like Emma, Lela, and Joseph, she married someone who is not Latino (her ex-husband is white). Though Ava was employed part time when she married, the parents of Ava's spouse actually financially supported her and her husband in their less-than-one-year marriage.

Ava described her own parents in the following way:

> My dad had a lot of drive. He was a very bright man. He went on to the Maritime Academy, became a captain of the ships, and he was a successful man. My mother, in her own way, she didn't have the drive that he had. She was more concerned with being beautiful and lounging around.

In Ava's case, like Madison's—a white baby boomer whose parents' marriage was also based on a very much romanticized version of the male breadwinner model—Ava's mother fit the description of the very beautiful glamour girl of the mid-twentieth century (Parsons 1943). The daughters did not see their respective mothers treated in a negative manner, and they did not observe any negative consequences of the traditional gender roles in their childhood. Both Ava and Madison perceive the gender differences in their childhood families to be voluntary—based on the individual preferences of their mothers and fathers. As a source of esteemed value (and, thus, power), it may be that a woman's beauty softens the effects of the gender inequality that typically is associated with the traditional sexual division of labor. However, in both cases of Madison and Ava, the "beautiful" mothers also had at least some college.

Despite that Ava did not report personally having negative perceptions about the traditional household model of her parental household, she reported there to be some economic insecurities of the male breadwinner model in case of marital dissolution or death. She said in regard to it being important for a woman to gain an education [before marrying], it's so "she can survive quite well without [the husband], should they divorce, should the marriage fall apart, should he die." Thus, for Ava, she too thought it important to pursue an education before marrying. Possibly because her parents' spousal relationship and ideology was socially (though not financially) more gender egalitarian, Ava's educational pursuits were also encouraged by her parents. Ava said,

> I considered education my most important goal... Education was the key to a successful career, which I wanted more than anything. Also I was very interested in academics and learning about literature, science, arts, and the law. This was instilled in me at a young age.

Even when there are not negative experiences associated with the male breadwinner model due to unequal gender relationships or men's increasing precariousness in the labor market, Mexican American sample participants report that there are concerning financial risks (beyond the relationship risks) of the male breadwinner model. The now widespread perception of the risk of divorce and the perception of the ever-present chance of death makes women who experienced positive personal experiences with the model still weary of the prospects for a stable and secure traditional male breadwinner household. Yet I find that these concerns about financial risks are not as deeply felt or evaluated as negatively as those who hold negative experiences of gender unequal relationships or who experienced the financial breakdown of the male breadwinner model personally.

I find that having personally faced one's own father experience extended bouts of joblessness, death, and divorce or having personally observed unequal gender relations in the parental household more directly and more deeply discourages the internalization of the male breadwinner norm as an ideal. Sample participants who report having experienced these circumstances express such conditions to be a primary motivator in coming to evaluate women's earning power as positively related to marrying. For those with these experiences in the parental household, a women's acquisition of a minimal level of earning power is a prerequisite for being considered ready to marry. Further, Mexican Americans generally value women's earning power as a basis for establishing more gender-egalitarian spousal relationships.

GENERATION X: MODERN CRITIQUES OF LAGGED PATRIARCHY

In generation X, Mexican Americans report more negative views about their experiences of patriarchy in their parental household and more positive views about the relation between women's earning power and marrying. Because they perceive shifts in broader society toward more gender-egalitarian households, Mexican American sample participants in generation X report being even more averse to their experiences of unequal gender relations in laggard Latino households that maintain traditional authoritarian and patriarchal structures. Indeed, Mexican American women in generation X more explicitly report delaying marriage in order to avoid such arrangements.

Generation X Latinos who have highly salient negative memories of gender inequalities in their childhood households purposely seek gender-egalitarian relationships as adults. Being disinclined to enter a male-dominant household structure, many I interviewed report preferring to stay single for an indeterminable period than to replicate the gender-unequal households of their childhoods. The data suggest that Latinos may seek interracial (Latino and non-Latino) marriages due to concerns that a Latino spouse may uphold traditional gender ideology.

However, in generation X, there are more cases where Mexican Americans have not experienced a traditional household structure based on either a sole male breadwinner model or a household with the husband/father as the dominant (but not sole) earner. Some Mexican Americans of generation X report growing up in gender-egalitarian dual-earner households. These sample participants report more positive views about the relation between women's earning power and marrying based on the greater financial advantages of having two earners in the household.

Alex is a Mexican American generation Xer born in 1973. Both his parents are native-born Mexican Americans, and each completed a bachelor's degree. Since his birth, both his parents were regularly employed, and he considers his family to be middle class. Married, his parents never divorced, but they did have a one-year separation when Alex was sixteen years old (and then his parents reconciled and remained married until his father's death). Alex does not have a religious affiliation. He considers his political views to be moderate.

At age forty, Alex has never been married. He did not report any negative experiences with observing unequal gender relations in his parents' household. Rather, he reported that the high cost of living has eroded his ideals about the traditional male breadwinner model. He perceives that his positive views about the dual-earner model are shared among other Latinos of his generation. Alex said,

> I would say, among my friends, at least, um, and even the ones that I know now, and thinking back to the ones that I've had, going back to the time of when people started getting married, I guess, um, most of the time they wanted that dual income. I mean, that was kind of a big thing, especially nowadays with the economy tanking, you know, and jobs are harder to get, um, I think a dual income is [needed]…I almost feel like there's a shift going away from that line of thinking…with the old traditional Hispanic role of the mom being able to stay at home, cook, clean…I mean…that might still exist, and I'm sure it does, but I think it's probably going away quickly. Um, and that's all relative, I mean, I guess I should say, because I can think of one…person back in my childhood that had that, one or two people that were like that, where the mom stayed at home. Nowadays…I have

a hard time trying to think of somebody now that the female, uh, Hispanic or not, stays home and does nothing but clean. Well, does the housework, I should say, stay-at-home-type mom. Um, everybody I know works.

Alex evaluated these changes positively as a change that Hispanic women and men alike embrace:

> I think the women's attitude is a good thing that they think that working is a good thing. Um, because I know even…a couple of my friends, I think they had the female spouse say, uh, they may have said at one point…their mom was kind of the…not maybe a complete 100 percent stay-at-home-type mom, but they were more the type that they would do the cooking, do the laundry. Maybe they weren't working full time. They worked part time. Um, when the…when there would be a get-together, all the ladies would be in the kitchen. The guys would be out in the back barbecuing, drinking beer, um, so there was that kind of traditional separation there, but nowadays, I mean, like I said, my friend…the two people I could think of, they were both like, "Well, my mom was kind of like that, but I'd never be like that. Screw that. I'm going to be a bread earner too, you know, and God knows we need it because stuff is just so expensive these days."
>
> So…I guess in my experience and from the people that I know, uh, yeah, that's a dying breed of person

who is the mom that…or the dying breed of family, I should say, is the mom that stays home and is just a house mom…I'm trying to think of any stubborn Hispanics that I know that would disagree, but, um, even the most…even the person that I would think of as a more traditional Hispanic person would probably want the mom working, the spouse working, and he would probably agree that the money is more important than that traditional role, I guess.

Alex connects the economic pressure to afford what he perceives to be higher costs of family life to his ideas that he and any potential spouse should have comparable incomes and a stable basis of earning power before marrying. Alex said,

Stable full-time job implies I have completed schooling, current education goals. If I can't feel confident supporting myself, I have no business trying to support a wife/family…Spouse should be at least at a stable/steady point in their life. [My personal philosophy] is marry within your own salary range.

The theme that potential spouses should be at the same level in terms of earning power is reported across gender in generation X. Furthermore, the data suggest that Mexican American women may increasingly be having experiences with men who are not financially stable or who have relatively lower earning power. This is a perspective that is not reported among Mexican American baby boomers. Carmen, a Mexican American generation Xer (born in 1977), wrote,

I do not want to be anyone's sugar mama. I do not want to stress/worry about living pay check to pay check, but rather enjoy each other comfortably. I want to feel cared for as well, but not by obligation ever. I don't want to ever be used either. I want to be as equal as possible but compliment/appreciate each other's strengths and build off those together. I am not a good cook, but I don't mind trying. My job requires much of my time so I hope he would understand…I think many men may want to earn more than his woman, but I am indifferent. I just want him to make consistent money at least above $75,000 per year. I don't want to struggle with anyone…I want to just be comfortable, not rich. I enjoy traveling and helping others, family so I'd want to do [and afford] this.

Like Alex, Carmen grew up in what she considers to be a middle-class home. Both her native-born Mexican American parents completed a bachelor's degree. However, her father was the primary breadwinner, and her parents maintained a traditional sexual division of labor, where her mother was the primary homemaker. The mother balanced working in the family restaurant with her primary responsibility of taking care of the children. Carmen and her family religiously identify as Catholic. At age thirty-seven, Carmen has never been married and she has no children.

In generation X, as with the baby boomer generation, Mexican Americans who observe the traditional sexual division of labor in their parental household associate traditional household structure with great (and regretful) sacrifices by their mothers. For example, Carmen described the case of her own mother and how it affected her attitudes about marrying:

> When [my mother] finished [college], she was like, "Oh, I'm going to be able to go to law school, maybe," and my grandparents were like, "No, what are you thinking? You're going to take over [the family's] restaurant." And [my mother] was, her life was shattered. But because she had already had two daughters, and she was pregnant with me, um, she thought, well, let me do this for my family. Because both my grandparents and my father were, like, "What are you thinking?...You have two daughters, and you have one on the way, and the restaurant's here. And you can bring the kids to the restaurant. And why would you want to do that...go to school and get in debt? Go to law school?"...Um, so whenever my mom tells the stories, it makes me so sad...I'm sad for her because...I wouldn't have wanted her to do that.

Carmen's parents eventually divorced, and Carmen observed the lack of marital fulfillment in her parents' home even before the divorce. She continued,

> My parents got divorced when I was in high school. So [my dad] wasn't really—he wasn't much in the picture at all much. So when he finally—when [the divorce] finally happened in my junior year, senior year of high school, I didn't really see him ever again after that much. Like, maybe once a year...I'm like, "Why did you marry

him?" [My mother and I] had a conversation like that. She was like, "You know, I wanted to get out of the house." I'm like, "So you married somebody?" Like, what—that sounds so crazy. And she's like, she, she couldn't explain it. But then she remarried. So, um, both my parents had, ah, multiple affairs on each other. And we saw that, too, the children. So, you know, they got married. They stayed married because of us, but really that was still an injustice to us daughters. Because we saw them with other people.

Though her parents did not directly discourage her to marry, the conflict Carmen observed in the household formed very strong negative memories in her mind. Carmen internalized the tensions of her parental household and developed pessimistic ideas about the high level of risk that marriage holds due to the mistrust that characterized her parents' relationship. Carmen reflected on this in the following way:

Dealing with a divorce, I think, was a pivotal, a big thing in my life. Um, because at that point, after that, I really didn't want to be in any relationship. I didn't trust any men, and—and I still have issues today… Um, but so, when it comes to relationships, I'm pretty pessimistic…I know that stems back from not having a really healthy male figure besides my grandfather.

When I asked Carmen why she feels her generation has delayed marriage, she responded,

> I think it's definitely a generational thing. I don't know if I can really pinpoint it as a historical moment for my generation. I think it, it's more so, um, like even in this, my department here in this office…We're all in our thirties, and we're all single. And I don't think—I know we've had multiple conversations about this kind of stuff, and we really don't pinpoint it to a, like a civil rights or a historical thing. But I think seeing our own peers, like, not rushing into marriage…I think it's more a personal experience. [For example,] I didn't want to depend on anybody, and then have to be in the situation to feel trapped in a relationship…because I couldn't make my own money.

Yet Carmen still wants to get married, and much so based on the incentives of the dual-earner marriage. She said,

> It would be so great to have an additional income, not have to worry about [paying the rent alone], well…maybe I need a roommate. But I do want to get married…A perfect scenario would be a man… who already has a kid, and I don't have to pop one out of my body, and I can help raise a kid. And we have both incomes, and we both graduated. For me, that's perfect.

Part of her statement can be explained by Carmen learning a few years ago she cannot have children. She continued,

I was going to freeze my eggs, and we then discovered that my eggs were not healthy…I know I'm not able to have children now. But I'm okay with that.

For Carmen, her fears about entering the wrong kind of marriage or the dim prospects for a stable marriage disrupted her ability to form the type of romantic relationship that might lead to marriage and motherhood. She said she "sabotages healthy relationships" due to the mistrust of men she formed based on observations of her parents' marriage. She prefers to stay single than to enter a union that might be like that of her parents or one in which she is not financially self-sufficient (in case the union dissolves). Thus, Carmen has adjusted to alternative life options that she must consider as her delay in marrying is apparently indeterminate (e.g., she thinks maybe she'll just get a roommate; she reports that she's okay with not bearing children).

Like Carmen, other Mexican American women would rather stay single than enter a marriage that might dissolve when they are financially unready or that might be based on unequal gender relations (either because the women is dependent on the man or, even, because the man is dependent on the woman). Graciela is a Mexican American female generation Xer born in 1976. Graciela was born in the United States. She religiously identifies as Catholic. At age thirty-three, she has never been married and has no children. She has cohabited with a boyfriend before, but at the time of the interview she was not living with a romantic partner. Both Graciela's parents, who never completed high school, were born in Mexico. Never divorcing, her parents' marriage remained intact. Nevertheless, Graciela reported pessimistic views about the stability and security of the traditional male breadwinner model. In discussing the male breadwinner research vignette I use during interviews, she said,

> I think it'd just be hard for them both just having one sole income earner. It can be, I would say, problematic in the future, I guess, with some kind of resentment towards her. I mean, I don't know what her…like what would her contributions be to the relationship? Then, too, well, if it weren't to work…Like if they get married, if it wasn't going to work out, then how is she going to be able to stand up on her feet? I don't know if she'll form some kind of dependency on [the husband] and, uh, and I think for her the big thing is for her to be financially independent…I mean I guess that'd just be a disadvantage for her, like, will she be able to stand on her two feet if something were…if it weren't going to work out?

Carmen continued,

> I think it's very important for [a woman] to be financially independent…You can't be depending on a man to support you…because if things don't work out…I don't know—I feel like marriage is like…I don't know—I just have, like, this view of marriage, like it just wouldn't work out just because of my… of, you know, what I'm surrounded with, but no, it's

just I feel, yeah, that [a woman] should be able to be financially independent.

As an indicator of her undergoing transformative socialization in the parental household, Graciela's family did not encourage her to get married, though her own parents were married. Graciela reported,

> Once I got older, [my mother] just told me don't ever get married. [She said,] "Don't do it. You don't have to get married to be happy"…Well, I understand it from that aspect because, one, my sister, and then, two, my mom had a rough marriage. I mean, it was rough. It was…uh, my dad wasn't…My dad, I mean, yeah, he's a laborer, but he was also a big alcoholic, uh, abusive alcoholic throughout my younger years…I think that in a sense I'm cautious…I feel like if I were to get married, I want to make sure that it's…if I do it, I want it to work out. I don't want it to be a failure because I see what my sister's [and my mom's] gone through…I'm just definitely more cautious about it. Like even with my family, like my aunts…A lot of them have been single moms. And my mom…my sister, too, was a single mom, but, you know…a lot of them are divorced or a lot of them…you know about infidelities.
>
> So I don't know…In a sense, like I'm very cautious about [marrying]…I think the only thing that I do remember [about my parents' marriage] was just the bad things, and they always kind of like argued and,

yeah, it was very chaotic. And like as far as with us, I mean, my mom only talked to us, like we didn't really have much interaction with my dad...He was the sole breadwinner there, and he, uh...I guess he, uh...he was just able to provide us with the things that we needed, like material things, but as far as like emotional support and whatnot, he didn't do that. We didn't...[interact]. I guess that's still...that's still with me, I suppose.

Though Graciela considers her family growing up to be lower middle class, it is the observation of her parents' abusive relationship, which included infidelities, as well as her observations of divorce and single motherhood that cautions her from entering a marriage unless she is financially self-sufficient. She prefers to stay single rather than enter into a gender unequal union. This is partly due to advice from her mother and family of the prior generation discouraging her from marrying due to their own negative experiences while married.

I characterize Graciela's case as rejecting the traditional male breadwinner model and traditional gender ideology due to social considerations because she is primarily concerned about achieving her generation's now normative standards of gender-egalitarian relations rather than being primarily concerned with the financial advantages of the new economics of modern marriage or due to the economic pressures of a higher and harder marriage bar. Of course, her being able to wait for a suitable prospective spouse who may offer her a more gender-egalitarian relationship has an economic basis. That is, women's higher earning power allows them to wait. However, her decision about delaying marrying is not fundamentally based on the modern financial gains of marrying. Rather, the decision is due to the expected social gains of marrying based on the dual-earner model and earning power across gender—that is, she wants to wait it out until she feels confident she can establish a more gender-egalitarian and more stable marriage than that of her parents'.

As another illustrative case, Robert is a male Mexican American generation Xer born in 1974. Both his native-born Mexican American parents completed college. Each parent worked regularly when he was growing up, and their marriage remained intact without any bouts of separation. He and his family religiously identify as Catholic. At thirty-nine, he has never been married and has no children. Robert has cohabited with a girlfriend before, but at the time of the interview he was not living with a romantic partner. His responses demonstrate that the social basis of marrying and the new economic basis of marrying do not alter the presumption that a male's economic readiness is part of the modern expectations of marrying among Mexican American generation Xers.

Robert reported financial readiness to be the most important thing for him to have set before marrying for himself. For his potential spouse, he thinks it's most important for the person to be in love with him. He said,

> If I were to ever marry, the ability to provide for my family would be the very most important factor in getting married. I would not want to fail as a man or loved one, especially if children were involved.

However, in regard to his potential spouse, Robert responded,

> I would need to feel that I was loved or needed as a partner in a relationship to want to marry someone... Being in love would be the most important to me. I've seen divorce in my family [outside my own parents], and I can't see marrying anyone for any other reason other than love or being in love with someone.

As with sample participants from other racial groups, Robert reported highly valuing romantic love as a basis of marrying, but Robert also thinks he must be established as a successful provider prior to marrying. Yet he also supports that family women work to earn income for the household and to establish more gender-egalitarian relations. He links his views about marrying and gender roles with the negative experiences of gender inequality in his parental household despite that both his parents were college educated. He said,

> My mother was a schoolteacher, and she only taught when my father allowed her to go back and teach. So there were times when he wanted my mother to stay home with my sister and I [sic] to make sure we grew up and she was there. There were times when she wanted to go teach, and we were older, but my father said no, you need to stay at home...It was definitely negative...He was the successful domineering type, and my mother, even though she was educated, she

really didn't have much say, and I think she felt less of a woman, I think. Because she couldn't do what she wanted to do. It was a very dominant relationship…He often took it out on her…You know, he would belittle her…verbally and physically. But more so, it was more mental abuse. He would remind her that he was more successful than she. But she was just as successful—she just couldn't work. She couldn't do what she wanted to do because he told her to stay at home.

He added,

> [My dad] was very macho. He said, you know, don't just have one girlfriend, have several. And then my mom would come in and say, don't listen to your father, and I didn't really. I haven't spoken to my dad in ten years, and we don't have a very good relationship. But a lot of those things really were about his upbringing or trying to raise me as a son to be a man. And then the way that my mother wanted to raise me, so it was very conflicting…I think [my dad] always felt like the man should be the shot caller, somebody that is the dominant one. You know, he always told me that it just wasn't possible to have one sexual partner.
>
> Mind you, I'm a teenager; I'm like a preteen, teenager hearing all of this, so I'm just trying to process all this information. I was like, is this really how it's supposed to be, and then my mom would pull me aside and tell me don't listen to your father,

that's not how it's supposed to be...She would just say that's not how you're supposed to treat a woman. You know, you're not supposed to treat somebody like that. You're supposed to treat them with respect. You're supposed to honor them. If you're in a relationship, you're in a relationship; you're in a committed relationship.

But my dad always joked...and I always had girlfriends, like I would be in a committed relationship with one girl, and my dad...he would almost be disappointed in me. He would say, you know what are you doing? And that's...I knew right from wrong, because I saw what my dad did to my mother. You know the infidelities and everything growing up.

Though the cases of Graciela and Robert are very different, gender inequalities in the parental household were similarly perceived as very negative and influential to their later attitudes as adults about marrying. Though Robert is male, he felt empathy and rejected the negative treatment of his mother by his father, just as Graciela did with her father. In both cases, the mother instructed the child not to replicate the type of gender-unequal relationship that was experienced in the parental home. Again, we see an illustration of transformative socialization where at least one, if not more, members of the prior generations directly instruct and often indirectly influence (by modeling negative experiences) the successive generation's departure from traditional gender roles (despite that those traditional gender roles were practiced by the parental generation).

For Sara, a Mexican American generation Xer born in 1967, she stressed the importance of financial readiness across gender. Divorced, her father had vocational training while her mother completed high school. Married, Sara said what was most important to her to have set before marrying was being financially self-sufficient. Sara said it's important to be

> established financially and [have] a strong sense of trust. Growing up, we always had some sense of financial stress. I thought that when I'd get married, I would be both self-sufficient financially and my spouse would be too. In addition, I viewed marriage as a partnership of equals—in love, yes, but also able to contribute equally to the household. I wasn't going to get married until I was financially secure and had completed my educational goals. I didn't want to depend on anyone.

Like other Mexican American sample participants, she was very much affected by negative experiences of gender inequality in her own family. She reported,

> [My] dad graduated with a little bit of, um, not college, but he went to the army, and they did technical training, so he got certified as a sort of an electronic technician. Um, mom got high school, um, but he didn't want her to go [further]…She wanted to do some community college, but he wanted her to stay and watch the three of us…She told me later. I asked because I…Later on when I was in college, I

asked her about college because I knew she was really smart…and she said, "Well, it's because your dad always wanted me to…I tried going to [community college]. I took a class, but he said it was interrupting dinner being ready on time and the kids and all this stuff," so he was very traditional about the role of the woman and my mom.

Sara noted,

[Father] thought [my mom's] biggest value was to stay home and take care of the three of us…No, I never heard it from him, never heard it from him. She told me later on, yeah, and they divorced, also. Um, so I would say that…my parents' marriage is probably most like that, and also why I believe so strongly that, um, you don't…you don't, especially women, shouldn't depend on anyone, right? You shouldn't allow yourself to be in a position…Not that my mom put herself in that position, but the fact that when they got divorced and we were left with very little, um, and she didn't have all…you know, a degree—she had high school but she didn't have much more than that—that we very much struggled.

We thought we were middle class when they were married, and then when they got divorced, we really felt like we had dropped to like working [class]…You know, just we felt it a lot more. Uh, we didn't have help. We didn't have a babysitter. We didn't have someone to come and clean once in a while. Um, we were doing all of it ourselves, and so, you know, we went from shopping at Kmart to shopping at the secondhand store. You know, you sort of…things changed…The divorce was…I was thirteen. I was very…cognizant on what was going on, and I always felt, you know, that personally I'm never going to…allow myself to be in the position of having to depend on someone financially, and that was always my goal…[My] drive is just to be financially secure.

Sara's grandmother, a widow, actually, would always tell Sara not to marry. Sara recalled, "I remember [my grandmother] saying, 'No te cases. Ten muchos novios. No te cases.'" ("Don't marry. Have lots of boyfriends. Don't marry.") Her other family members also discouraged her from following in her mother's footsteps. Sara continued,

> I had a couple of uncles, both on my dad's and my mom's side, that always said, you know, uh, make it on your own, you know, don't rely on a man, you know, those kinds of messages. I think all of them resonated with what was happening to my mom, you know, who had relied so much on my dad, and my dad telling her, "No, no, don't go to community college. I need you to be at home."…And then, you know, then he divorced [her]…They get divorced, and then she was sort of at a huge disadvantage.

Sara's observations of her parents during her childhood were deeply impactful. She reported,

> My dad was extremely unfaithful, and so there were all these levels and layers of not trusting men that I grew up with and dealt with, with boyfriends that I always suspected were cheating, and so that was a good enough reason for me to hold off, too…Mom told me about [the infidelity] and Dad was gone a lot on Friday nights and Saturday nights and would come home late.

Like the other Mexican Americans I interviewed, Sara's case in terms of the primary basis of her rejecting the traditional male breadwinner model and traditional gender ideology is due to the same social considerations of wanting to avoid a gender-unequal marital union. She associates becoming financially set before marrying more so as a basis to establish an equal standing in the marriage and to be ready in case the marriage dissolves. She does not perceive the male breadwinner model to be a gender-egalitarian arrangement. Because of the mistrust she developed by observing the infidelities and a divorce in her parental household, she distrusts that a marriage of her own is likely to last.

I find that among Mexican Americans I interviewed, negative experiences regarding gender inequalities in the parental household and the related negative treatment of their mothers (e.g., belittlement, infidelity, or gender-unbalanced family sacrifices) influenced Latinos to perceive the male breadwinner model to be inadequate. In this way, social concerns about gender relations rather than economic concerns about the financial advantages of alternative household models are shown to be most salient in motivating Mexican American generation Xers to reject the traditional male breadwinner ideal and traditional gender ideology.

With great esteem toward their mothers' functions in the households, men and women—the sons and daughters—negatively evaluate the damaging effects of authoritarian patriarchy associated with the traditional sexual division of labor. In this way, the traditional values of familism (highly valuing family roles, including the mother's role) conflict with the traditional male breadwinner model in a way the results in nontraditional patterns of family formation in the successive generation (that is, the children delay marriage and/or enter dual-earner arrangements in order to avoid the model established by their parents).

Fearing a woman is vulnerable to misogyny and inept to face potential abandonment without an adequate level of gender parity and self-sufficiency in terms of earning power, the Latinos I interviewed rejected the male breadwinner ideal that involves a women being financially dependent on a man. Mexican Americans positively evaluate a women's earning power in relation to marrying as a way to better balance the gendered basis of financial power in the household. Further, a women's earning power is a means of insurance that she, with her children, may be able to be self-sufficient, if necessary, due to marital dissolution.

From this perspective, Mexican Americans are not necessarily redefining the male's traditional role in the household due to observed failure of a man being able to be an adequate sole provider (as we observed among blacks). Conversely, Mexican Americans are not necessarily redefining the female's traditional role in the household due to the much greater gains of a woman with higher earning power working outside the household (as we observed among whites). Yet as we saw with whites and blacks, there is an indication that Mexican Americans feel that the dual-earner household model allows families to meet a higher and harder marriage bar and the accompanying higher standard of living that is now broadly sought by Americans.

Among Mexican Americans, there is a distinctly more salient concern for gender equality as driving the reports of positive attitudes about the relation between women's earning power and marrying. That is, for the Latinos I interviewed, there is a more social basis (the negative evaluation of unequal gender relations) that explains the shift from the traditional male breadwinner ideal to the modern dual-earner ideal. The social basis of the transition from traditional gender ideology (about the sexual division of labor) to more egalitarian gender ideology among Mexican Americans is in contrast to the primarily economic basis for the same transition among whites and blacks.

Generally speaking, whites in generation X see the greater relative advantages of the modern dual-earner model due to white women's higher earning power, while blacks across the two generations see the economic imperative of the dual-earner model due to black men's unstable or lower earning power. Further, the social basis of concern for gender inequality in the household is not as frequently reported among white and black generation Xers compared to Mexican American generation Xers. Due to the profound changes toward gender egalitarianism in the private sphere—that is, in the homes of many whites and blacks—it is not as common that black and white generation Xers experience the magnitude of unequal gender relations that Mexican American generation Xers experienced while growing up. For more whites and blacks, their mothers—and in some cases grandmothers—had already entered the labor market and had already established more gender-equal relations in the family.

Conversely, though it is not found to be primary, the economic basis of the male breadwinner model being perceived as an inadequate model is reported among Mexican Americans of generation X. Some Mexican Americans I interviewed share the perception that the US economy is more precarious in general and that a women's earnings are increasingly important to help households achieve the higher modern standard of living. As mentioned, however, the economic incentives or benefits appear to be secondary or less important than the more deeply held concerns about women's unequal position. For many Mexican Americans, the negatively evaluated social concerns about the male breadwinner model (i.e., gender inequalities) are more salient relative to the economic concerns (i.e., men's employment precariousness and the higher economic marriage bar).

Yet it is possible, as Mexican American men face more fragile employment conditions due to broader economic forces and Mexican American women make greater strides in narrowing gender and ethnoracial disparities in the labor market, that the economic disadvantages of the traditional male breadwinner model and the economic advantages of the dual-earner model will become more apparent to Latinos. For example, some explain that Latinos have historically had higher rates of employment due to a lower reservation wage (Landale and Oropesa 2007). Yet if native-born Latinos, including Mexican Americans, adopt a reservation wage on par with native-born blacks and whites, or if more recent Latino immigrants have even lower reservation wages, then native-born Mexican American men may start to face more unstable employment patterns and the effects of harsher business cycles, as was observed during the 2007–2009 Great Recession (Kochhar, Espinoza, and Hinze-Pifer 2010).

On the other hand, as Latina women become higher earners, the financial advantages of the dual-earner model might become more apparent among Mexican Americans. This would then, to Mexican Americans, make more evident the financial disadvantages of the traditional male breadwinner model and also make more evident the financial advantages of the dual-earner model. Thus, successive generations of Mexican Americans may perceive the male breadwinner model to be neither viable nor the best alternative form of household structure due to increasingly economic rather than social reasons. This suggests that in the future there may be an even closer trend of convergence in gender ideology and household structure across race and ethnicity as economic conditions more closely converge across race and ethnicity in the United States.

Graph 8. Income Levels Low among Latinos and Lowest Among Latina Females

Relative Individual Income as Percent of White Male Income, 1980 – 2000

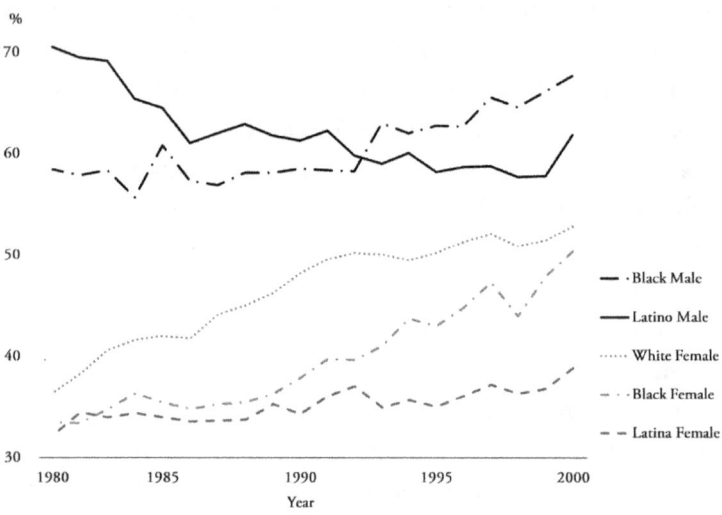

Source: Author's display of Current Population Survey (CPS) data.

Graph 9. Relatively High Employment Levels among Latino Males

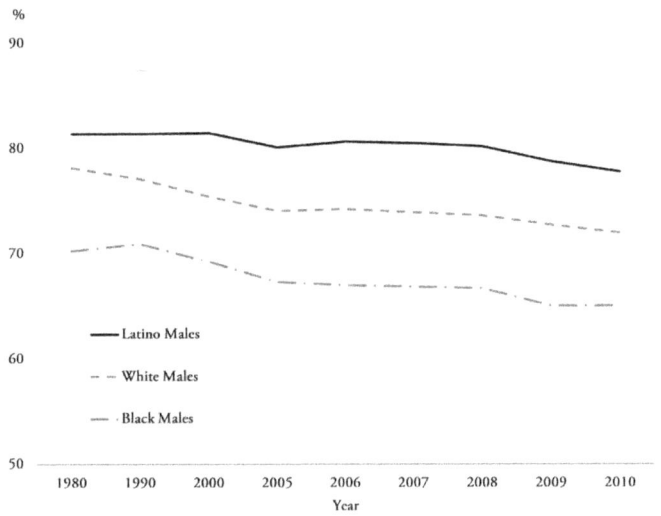

Source: Author's display of Current Population Survey (CPS) data.

Graph 10. Relatively Low Employment Levels among Latina Females

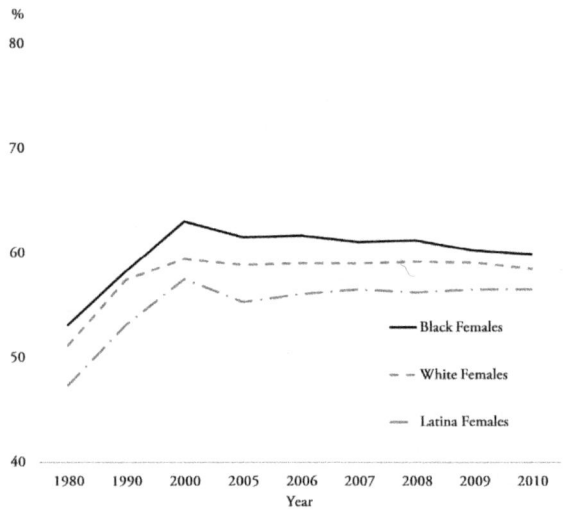

Labor Force Participation Rates of Women by Race, 1980 - 2010

Source: Author's display of Current Population Survey (CPS) data.

Graph 11. Decline in Traditional Model of Marriage among Latinos

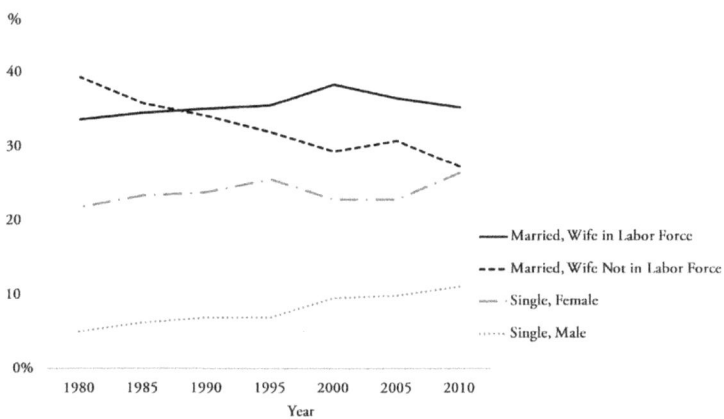

Type of Household Structure
among Latino Families, 1980 – 2000

Source: Author's display of Current Population Survey (CPS) data.

Graph 12. Gap in Relative Advantage of Household Structure, Latinos and Whites

Median Income by Traditional Male Breadwinner Versus Modem Dual-Earner Models, 1980 – 2010

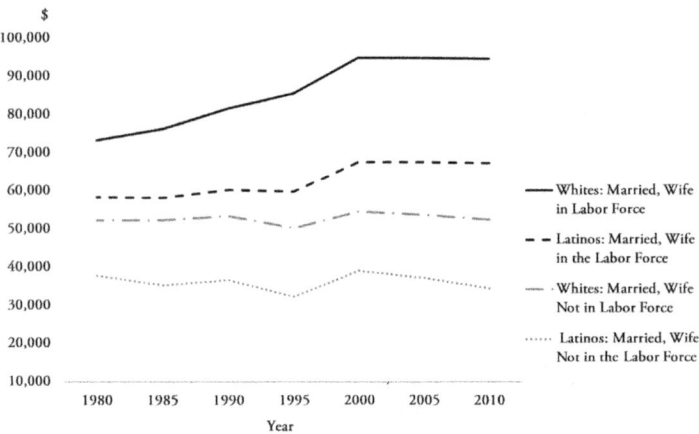

Source: Author's display of Current Population Survey (CPS) data

6

ECONOMIC RESTRUCTURING AND MARRYING ACROSS THE BUSINESS CYCLE

In this research study, I collect data after one of the most severe recessions since the Great Depression, the Great Recession. Therefore, in this chapter, I conduct an analysis of the relation between earning power and marrying across recent recessions to inform how my findings might be affected by the economic context and specific period of the study. Since the mid-twentieth century, there have been deep shocks in the business cycle in the United States. Over this same period, we have seen changes in the historically gendered structure of the labor market and an increase in the proportion of dual-earner households. While there is much scholarly attention on how these profound shifts in the macroeconomy have affected the labor market and economic status of males disproportionately, the changing context of work and marrying brings serious challenges in new and more complex ways to families and the larger segment of female workers.

Based on the empirical analysis of this chapter, I find that the business cycle does not account for distinct marrying patterns in recession compared to nonrecession periods, but the probability of marrying is observed to be higher in the Great Recession compared to the nonrecession years of the 2000s. I find the effect of women's earning power on marrying during a recession to be ambiguous, with the effect of having a college degree and the effect of earnings to not be statistically more positive in the Great Recession compared to the nonrecession years of the 2000s. I interpret these findings further in the discussion section of this chapter. The findings suggest that my overall study of attitudes about the relation between women's earning power and marrying does not necessarily reflect attitudes distinct to the recession event prior to the period in which I conducted the study.

BACKGROUND

For this analysis, I take the most recent nonrecession period in the data as the baseline reference (the years 2004–2007 and 2010). I make a comparison between the pattern of marrying in this period to the nonrecession period at the start of the observation period (1983–1989) and the adjacent recession periods of the Great Recession (2008–2009) and the early 2000s recession (2001–2003). I then examine the changes in the relation between earning power and marrying across these periods. By examining recession and nonrecession ("period") effects on recent marrying patterns, I demonstrate how the economic determinants of marrying may be changing in the contemporary gender regime of the postindustrial economy across the business cycle.

I analyze the period effects interacted with micro-level earning power to examine whether these periods—each with distinct macroeconomic conditions—have effects on the microeconomic determinants of marrying. The observation period covers pivotal transitions in the structure of the labor market and business cycle. I control for the national unemployment rate among males, an underlying historical (linear) time trend and personal time (age). I consider not only that the United States has transitioned to a regime of more gender-equal levels of earning power and labor force participation, but also that the nation has simultaneously experienced profound male-specific as well as gender-shared economic shocks.

In the modern era of more gender-equal earning power, the benefits of the dual-earner household can make entry into marriage especially more attractive (and viable) given the instability of the macroeconomy. The increased security dimension of the dual-earner model might be particularly appealing to someone who has experienced economic setbacks due to job loss or underemployment (as would be more likely experienced during a weak labor market). Underlying the testing of whether a recession period may affect the outcome of ever marrying, I theorize that the context of a recession may induce a generalized sense of economic insecurity irrespective of an actually experienced job loss or other personally experienced losses. (I cannot test individual employment status directly because appropriate variables are not available in the data.)

Per Groshen and Potter (2003), the structural component of total employment across recessions has increased from 51 percent during the early 1980s to 79 percent in the early twenty-first century. The United States has experienced "jobless" recoveries from economic downturns since the 1990s, with permanent job losses in certain sectors of the economy (Gordon and Baily 1993; Groshen and

Potter 2003; Bernanke 2009; and Berger 2012). Further, there have been multiple sources of deep economic shocks with concurrent crises in the housing market, banking, and finance.[19] The foregoing motivates the first part of my research question: Does the increasing severity of the structural component of economic downturns in the United States result in an increasingly negative or positive relation between recession period and marrying at the macro-level?

At the micro-level, the focus of this chapter's analysis is to examine whether the relation between women's earning power and marrying emerges as increasingly positive across the recession periods. The observed 1978–2010 time frame involves the transition to most women serving a wage-earner role in the household across education levels (Fry and Cohn 2011). As discussed in previous chapters, in the 1970s there was a shift in American social attitudes away from the presumptive norm that (white, middle-class) women take on the traditional housewife role. After the 1970s there was broad public support and a widespread expectation that women (across the class distribution and race) work in the labor market irrespective of family status as a wife and/or mother (Cherlin 1980; Spitze and Huber 1980).

With the apparently persistent negative impacts of recurrent macroeconomic downturns, I would argue that it might be expected that both men and women would adjust to the experience and observation of the increasingly

---

[19] For example, the effects of the Great Recession are often characterized as being particularly profound not only due to prolonged unemployment but due to the recession being simultaneous to deep housing market, banking, and financial crises (Gascon 2009).

apparent financial insecurities of the sole male breadwinner model. I test whether in the United States there has been an adjustment to such economic uncertainty whereas, on balance, individuals increasingly marry more so based on the gains of the dual-earner model (Oppenheimer 1988, 1997) than the specialization model of household structure (Becker 1973, 1974, 1981) with each successive recession. Given women's mass entry into the labor market and a trend toward more gender-equal earning power, there is growing potential for a woman to make household consumption higher and more secure as a second earner in the household. I expect to observe in this analysis that a woman's earning power has an increasingly positive relation to marrying across the observation period.

Based on the available data, I analyze individual earning power (via the proxies of education level and earnings), distinct recession/nonrecession periods, and interactions between the two as indicators of the modern macro- and microeconomic determinants of marrying. I theorize about whether the observed patterns more so support the modern perspective of household economics that contemporary marriage is increasingly a strategy pursued based on the gains to pooling resources and social insurance versus the specialization perspective that marriage is a strategy pursued based on the gains to establishing an earner and nonearner exchange in the household (traditionally, the male breadwinner model).

This chapter's analysis starts with the recessions of the 1980s because the data is available starting in 1978. However, this is an appropriate period to study because it covers the era after American women had entered the labor market en masse, irrespective of family status (Oppenheimer 1982 and Bureau of Labor Statistics 2008). The observed time frame involves a much more gender-egalitarian US regime of work and family—a period when for the first time in history the typical American married household is based on the dual-earner model. Most mothers and most wives were working in the labor market across the three largest US ethnoracial groups of whites, blacks, and Latinos by 1978 (Hayghe 1981).

Amid the more gender-egalitarian norms and arrangements of work and family, each postindustrial US recession has unique contextual factors. The early 1980s (1980–1982) recession period involved a double-dip recession that included the 1980 recession and the 1981–1982 recession. The first recession dip was marked by a decline in consumer credit and personal consumption, while the second recession dip involved some banking panics and, subsequently, the infamous savings and loan crisis (Bordo and Haubrich 2012).

The early 1990s recession (1990–1991) was the first postindustrial recession dubbed a "jobless recovery" (Groshen and Potter 2003). This was accompanied by a credit crunch and a minor housing bust. Yet after less than two years, the 1991–1992 recovery had strong employment growth, and the early 1990s recession was followed by the longest economic expansion of the late twentieth century (Bordo and Haubrich 2010). In addition, the 1990s is a notable time period for gendered changes in work and family because it was the context of a dramatic and publically contentious welfare reform campaign, which resulted in welfare-to-work mandates to compel non-self-sufficient women with children into the labor market and an end of public assistance to children and families as a grant entitlement (Bane 1994; Loprest et al. 2000).

The early 2000s recession (2001–2003) was a more moderate economic downturn, and following the "tech boom," the dip was initially accompanied by a somewhat tight labor market (Bordo and Haubrich 2012). Still, the recession at the turn of the century was notable in the predominance of permanent job losses over temporary layoffs. Most recovery jobs were due to new jobs in different firms and industries rather than rehires. Economists point to this recovery as representing the emergent pattern of permanent restructuring in production as a result of economic shocks (Groshen and Potter 2003).

Fortin (2009) finds that, after accounting for life-cycle and cohort effects, full-time labor force participation since the 1980s peaked and then started a slight decline in the 2000s. She finds the decline to be sharper for women than for men—a finding that Fortin conjectures may imply an increase of women "opting out" of the labor force in the first decade of the new century.[20] However, this also was the first postwelfare reform recession and a recession subsequent to the dot-com bubble. Given the likely gender-uneven effects of the tech "bust" and any effects specific to the new welfare context, I would argue

---

20 It is important to note that Fortin (2009) and Blau, Ferber, and Winkler (2006) argue that women's labor-force participation is in recent times only slightly and increasing less so driven by a husband's actual income or employment prospects. Other extensions of my research (upon access to appropriate data) would be to test whether women's marrying behavior is increasingly based on the national unemployment rate of women and women's own employment status during a recession.

that additional research is necessary to understand the gendered relations between changes in labor force participation across the income distribution during this time.

Proceeding to the Great Recession (2008–2009), the steep fall in home prices and rise in home foreclosures were unique in magnitude (Gascon 2009). Per Bordo and Haubrich (2012), the most recent economic downturn was the only post–World War II recession accompanied by the trifecta of a banking crisis, stock market crash, and housing bust. Unusually sluggish, the recovery involved an increase in economic growth but with continued high unemployment and high home foreclosure rates (Roubini 2009). Job losses continued after the official NBER-determined end of the Great Recession in 2009 until February 2010 (Goodman, Christopher, and Mance 2011).

This chapter's analysis explores the empirical evidence for two competing hypotheses about the relation between recession periods and marrying. The classical hypothesis is that recessions have the effect of reducing the economic readiness for and economic gains of marrying (due to lower earning power). As the counter perspective, however, Shore (2009) argues there may be an increase in familistic behavior during a recession. If so, the data may show that Americans are increasingly more likely to marry during the recession. Following more modern economic theory on marriage, it is argued that pooling resources and risk via marriage may emerge as a coping strategy during a recession. Thus, I would argue further that women's earning power should become more positive during a recession.

Alternatively, it may be that these two forces operate simultaneously. If so, then the effect of a recession may be ambiguous.

That is, some may pursue marriage more so (as a strategy of social insurance) while others less so (due to lower economic prospects). If a decline in marrying is not observed or if there is an increase in the likelihood of marrying during a recession, then I would argue that this at least suggests that the modern economic approach to marriage may balance or even drive more so the relation between recession periods and marrying (this then would counter the classical hypothesis that there is a negative relation between recession periods and marrying).

In this chapter's analysis, I endeavor to advance the understanding of the macro-micro link of the economics of family formation. I explore the macro- and microeconomic determinants of marrying across increasingly structural economic downturns in the United States, which occurred amid women's increasing earning power. Per prior research, I expect to find a linear time (calendar year) trend of declining entry into marriage, a quadratic age effect of entry into marriage increasing and then decreasing over the life cycle, and a negative linear relation between the national unemployment rate of males and the probability of marriage. Here, the national unemployment rate among males speaks to the theory that changes in the decline in marrying are driven by shifts in male employment.

My focus is on capturing the distinct contextual effects of each recession/nonrecession period. I am interested in looking at the generalized context and social marker of the recession period as an indicator that may relate to specific ways in how individuals may respond to weak macroeconomic conditions in particular periods. I use distinct recession periods as not only being recognized markers of downturns in production but also as generalized indicators of the broader economic changes during each recession, such as the market conditions across banking, finance, and housing.

As a new contribution to the literature, the focus of my research is on testing the hypothesis that as the structural component of the downturn in the business cycle becomes more dominant and as concurrent contextual shocks become stronger, the effect of a recession on marrying might become more salient. I test whether the direction of this change might be negative or, alternatively, emerge as positive given the potential of marriage to act as a form of social insurance. Secondly, I test the proposed hypothesis that women's earning power should become increasingly positive in relation to marrying during each consecutive recession (as women have entered the labor market en masse). I operationalize earning power with proxies for education level and earnings.

I focus on individuals of the ages fifteen to thirty-five in order to observe the decision to marry from the initial life stage of adolescence when individuals begin to marry (legally and by custom) and across the transition from being a youth to adulthood. Further, the period and age range examined herein are important because it is during the Great Recession that for the first time there were more US adults aged twenty-five to thirty-five that were never married than ever married (Mather and Lavery 2010).

DATA

The data set for this chapter's analysis is based on merged data from the Census Bureau's Survey of Income and Program Participation (SIPP) survey and confidential lifetime earnings data from the Social Security Administration

(SSA). The public-use version of this data is the SIPP Synthetic Beta (SSB) data product.[21] The restricted-use data I use in this chapter's analysis is the SIPP Gold Standard File (GSF), Version 6.0. These data are produced as a project of the US Census Bureau in collaboration with the SSA and the IRS.

The merge of the survey and administrative data is based on protected identification keys (PIKs). These are anonymous person-level identification numbers assigned by the US Census Bureau's Person Validation System (PVS) using person-level data such as a verified social security number and date of birth. The survey data and sample persons included are from the 1984, 1990, 1991, 1992, 1993, 1996, 2001, 2004, and 2008 SIPP panels. Because this is an analysis that focuses on period effects and includes the recent Great Recession (controlling for age), at each age I observe the full range of calendar years (1978–2010) but not the full range of birth cohorts (1943–1995).[22]

The marital, education, women's fertility, and earnings data is collected across a person's life history. The data on gender, race, marriage, education, and women's fertility are from the SIPP. The SIPP life-history data are mostly retrospective except for the years in which the respondent was in the SIPP panel. The unemployment-rates data are from

---

21 The US Census Bureau uses a synthetic data procedure based on Rubin (1987) to make this data publicly available.

22 Since a person may be observed for only a partial segment of the age range, the data is unbalanced at the person level (each person has a different number of person-year observations). However, the event-history data structure accommodates right censoring, and only persons who have never married prior to observation or at first observation are observed (i.e., left censoring is addressed using each person's available marital life history).

the Bureau of Labor Statistics (BLS), and the recession period indicators (by year) are guided by the official recession determinations made by the National Bureau of Economic Research (NBER).

DESCRIPTIVE STATISTICS

For the analysis, I only include native-born whites, blacks, and Latinos because my theoretical framework is focused on the US socioeconomic context.[23] Never-married sample persons are observed from age fifteen up to first marriage or up to age thirty-five if never observed to have married by the end of the analytic period (year 2010). Based on the constructed event-history data structure, the large person-year level sample includes 932,567 person-year observations of women and 967,914 person-year observations of men (see tables 1 and 2).[24]

By race, 78.0 percent of these observations are among whites, 14.7 percent are among blacks, and 7.3 percent are among Latinos. In the distribution by highest educational level, 24.5 percent of these observations are among those with less than a high school degree, 23.9 percent are among those with high school degree, 28.9 percent are among those with some college, and 22.7 percent are among those with a bachelor's degree or higher.

At the person level, the sample includes 266,482 persons, of which 137,263 are women and 129,219 are men (see table

---

[23] National origin is not available in the data, so I use the pan-ethnic variable for Hispanic/Latino.

[24] The case and full series of person records for any respondent who died during the fifteen to thirty-five age range of analytic observation were dropped prior to the analysis.

2). By race, 80.8 percent of the sample persons are white, 12.2 percent are black, and 6.9 percent are Latino. For highest educational level, 24.9 percent of the sample persons had less than a high school degree, 26.2 percent had a high school degree, 28.5 percent had some college, and 20.4 percent had a bachelor's degree or higher.

METHODS

I conduct the analysis of event-history data using a discrete-time hazard model for first marriage as a single, non-repeatable event. Here, the dependent variable is a binary (0/1) for the outcome of first marriage. My approach accommodates the use of time-varying and time-constant predictors as well as right censoring (the event may not occur within the observation period). Modeling for a conditional probability, I observe individuals transition from the state of being never married to the state of being ever married. With the analysis over the age range of fifteen to thirty-five years old, I specify the baseline hazard to be an age quadratic function.

For the entry variable of marrying, I code the outcome as 0 for being never married and 1 for when a person becomes married for the first time. That is, across person-year observations, the event outcome variable for marrying is equal to zero for all sample person years prior to first marriage and equal to one for the person-year observation when the sample person first marries. All person-year observations for the ever-married sample persons are omitted subsequent to the first observation of having married.

In event-history analysis, there is generally a concern about dependence within the person-year observations of persons and unobserved heterogeneity between persons (Allison 1982, 1995 and Yamaguchi 1991). For the first concern, I make adjustments for the grouped data with standard error adjustments (I use robust standard errors for clustering at the person level). Further, the use of period indicators addresses the temporal dependence of observations within persons. I also use person weights that take into account sample design. My approach is then not compatible to the tests for unobserved person-level characteristics using random-intercept (random effects) or fixed-effects models. I report the results based on ordinary logit models in the subsequent sections.[25]

In equation 1, I represent a simplified form of the equation for the ordinary logit model.[26] Here, β is the row vector of observed time-varying (and time-constant) regression coefficients and $\alpha(t)$ is a function of personal time (age). The conditional distribution of the outcome variable is Bernoulli, with probability following a standard logistic regression model.

---

[25] Per Allison and Christakis (2000), problems can arise in fixed-effects logistic regression to discrete-time event-history data with nonrepeated events. The random-intercept model is also not generally a superior approach to the ordinary logit model for discrete-time event-history data with nonrepeated events. Further, this alternative procedure is not permitted when using person weights. Thus, I do not apply these methods to address person-level heterogeneity.

[26] Here, I do not provide distinct notation for time-constant or time-invariant covariates for the sake of simplicity. Final working model with a quadratic time function for the baseline hazard is described in the subsequent text.

$$\text{logit}(\pi_{it}) = \alpha(t) + x'_{it}\beta \tag{1}$$

In the first step, I use separate models by gender to regress the log odds[27] of first marriage with each recession/nonrecession period and highest education level as a proxy for earning power (see tables 3 and 4). I also report the results for the person-level proxies for earning power interacted with each period (see tables 5 and 6). In the second step of the analysis, I replicate the analysis with the interactions between earning power and each period using gender-separate models for college-educated persons with logged annual earnings as a proxy for earning power (table 7).[28]

In the reported logit models, I use a uniform set of control variables. I regress the log odds of first marriage on the concurrent national unemployment rate of males; the age quadratic function; a linear trend for calendar year; three-category race (black, Latino, and with white as the baseline group); four-category educational levels (less than a high school degree, a high school degree, some college, and with a bachelor's degree or more as the baseline group); an in-school indicator (with not being in school as the baseline group); and, for women only, an indicator for motherhood (with not having ever had a child as the baseline group). As mentioned, the measure of the underlying event-history

---

27 The odds of marrying at the observed time is the ratio of the probability of marrying to the probability of not marrying at that time (given that marriage has not already occurred prior to that time).

28 Due to concern for reverse causation, I tested lagged and nonlagged variables for motherhood, being in school, and earnings. I find consistent results and maintain the nonlagged variables due to concern for the bias that misspecified lagged variables may induce.

time function is each year of progressive age. Following my prior work (Espinoza 2013), I employ the quadratic function for age.[29] Prior research has also established that a quadratic in age best captures the expected diminishing increase in the probability of first marriage across age (Hernes 1972). The age quadratic is interacted with education level to accommodate that marrying behavior may follow different life-course patterns for the different education groups.

I use eight-category recession/nonrecession periods. There are four distinct nonrecession periods (in the late 1970s, 1980s, and 1990s, with the 2000s aggregated nonrecession years as the reference). These are in addition to the four distinct recession periods (the early 1980s recession, early 1990s recession, early 2000s recession, and the Great Recession). I examine interaction terms between each period and microlevel proxies for earning power to test my hypothesis that the effects of earning power on marrying are conditional to period-specific effects and, more specifically, US recession period.

As controls, the models I present include two time-invariant covariates (black and Latino) and six time-varying covariates (unemployment rate for males, calendar year, recession period, and being in school). For women only (due to the available data), I include an additional time-varying covariate (motherhood). In the first step of the analysis, I focus on the

---

29 I tested the performance of age indicators and linear, quadratic, and cubic spline age functions. The age quadratic and cubic spline age functions are about equivalent in fit to each other yet superior in fit to age indicators or a linear transformation. I use the quadratic function for simplicity and to follow prior work.

analysis of the time-constant variable for a person's highest education level.

In the second step, I focus on the time-varying logged variable for individual-level annual earnings. In the data, the dollar unit for the earnings variable is converted from nominal dollars to 2010 real dollars using the Consumer Price Index for Urban Consumers, Research Series (CPI-U-RS). Earnings data are from IRS form W-2 and SSA self-employment records, and they include employee contributions to deferred compensation plans. I use the log of the variable for annual earnings due to the positive skewness in the distribution of that variable (zero earnings are recoded to one).

I test both lagged and nonlagged earnings as predictors. I report the findings from the model for nonlagged earnings based on the preference to use nonlagged predictors, unless the time lag is clearly appropriate and superior. Prior research suggests careful and cautious use of lagged predictors (De Boef and Keele 2008). Under my theoretical framework, I consider the logged earnings in the year of marriage to be an adequate indicator.

Though I test the conventional procedure, one-year lagged earnings may not be a superior option. On the one hand, I assume a person makes the decision to marry based on anticipated earning power once married. In the case of an unanticipated earnings shock in the year of marriage (e.g., an involuntary job loss), capturing this is the approach I take to test how earning power in a recession affects the likelihood of marrying. However, I would pursue comparing alternative earnings specifications (e.g., lagged non-recession-year earnings, average earnings, or earnings quintiles) as well as pursuing alternative methods to better address concerns for simultaneity or reverse causation in the future.[30]

A lower Akaike Information Criterion (AIC) and Bayesian Information Criterion (BIC) indicate better fit. Per this criterion, I report the models that provide the best fit. The AIC and BIC are reported for all models.

FINDINGS

To discuss the results of this chapter's analysis, I interpret the logit coefficients by sign and significance in order to examine the qualitative relation between covariates and marrying (i.e., a positive or negative relation) and to make qualitative comparisons of the magnitudes of selected covariates (i.e., higher or lower relations). Based on a one-unit change in the explanatory variable, a statistically significant positive (negative) sign on the coefficient implies an upward (downward) shift in the logit—an indicator of the conditional probability of marrying. Thus, a statistically significant positive (or negative) coefficient is interpreted as indicating an increase (or decrease) in the likelihood or propensity to ever marrying (relative to the baseline reference). However, for time-varying covariates, a one-unit increment shifts the logit function relative to the reference starting only from the time period when the covariate changes.

---

30 I do not pursue an instrumental variables (IV) estimation because it relies on the untestable assumption that the instruments are uncorrelated with the error term of the model, which I consider to be an unsuitable alternative here. Instead, my approach is to pursue robustness checks to garner greater confidence based on establishing consistent results.

My central interest is to examine meaningful period-specific time effects by recession/nonrecession indicators. I employ stepwise modeling to examine how adding different specifications of time indicators contribute to the fit of the model. Based on the results of the stepwise modeling, the eight-category recession/nonrecession aggregation of years with an age quadratic is the best fit model (table 8). All comparative statements in the analysis have undergone statistical testing, and unless otherwise noted, all comparisons are statistically significant at the 5 percent significance level. The z test is used for the test of a single variable, and the Wald test is used to jointly test more than one variable or comparisons between variables.

I first focus on describing the results for the separate models for women, and then I discuss the results for the separate models for men. Looking at the preliminary model (without an interaction for earning power-period effects) for women (table 3, model 1), I first compare the likelihood of marrying for the baseline category to other select nonrecession and recession periods. The baseline is the period of the nonrecession years of the 2000s, first decade. Comparing the baseline period to the earliest nonrecession period observed, there is a higher likelihood of marrying in the baseline period (controlling for the linear trend). That is, there is a downward shift in the log odds of marrying in the earlier 1980s nonrecession period. In the early recession of the 2000s (first decade), there is a downward shift, but then we see an upward shift for the period of the Great Recession.

The period-specific effects are all statistically significant, and we do not see support for the hypothesis of an ever-increasing negative effect of each successive recession on marrying. Instead, the likelihood of marrying in each prior recession period is relatively lower than the likelihood of marrying in the Great Recession. In addition to the other controls for this model (not shown), I display the results for the negative linear time trend and the negative effect of the national unemployment rate among males.

While there is not enough data to establish a conclusive trend, these findings do not support the hypothesis that as recessions have become increasingly structural and more complex, there is an increasingly negative relation between the contextual effects of successive recession periods and the likelihood of marrying. As this pattern is not observed in the period after women have entered the labor market en masse, I am further motivated to test how this pattern holds when interacted with micro-level earning power by gender. In the subsequent sections, I first proceed to discuss the marrying patterns across the observed periods among men and then by gender-education categories

Looking at the preliminary model (without an interaction for earning power-period effects) for men (table 4, model 2), I first compare the likelihood of marrying among men for the baseline category to other select nonrecession and recession periods. There is a higher likelihood of marrying in the baseline nonrecession period than the earlier 1980s nonrecession period. Compared to the baseline period, there is a downward shift in the log odds of marrying in the early 2000s recession. As observed among women, the likelihood of marrying in the

Great Recession shifts upward, and this shift is statistically higher than not only the baseline period but each prior recession period. As with women, among males we see a negative linear time trend and a negative effect of the national unemployment rate on marrying.

Again, there is not enough data to establish a conclusive trend, but among men—as among women—the findings do not support the hypothesis that there is an increasingly negative relation between the contextual effects of a recession period and the likelihood of marrying. Next, I discuss these patterns, adding interactions for earning-power-period effects to the models, with education level serving as a proxy for earning power. In addition to discussing the "college effect," I also test the difference between the coefficients for holding a college degree, or more, compared to having less than a high school degree as a measure of the "college advantage" in marrying.

I analyze the results from the model with an interaction for earning-power-period effects for women (table 5, model 3) and then for men. Firstly, I compare the likelihood of marrying among college-educated women in the nonrecession period of the early first decade of the 2000s to the nonrecession period of the 1980s. For this comparison, women with a college degree in the more recent period have a higher likelihood of marrying than women with a college degree in the earlier period. Within the same nonrecession period of the 2000s, the baseline category of college-educated women has a marrying advantage when compared to women with less than a high school degree. However, the likelihood of marrying for college-educated women is higher in the Great

Recession than in the baseline period (the nonrecession period of the 2000s, first decade).

Additionally, I compare the college advantage of the nonrecession period of the 2000s (first decade) to the college advantage of the nonrecession period of the 1980s. For this comparison, the college advantage is higher in the more recent period than the college advantage in the earlier period. Yet the college advantage in the baseline period (the nonrecession period of the early first decade of the 2000s) is not statistically different than the college advantage of the Great Recession. However, the college advantage of the baseline period is lower than the college advantage of the early 2000s recession and the 1990s nonrecession period. The college advantage in the Great Recession is also lower than the college advantage of the early recession period of the 2000s, first decade.

Though not conclusive, these comparisons suggest that among women, there are important period-specific effects that condition the relation between having a college education and marrying as well as between the relative relation of the college advantage and marrying.[31] Given the lower college advantage in the most recent recession compared to the penultimate recession, not only do we not see evidence that there is a negative relation between women's earning power and marrying, but there also is a lack of evidence for the claim that there has been an ever-increasing marrying disparity by education level in the United States. The data

---

31 The relative relation of the college advantage and marrying is a function of the effect of having a college education on marrying compared to the effect of having less than a high school degree and marrying.

do not reveal the emergence of (continuously) increasingly positive or negative trends, but rather distinct contextual effects for each observed period.

Next, I analyze the results from the model with an interaction for earning-power-period effects for men (table 6, model 4). In the first comparison, the likelihood of marrying among college-educated men in the (nonrecession) baseline period is compared to the nonrecession period of the 1980s. For this comparison, men with a college degree in the more recent period have a higher likelihood of marrying than men with a college degree in the earlier period. Within the same baseline period, the baseline category of college-educated men have a marrying advantage when compared to men with less than a high school degree. The likelihood of marrying for college-educated men is higher in the Great Recession than in the baseline period.

In addition, I compare the college advantage of the (nonrecession) baseline period to the college advantage of the nonrecession period of the 1980s. For this comparison, the college advantage is higher in the more recent period than in the earlier period. The college advantage in the baseline period is not statistically different than in the Great Recession. However, the college advantage of the baseline period is lower than in the early 2000s recession and the 1990s nonrecession period. As was observed among women, the college advantage in the Great Recession is lower than in the early recession period of the 2000s, first decade.

These comparisons suggest that among men, as was observed among women, there are important period-specific effects that condition the relation between having a college education and marrying as well as between the relative relation of the college advantage and marrying. Again, these preliminary results do not support the argument that the marrying disparity by education level is necessarily continuously increasing (or decreasing) in the United States.

In the next step, I analyze the results from the model with an interaction for earning-power-period effects for college-educated women (table 7, model 5). This model uses logged annual earnings as a proxy for earning power. Looking at the combined effects of earning power in each period, there is a positive relation between log earnings and the log odds of marrying in the baseline period as well as in the nonrecession period of the 1990s. The combined effect of log earnings on marrying is not statistically different than zero in the other observed periods. Other than for the Great Recession and 1990s nonrecession periods, this is due to a downward shift in the interaction effect of log earnings. In the Great Recession, change in the interaction effect of log earnings is not statistically different than zero.

Although there is not enough data to make a conclusive interpretation of the trend, the data suggest that there is a lack of support for the model of specialization that predicts a lower probability of marrying for women with higher earning power. On the other hand, in some of the periods we see a positive relation between logged earnings and the log odds of marrying, but we do not see evidence that the relation is increasing in each successive period.

When applying this model to the sample of college-educated men, the interaction between log earnings and period is not found to be statistically significant in any period (model not shown). I interpret this to suggest that while there are some period-specific changes in the effect of log earnings on marrying among women, the (positive) effect for men is consistent across the analytic periods. This suggests additional (preliminary) support for the theory that the micro-level economic basis of marrying changes toward being positive among women (as it is with men) in the period after women's mass entry into the labor market. However, the results relate to my initial hypotheses in a mixed fashion, since the relation between earning power and marrying is not clearly observed as increasingly positive across each successive period for the proxies of education level and earning power.

As mentioned previously, it may be that there are ambiguous effects masked within each distinct recession period. Some may marry more due to social insurance, while others may not marry due to a lower ability to meet some standard for economic readiness, the economic marriage bar. The balance of these two effects may be different in each recession (for example, based on the severity of credit or housing market downturns). If so, then further research should focus on disentangling what may be multiple and countervailing effects operating during specific recession (and nonrecession) periods.

Overall, I find tentative support to the theory that once women entered the labor market en masse, women's earning power is a positive determinant of marrying, including (but not necessarily more so) during a recession period. However, the relation does not appear to be stable or ever increasing across the observed periods, and further analysis would be necessary to establish a trend. Given that the changes in the labor market and household structure are recent, the analytic time frame may cover a period of social and economic adjustment. Long-term permanent shifts in the trend may be yet to materialize.

However, it is important to especially highlight that I do not find any evidence that women's earning power has a negative relation to marrying (per specialization theory) and that the balance of the findings suggest support for the modern perspective on household economics. The data more so reconciles with the theory that a women's earning power (and a man's earning power) makes marrying more affordable, enhances economic security, and increases the gains to marrying despite (if not necessarily due to) a recession. Further, the negative effect of the national unemployment rate among males suggests that future studies look at both conventional and supplemental male-specific and female-specific economic determinants of marrying. There may be countervailing effects of multiple gender-shared and gender-specific economic changes that more fully explain marrying patterns across time when considered jointly.

LIMITATIONS

The data set used in this chapter's analysis provides a unique opportunity to conduct an analysis with a large sample across multiple recession/nonrecession periods. While there are substantive benefits derived from the nature of this life-history data that covers a long historical period, there are also major trade-offs. Firstly, there are a limited set of variables that are available. Thus, the findings should be considered with caution because a model specified with a fuller set of variables may support different conclusions. Indeed, the interpretations of the findings should be considered tentative because the analysis does not separate the three measures of time—age, period, and birth cohort.

This chapter's analysis takes a period-analysis approach, while I have also conducted prior research with a birth-cohort approach. My prior empirical work (Espinoza 2013) finds dramatic shifts in the effect of earning power on marrying by US generation. Studying the shift in the effects of time-varying education level and time-varying earnings on marrying across the lucky few generation, baby boomers, and generation Xers, I find that the earning-power advantage for marrying among women first emerges among generation X women—women who are at the prime age for marrying in the first decade of the 2000s. I would argue that this prior finding is congruent with the findings of this current study, and I do not attempt to disentangle the age, period, and cohort effects here.

An analysis that focuses on identifying period and age effects confronts challenges in simultaneously identifying birth cohort (generation) effects. In addition to the issue of adding conceptual complexity that may be overwhelming, including within any model specification all three concepts—personal time (age), historical time (period), and generation (cohort)—can cause identification problems and severe multicollinearity (Buss 1974 and Hagenaars 1990). Following other scholars, I would argue that the theoretically driven period-analysis approach should garner some confidence despite that it does not isolate each of the three time-related concepts (Rabe-Hesketh and Skrondal 2012).

Further, there are limits to the analysis I conduct using crude measures of earning power. My methods do not cancel concern for reverse causation or unobserved dimensions of earning power. Yet even in reality, there is a lot of uncertainty, simultaneity, and asymmetrical information in the observable measures available when evaluating whether a person is economically ready to marry. Much of the theory about the effect of earning power on marrying acknowledges the limits in the analysis of earning power not only in empirical analysis but also subjectively at the personal level (Oppenheimer 1988). Thus, I would argue that using commonly available measures of earning power that are generally accepted is useful despite their lack of exactness or completeness.

Despite that each panel of the SIPP survey[32] is a nationally representative survey and I use weights that take into account the sample design, without the application of replicate weights in the calculation of the standard errors and a fully specified model (i.e., a model without omitted variable bias), we must treat these findings as suggestive.[33] Because

---

32 Statistics from surveys are subject to sampling and nonsampling errors. For further information on the source of the data and accuracy of the estimates, including standard errors and confidence intervals, see <http://www.census.gov/programs-surveys/sipp/tech-documentation/source-accuracy-statements.html>.

33 Replicate weights are still in development for the data (Gold Standard File) used in this chapter's analysis.

there remains concern that possible endogeneity and selection issues may result in biased estimates, I am cautious about the conclusions that are drawn from the findings. I do not present the results as precise quantitative estimates for the US population, but rather I discuss qualitative relationships that appear to be robust across various analytic strategies and model specifications.

The robustness of my findings suggest that the magnitude of any bias may be low, and though alternative methods may lead to more precise estimates, they may not necessarily reverse or counter the qualitative findings of this chapter's analysis. I present the conclusions in the next section as theoretical arguments made based on the suggestive findings of the analysis. Further data and analyses would be necessary to make the interpretations conclusive.

DISCUSSION AND CONCLUSION

In this chapter's analysis, I examine the period-specific effects of earning power on marrying conditional to shifts in the macroeconomy in the period after women's mass entry into the labor market (1978–2010). The objective of this chapter's analysis is to provide an exploratory analysis of how gender-shared and gender-specific economic shifts may drive changes in the basis of marrying and household socioeconomics in the United States. This period covers what may be a pivotal transition in the labor market and household structure, and a longer time series would be necessary to conclusively establish the permanent trend. However, I find in this chapter's analysis further encouragement for research that advances a new framework for understanding household socioeconomics in the United States—one that incorporates the gains to marrying as operating more so based on the dual-earner household structure (than based on specialization theory).

The results generally support the theory that the economic basis of marrying has shifted in the United States to one that is based on women's earning power being a positive determinant of marrying. Especially during a recession, a women's financial contribution and the greater security of a dual-earner household can help make marrying more economically viable and advantageous. With women garnering a more gender-equal level of earning power, I would argue that a couple can more likely meet an aggregate earning potential that is high (and secure) enough to make more attractive the gains of the dual-earner household structure as compared to staying single (or, alternatively, entering a sole-earner union).

With many of the traditional functions of marrying increasingly delinked to being married (e.g., sexual activity and procreation), I would argue that—along with companionship—the economic gains to marrying are increasingly central to the decision to marry in the United States. While the stigma of divorce and some of the provisions of divorce law have weakened over time in the United States, there is still a greater protection of the investments one makes in a formalized relationship within the context of marriage compared to within an informal relationship. I theorize that marriage may serve as an attractive and voluntary contract that allows couples to manage risks and make investments and commitments to each with greater confidence about the potential returns to such arrangements.

By observing a positive college effect among women across the analytic periods (and a nonstatistically significant or positive earnings effect among the college educated), I provide some empirical evidence that bolsters the theory that marrying is now based on the gains derived from women's earning power and the dual-earner model. Rather than showing a consistent trend, however, the results across time are mixed. It may be that singlehood, including cohabitation, may be a more attractive option than the alternatives of a specialized marital union or, even, the dual-earner arrangement, when a person does not meet the economic threshold for marrying. In this way, it may be that the effect of the marriage bar, and also increasingly viable alternative household arrangements as a nonmarried adult, mediate the gains to marrying based on the dual-earner model.

A recession may preclude more women as well as more men from being economically ready to marry (at the exact time when the increased security and economies of scale of marriage should be most at play). If so, the degendering of the economic basis of marriage may operate more so like double jeopardy during hard economic times. With potentially countervailing effects, additional data is necessary to disentangle the net effect of a recession on marrying. Further research should examine whether cohabitation and the marriage bar may help advance our understanding of the modern economic determinants of marrying and household structure across the business cycle.

Table 1. Distributions of Variables, Person-years (NT)

	Women		Men		Total	
	NT	% (NT)	NT	% (NT)	NT	% (NT)
Analytic Sample	932,567	100	967,914	100	1,900,481	100
Categorical Variables	Frequency	Percent	Frequency	Percent	Frequency	Percent
Marital Status						
Ever Married	87,617	9.4	75,794	7.8	163,411	8.6
Never Married	844,950	90.6	892,120	92.2	1,737,070	91.4
U.S. Recession						
No Recession	675,363	72.4	698,088	72.1	1,373,451	72.3
Early 1980s: 1980 - 1982	113,997	12.2	120,346	12.4	234,343	12.3
Early 1990s: 1990 - 1991	68,960	7.4	72,602	7.5	141,562	7.4
Early 2000s: 2001 – 2002	54,683	5.9	56,057	5.8	110,740	5.8
Great Recession: 2008 - 2009	19,564	2.1	20,821	2.2	40,385	2.1
Highest Education Level						
Less Than High School	224,739	24.1	241,043	24.9	465,782	24.5
High School	208,351	22.3	246,547	25.5	454,898	23.9
Some College	278,915	29.9	269,441	27.8	548,356	28.9
Bachelor's Degree or Higher	220,562	23.7	210,883	21.8	431,445	22.7
Race						
White	700,251	75.1	781,256	80.7	1,481,507	78.0
Black	161,429	17.3	118,746	12.3	280,175	14.7
Latino	70,887	7.6	67,912	7.0	138,799	7.3
Motherhood						
Ever Given Birth	153,040	16.4	n/a	n/a	n/a	n/a
Never Given Birth	779,527	83.6	n/a	n/a	n/a	n/a
School Status						
In-School	460,764	49.4	443,468	45.8	904,232	47.6
Not-in-School	471,803	50.6	524,446	54.2	996,249	52.4

Data sources: US Census Bureau, Survey of Income and Program Participation (SIPP) 1984, 1990, 1991, 1992, 1993, 1996, 2001, 2004, 2008 panels and SSA earnings data—Gold Standard File (GSF), Version 6.0
NT: Person-year level observations (unweighted)

Table 2. Distributions of Variables (Event-History Data Structure), Persons (N)

	Women		Men		Total	
	N	% (N)	N	% (N)	N	% (N)
Analytic Sample	137,263	100	129,219	100	266,482	100
Categorical Variables		Percent		Percent		Percent
Marital Status (at Last Observation)						
Ever Married	87,617	63.8	75,794	58.7	163,411	61.3
Never Married	49,646	36.2	53,425	41.3	103,071	38.7
Highest Education Level						
Less Than High School	32,529	23.7	33,955	26.3	66,484	24.9
High School	36,106	26.3	33,626	26.0	69,732	26.2
Some College	40,999	29.9	34,974	27.1	75,973	28.5
Bachelor's Degree or Higher	27,629	20.1	26,664	20.6	54,293	20.4
Race						
White	108,954	79.4	106,447	82.4	215,401	80.8
Black	18,609	13.6	14,033	10.9	32,642	12.2
Latino	9,700	7.1	8,739	6.8	18,439	6.9

Data sources: US Census Bureau, Survey of Income and Program Participation (SIPP) 1984, 1990, 1991, 1992, 1993, 1996, 2001, 2004, 2008 panels and SSA earnings data—Gold Standard File (GSF), Version 6.0

N: Person-level observations (unweighted)

Table 3. Ordinary Logit Specifications on Marrying, Women

	Women						
	Model 1					NT	932,567
	coefficient/(standard error)					ll	-66539
Selected Coefficients						aic	133120
						bic	133366
						Pseudo R^2	0.2644
Year (linear trend)	-0.093***						
	(0.00)						
U.S. Unemployment Rate, Males	-0.037***						
	(0.00)						
Less than High School	-1.153***						
	(0.02)						

	1980s		1990s		2000s		
	Early Recession	No Recession	Early Recession	No Recession	Early Recession	No Recession	Great Recession
Period	-1.410***	-1.177***	-0.860***	-0.700***	-0.234***	(Baseline)	0.231***
	(0.09)	(0.08)	(0.06)	(0.05)	(0.04)		(0.06)
Wald Tests							
Difference-in-Difference Analysis							
Earlier Recessions							
Versus Great Recession	-1.641***		-1.091***		-0.465***		n/a
Prob > chi2 =	0.000		0.000		0.000		(Reference)

Legend: * p<0.05; ** p<0.01; *** p<0.001

Control variables (not shown): age quadratic, race/ethnicity (baseline: white), motherhood (baseline: never), and school status (baseline: out of school)

Omitted categories (not shown): 1978–1979 nonrecession period, high school degree, some college (age quadratic interacted with education levels)

Mean centering for continuous variables: year, age, and unemployment rate

Data sources: US Census Bureau, Survey of Income and Program Participation (SIPP) 1984, 1990, 1991, 1992, 1993, 1996, 2001, 2004, 2008 panels and SSA earnings data—Gold Standard File (GSF), Version 6.0

NT: Person year observations (unweighted). Weighted specifications.

Dependent variable: First entry into marriage (binary 0/1)

Table 4. Ordinary Logit Specifications on Marrying, Men

	Men		NT	967,914
	Model 2		ll	-66723
	coefficient/(standard error)		aic	133486
Selected Coefficients			bic	133721
			Pseudo R^2	0.2049
Year (linear trend)	-0.109***			
	(0.00)			
U.S. Unemployment Rate, Males	-0.066***			
	(0.01)			
Less than High School	-1.011***			
	(0.02)			

	1980s		1990s		2000s		
	Early Recession	No Recession	Early Recession	No Recession	Early Recession	No Recession	Great Recession
Period	-1.872***	-1.549***	-1.140***	-0.888***	-0.293***	(Baseline)	0.529***
	(0.10)	(0.08)	(0.07)	(0.05)	(0.04)		(0.06)
Wald Tests							
Difference-in-Difference Analysis							
Earlier Recessions							
Versus Great Recession	-2.400***		-1.669***		-0.822***		n/a
Prob > chi2 =	0.000		0.000		0.000		(Reference)

Legend: * p<0.05; ** p<0.01; *** p<0.001
Control variables (not shown): age quadratic, race/ethnicity (baseline: white), and school status (baseline: out of school)
Omitted categories (not shown): 1978–1979 nonrecession period, high school degree, some college (age quadratic interacted with education levels)
Mean centering for continuous variables: year, age, and unemployment rate
Data sources: US Census Bureau, Survey of Income and Program Participation (SIPP) 1984, 1990, 1991, 1992, 1993, 1996, 2001, 2004, 2008 panels and SSA earnings data—Gold Standard File (GSF), Version 6.0
NT: Person-year observations (unweighted). Weighted specifications
Dependent variable: First entry into marriage (binary 0/1)

Table 5. Ordinary Logit Specifications on Marrying with Period-Education Interactions

	Women					NT	932,567
	Model 3					ll	-66253
	coefficient/(standard error)					aic	132590
Selected Coefficients						bic	133083
						Pseudo R^2	0.2675
Year (linear trend)	-0.092***						
	(0.00)						
U.S. Unemployment Rate, Males	-0.036***						
	(0.01)						

	1980s		1990s		2000s		
	Early Recession	No Recession	Early Recession	No Recession	Early Recession	No Recession	Great Recession
Less than High School Degree (LTHS)	-3.221***	-2.872***	-2.792***	-2.722***	-2.771***	-1.561***	-1.480**
	(0.11)	(0.09)	(0.10)	(0.07)	(0.10)	(0.07)	(0.11)
College Degree or More	-2.105***	-1.703***	-1.263***	-0.874***	-0.172**	(Baseline)	0.250***
	(0.10)	(0.09)	(0.08)	(0.06)	(0.06)		(0.10)
Wald Tests							
Difference-in-Difference Analysis							
College Advantage							
LTHS versus BA or More	1.116***	1.168***	1.530***	1.847***	2.599***	1.561***	1.729***
Prob > chi2 =	0.000	0.000	0.000	0.000	0.000	(Baseline)	0.000

Legend: * p<0.05; ** p<0.01; *** p<0.001
Control variables (not shown): age quadratic, race/ethnicity (baseline: white), motherhood (baseline: never), and school status (baseline: out-of-school)
Omitted categories (not shown): 1978–1979 nonrecession period, high school degree, some college (age quadratic interacted with education levels)
Mean centering for continuous variables: year, age, and unemployment rate
Data sources: US Census Bureau, Survey of Income and Program Participation (SIPP) 1984, 1990, 1991, 1992, 1993, 1996, 2001, 2004, 2008 panels and SSA earnings data—Gold Standard File (GSF), Version 6.0
NT: Person-year observations (unweighted). Weighted specifications
Dependent variable: First entry into marriage (binary 0/1)

Table 6. Ordinary Logit Specifications on Marrying with Period-Education Interactions

	Men							NT	967,914
	Model 4							ll	-66589
	coefficient/(standard error)							aic	133260
Selected Coefficients								bic	133743
								Pseudo R^2	0.2065
Year (linear trend)	-0.108***								
	(0.00)								
U.S. Unemployment Rate, Males	-0.066***								
	(0.00)								

	1980s		1990s		2000s		
	Early Recession	No Recession	Early Recession	No Recession	Early Recession	No Recession	Great Recession
Less than High School Degree (LTHS)	-3.055***	-2.836***	-2.557***	-2.685***	-2.389***	-1.337***	-1.000***
	(0.12)	(0.10)	(0.10)	(0.08)	(0.10)	(0.07)	(0.10)
College Degree or More	-2.244***	-1.788***	-1.397***	-1.013***	-0.204***	(Baseline)	0.559***
	(0.11)	(0.09)	(0.09)	(0.07)	(0.07)		(0.11)
Wald Tests							
Difference-in-Difference Analysis							
College Advantage							
LTHS versus BA or More	.811***	1.048***	1.160***	1.672***	2.185***	1.337***	1.559***
Prob > chi2 =	0.000	0.660	0.000	0.000	0.000	(Baseline)	0.000

Legend: * p<0.05; ** p<0.01; *** p<0.001
Control variables (not shown): age quadratic, race/ethnicity (baseline: white), and school status (baseline: out of school)
Omitted categories (not shown): 1978–1979 nonrecession period, high school degree, some college (age quadratic interacted with education levels)
Mean centering for continuous variables: year, age, and unemployment rate
Data sources: US Census Bureau, Survey of Income and Program Participation (SIPP) 1984, 1990, 1991, 1992, 1993, 1996, 2001, 2004, 2008 panels and SSA earnings data—Gold Standard File (GSF), Version 6.0.
NT: Person-year observations (unweighted). Weighted specifications
Dependent variable: First entry into marriage (binary 0/1)

Table 7. Ordinary Logit Specifications on Marrying with Period-Earnings Interactions

	College Educated Women						NT	220562
	Model 5						ll	-16773
	coefficient/(standard error)						aic	33625
							bic	34027
Selected Coefficients							Pseudo R^2	0.2463

Year (linear trend)	-0.067***							
	(0.01)							
U.S. Unemployment Rate, Males	-0.054***							
	(0.01)							
Log Earnings (Main Effect)	0.105**							
	(0.04)							

	1980s		1990s		2000s		
	Early Recession	No Recession	Early Recession	No Recession	Early Recession	No Recession	Great Recession
Log Earnings*Period (Interaction)	-0.112**	-0.089*	-0.110*	-0.063	-0.127*	(Baseline)	0.002
	(0.04)	(0.04)	(0.05)	(0.04)	(0.05)		(0.08)

Wald Tests

Log Earnings (Combined Effect)	-0.007	.0167	-.005	.042*	-.022	.105**	0.107
Prob > chi2 =	0.655	0.136	0.815	0.002	0.451	0.010	0.139

Legend: * p<0.05; ** p<0.01; *** p<0.001
Control variables (not shown): age quadratic, race/ethnicity (baseline: white), motherhood (baseline: never), and school status (baseline: out of school)
Omitted categories (not shown): 1978–1979 nonrecession period
Mean centering for continuous variables: year, age, and unemployment rate
Data sources: US Census Bureau, Survey of Income and Program Participation (SIPP) 1984, 1990, 1991, 1992, 1993, 1996, 2001, 2004, 2008 panels and SSA earnings data—Gold Standard File (GSF), Version 6.0
NT: Person-year observations (unweighted). Weighted specifications
Dependent variable: First entry into marriage (binary 0/1)

Table 8. Ordinary Logit Specifications on Marrying Stepwise Modeling for Year Specifications, Women

	coefficient/(standard error)			
	(i)	(ii)	(iii)	(iv)
Age	0.210***	0.218***	0.210***	0.218***
	(0.00)	(0.00)	(0.00)	(0.00)
Age*Age	-0.015***	-0.018***	-0.016***	-0.018***
	(0.00)	(0.00)	(0.00)	(0.00)
Year (linear trend)	-0.129***	-0.089***	-0.134***	-0.111***
	(0.00)	(0.00)	(0.00)	(0.00)
U.S. Unemployment Rate, Males			-0.366***	-0.050***
			(0.00)	(0.006)
1980s, Early Recession		-1.222***		-1.651***
		(0.09)		(0.09)
1980s, No Recession		-1.048***		-1.418***
		(0.08)		(0.08)
1990s, Early Recession		-0.738***		-1.034***
		(0.05)		(0.06)
1990s, No Recession		-0.569***		-0.782***
		(0.04)		(0.05)
2000s, Early Recession		-0.128***		-0.208***
		(0.03)		(0.04)
Great Recession		0.097		0.284***
		(0.05)		(0.06)
NT	932,567	932,567	932,567	932,567
ll	-75120	-69927	-72452	-69909
aic	150248	139875	144915	139842
bic	150295	140005	144973	139983
Pseudo R^2	0.1695	0.2269	0.1990	0.2271

Legend: * p<0.05; ** p<0.01; *** p<0.001
Omitted categories (not shown): 1978–1979 nonrecession period
Mean centering for continuous variables: age
Data sources: US Census Bureau, Survey of Income and Program Participation (SIPP) 1984, 1990, 1991, 1992, 1993, 1996, 2001, 2004, 2008 panels and SSA earnings data—Gold Standard File (GSF), Version 6.0
NT: Person-year observations (unweighted). Weighted specifications
Dependent variable: First entry into marriage (binary 0/1)

7

Discussion and Conclusion

To conclude, when comparing my findings among blacks, whites, and Mexican Americans, I find three different waves of awareness and adjustment to the insecurities and disadvantages of the male breadwinner model and traditional sexual division of labor. Though distinct in the package of imperatives and incentives underlying the transformation, each wave results in a shift toward a degendered economic basis of marrying where earning power is positively evaluated in relation to marrying across gender.

As the first wave, the black baby boomer generation is a generation that appears to have nearly spontaneously adjusted to the perceived inadequacies of the male breadwinner model because the model was never presumed to be viable among blacks. Due to the relatively lower earning power and lower labor force participation rates of black men in comparison to white men, family women working was imposed on the black community as an economic imperative (even after the historical legal imperatives related to slavery and the Jim Crow era). Yet I find women's earning power is more positively evaluated among blacks in generation X than in the baby boomer generation due to the shift to the dual-earner model representing an arrangement that is much more financially advantageous and, thus, more voluntary (due to black women's higher earning power).

While black men's exclusion from family-sustaining wages resulted in the male breadwinner model never being broadly internalized as a normative household structure or as a viable ideal among blacks, the dual-earner model was not financially more advantageous than the white normative male breadwinner model in the baby boomer generation. I theorize that this resulted in black baby boomers maintaining elements of the male breadwinner model as an abstract ideal (though not a practical norm for blacks) and, thus, some elements of traditional gender ideology. For example, though black baby boomers in the sample report constructing alternative ideas about masculine roles in the household, they nevertheless internalized the ideal of male dominance in the household.

We see more positive attitudes about the relation between women's earning power and marrying among black sample participants as well as white sample participants in generation X. I argue that this is because the conditions that led to whites adopting more gender-egalitarian ideology and a degendered economic basis of marrying resulted in bigger advantages to the dual-earner model among blacks and whites. With the higher incentives of the dual-earner model among women with higher earning power (substantially higher consumption, upward mobility), I find family women working to be perceived as a more voluntary arrangement based on race-neutral considerations in generation X for both blacks and whites.

White baby boomers maintained the male breadwinner model as an abstract ideal and internalized it as a practical norm despite some having personally experienced its inadequacies because it was part of baby boomers' childhood socialization. However, due to the negative experiences related to the male breadwinner model in their parental household—such as divorce, death, and joblessness—generation X was made aware of the vulnerability of women's economic dependence on a sole male earner in the household. However, I also find that the substantively higher standard of living made possible by white women's greater gender parity in the labor market reframed the gains to the dual-earner model to be more voluntary (in addition to more financially advantageous) in generation X.

As the second wave, I find that whites in generation X underwent a twofold process in the shift to the positive evaluation of women's earning power in relation to marrying. Firstly, they experienced transformative socialization in their families of origin, such that they were discouraged from replicating the traditional male breadwinner model of their parents' generation, and so they failed to internalize traditional gender ideology. Secondly, whites in generation X were incentivized by the greater financial advantages and more voluntary basis of the dual-earner model to positively evaluate women's earning power in relation to marrying.

I would argue that the study of women's earning power in relation to marrying under the framework that the dual-earner model is voluntary (and results in economic mobility) is distinct from the study of women's earning power in relation to marrying under the framework that the dual-earner model is forced (and results in economic deprivation). The first framework, based on incentives, motivates a change in traditional gender ideology. The latter, based on imperatives, does not necessarily motivate a change in traditional gender ideology (and rather it may actually reinforce traditional gender ideology). This is because, when family women working is associated with economic deprivation, the comparison of the dual-earner model (as an economic imperative) versus the default normative ideal of the male breadwinner model is not evaluated to be a superior (or rewarding) arrangement.

Furthermore, based on my research, I find transformative socialization to be a process that explains what I refer to as a generational lag in behavioral and attitudinal adjustment at the micro-level in response to transformative societal change in material (external) conditions. This process is motivated by rapid changes in socioeconomic conditions (external forces) that are experienced by the parental generation beyond primary socialization. That is, the parental generation must adjust as adults to a new regime or historical context that contradicts their earlier internalization of values. Their childhood socialization is based on congruent social conditions and values but they then become antiquated and problematic within the life course.

In other words, learned norms and ideals are harmonious in the precursor social context of childhood but they become dissonant in the later stage of adulthood. Thus, social change is experienced as a cause of tension and the lagged values continue to be idealized (despite that they are now maladaptive in the new social context). In this way, the transitional generation may maintain the idealized values of their childhood while modeling (through negative experiences) or directly messaging for changes in the norms and ideals of the generation to follow.

In this study, the transitional generation is the baby boomer generation. Baby boomers' behavioral and attitudinal adjustments to a changing social context later in life conflicted with the attitudes they internalized during primary socialization. Among baby boomers, the tensions that result from the adaptive behavioral adjustment to the dual-earner model amid rapid social changes with the still-maintained traditional gender ideology from primary socialization cause the generation to directly or indirectly motivate change in the successive generation, generation Xers.

That is, baby boomers did not fully disavow traditional gender ideology, nor did they fully internalize modern gender-egalitarian ideology (to be consonant to the rapid social and economic changes in the context of marrying and family women working). However, I find that the parental generation of baby boomers did facilitate change among generation X, through a transformative socialization process. As an example, white baby boomers maintained traditional gender ideology and traditional gender practices in the household despite offering messages, models, and lessons that encouraged white generation Xers to depart from traditional gender ideology, the traditional sexual division of labor, and the traditionally gendered economic basis of marrying.

As the third wave, Mexican Americans reference a much more social basis for departing from the traditional male breadwinner model and the traditional sexual division of labor partly because of an observed lag in the baby boomer generation shifting away from patriarchal gender practices. I would argue that due to the delay in Mexican Americans adopting more gender-egalitarian practices in the private sphere, this group more often cites normative influences external to the family and disharmony within the family as having motivated them to depart from the gendered expectations or gendered norms of their parental household.

Mexican Americans report being influenced by the women's movement, gender-neutral expansion in public education, and models from their friends' homes as sources of their motivation to shift toward more gender-egalitarian ideas and household arrangements. These normative forces constructed alternative gender ideals that likely helped Mexican American generation Xers reject the gender-unequal relations they observed in their parental household.

However, Mexican Americans also report cases where their own mothers or other relatives of the prior generation discouraged traditional gender practices or dissuaded them from entering marriage at all. Thus, like whites and blacks, Mexican Americans also underwent a process of transformative socialization. Yet the process was more so based on the social incentive of gaining access to greater gender egalitarianism in the household. This contrasts to the transformative process of generation Xers from other racial groups, which I find to be more so driven by the economic imperative (among blacks) and economic incentives (among whites and blacks) of family women working outside the home.

For white and black families, the more gender-egalitarian regime of the post–civil rights era brought about rapid change in the public sphere and the private sphere. These changes included higher women's wages and more gender-egalitarian norms in the broader society and in the home. Women's employment based on substantively higher earning power provided—especially among white families—influential examples of the dual-earner model as a more voluntary and more financially (and socially) advantageous alternative in the home. In contrast, I find Mexican American generation Xers were relatively more motivated by the changes in the social context of the public sphere, since they do not report experiencing as much change in the private sphere.

Women's employment in Mexican American families is not reported as rendering the dual-earner model as an example of a voluntary and more financially advantageous alternative to the male breadwinner model. Rather, jobs held by Mexican American women in the baby boomer (parental) generation were generally characterized by generation Xers (as the child generation) to be low paying and clearly perceived as secondary to the man's income and the woman's own family role.

Conversely, jobs held by men in Mexican American families are not reported to render the male breadwinner model to be a less secure or less financially advantageous model than the dual-earner model. Generation Xers generally do not report Mexican American men as having unstable employment histories or relatively lower wages than Mexican American women (as was observed among blacks). Rather, I find that the negative experiences of gender inequalities in the parental home, which conflicted with broader social norms of gender egalitarianism, motivated Mexican American sample participants to reject the male breadwinner model and internalize new gender-egalitarian ideas that were consonant with evaluating women's earning power positively in relation to marrying.

In this study, I analyze change in the traditionally gendered economic basis of marrying. I find that sample participants in generation X perceive women's higher earning power to confer greater financial advantages than in the past, such that the dual-earner model is considered a more voluntary arrangement. However, I find that for some sample participants, there is a social basis (rather than new financial incentives) that underlies the shift toward a positive evaluation of the relation between earning power and marrying across gender. The social basis appears to be more salient among sample participants whose mothers did not have a higher level of earning power (due to nonemployment or secondary employment and/or low education levels). I would argue that developing a deeper understanding of the relation between the new package of economic and social forces can better explain both the convergence across race and gender in positively evaluating the relation between earning power and marrying, as well as the remaining nuance in marrying patterns by ethnoracial groups and class.

Based on the original research I have conducted across socioeconomic status, I have been able to show that the changes in American family structure have multiple dimensions and have transpired across class and race. Overall, I find that the degendered economic basis of marrying is of fundamental importance. Americans pattern their marrying decisions based on the perception of economic readiness due to economic and social reasons. Secondly, by better examining the ethnoracial disparities in earnings by gender and how such disparities may affect attitudes, I have developed an important typology of incentives and imperatives for family women to work that relates to the formation of gender ideology. Through this typology, we can theorize more deeply about ethnoracial differences in family patterns and predict how patterns may change based on different scenarios of changing economic conditions.

Though the dual-earner model is now prevalent across race, it is not equally prevalent. My findings demonstrate that there are racial disparities in the incentives and imperatives of modern marriage. Thus, I would argue that marrying patterns may widen as different groups' propensity to marry may be based on persistently disparate economic prospects. Indeed, without ethnoracial convergence in earning power across gender, the fundamentally economic basis of marrying suggests widening ethnoracial disparities in marrying that are structured by racialized patterns of earning power (i.e., class).

My research suggests widening class disparities within race. Within each racial group, men with low earning power and women with low earning power will find it increasingly unaffordable to meet what is a higher and harder modern marriage bar. With educational attainment emerging as a proxy for long-term economic prospects, those of low education will increasingly feel financially unready to marry not only for temporary periods but across the life course. Educational attainment is a much more durable indicator compared to past indicators of earning power, such as employment. The dual-earning power of high-income individuals, who have a higher propensity to marry, will magnify within race income disparities, as low-income individuals not only have lower incomes but are also more likely to stay single. Low-income single households will become increasingly more unequal relative to high-income dual-earner households.

Moynihan's influential report (1965), *The Negro Family: The Case for National Action*, claimed that unique cultural features of the black community were driving the changes in the black family away from the traditional nuclear male breadwinner model. Yet Moynihan neglected to include in his analysis the white counterparts to the mostly low-income black communities he studied. Arguably, he spuriously attributed the changes and negative indicators observed in the black family to be specific to race and the matriarchal family structure because his report was overly narrow in the population he studied (low-income blacks) and overly broad in his inferences about black culture (Furstenberg 2009). Subsequent studies (Rainwater and Yancey 1967; Moynihan, Smeeding, and Rainwater 2005; Furstenberg 2009) that analyzed low-income communities across race concluded that the economic pressures driving change in the black family were driving change in low-income populations irrespective of race.

However, by my analyzing data across class, race, and gender simultaneously, I find a broader array of economic and social pressures driving change in the American family not only across race among those who are low-income but also across class. Indeed, I am able to find new attitudes about the relation between women's earning power and marrying because I study research participants with higher earning power and across two US generations that experienced a shift in attitudes and the economic basis of marrying in different ways. By observing the evaluation of women's earning power when the financial advantages are bigger and the arrangement is more voluntary, we see a process by which women's earning power has become part of the fundamental economic incentives of modern American marriage (across class). Women's earning power is now fundamental to achieving the social and economic pressures of an inflated modern economic marriage bar across race.

Many studies that focus on change in the American family still attribute changes in family structure as being due to men's low earning power or men's increasing economic precariousness. Generally, these studies are still based on the premise that the male breadwinner model is a functional ideal for American society, but the ideal has just become less viable among those outside the American middle class. However, I argue it is important to expand the analysis across class. Research should take into greater consideration the pivotal shift to women's earning power being important to modern marriage in America across class. Indeed, just focusing on the underlying inadequacies of the male breadwinner model or, conversely, the model of a female-headed matriarchy within low-income communities provides a narrow perspective that misses the broader landscape of family change and the very nature of modern marriage realities in the United States.

My argument is that modern marriage is an arrangement in which women's higher earning power incentivizes marriage and results in a financially more advantageous dual-earner household structure. Further, even without the increases in women's earning power (as observed among Latinas), we see the shift toward a degendered economic basis of marrying and the dual-earner model due to normative forces and contemporary expectations of gender-egalitarian relations.

While Mexican Americans in the sample report rejecting traditional gender ideology and report negative evaluations of the male breadwinner model due to observing gender-unequal relationships in the household, other data suggest that Latinos still have the lowest prevalence of dual-earner marriages. My research suggests that this may be due to the disparate economic conditions of Latinos rather than the cultural continuity of traditional gender ideology. Latino men have historically high employment levels, which weaken the economic imperative of the dual-earner household, and Latinas have historically low levels of earning power, which weakens the economic incentives of the dual-earner household. Latinas with low earning power may not be able to incentivize the dual-earner model, as has been observed among whites. This may foretell of continued patriarchy in low-income Latino households unless Latinas' stalled advances in earning power improves.

Across women and men in generation X, the findings of this study and other qualitative research suggest that the modern expectation is that individuals should postpone marrying until they feel that that they (and their partners) can meet the economic marriage bar and be financially self-sufficient in case of marital dissolution. Americans perceive modern marriage to require a minimal level of economic readiness that is often defined by educational attainment. This renders the marriage bar to be harder (more durable), and the inflation of household income due to most households having two incomes means the threshold is also much higher. Furthermore, to a certain degree, earning power now is a proxy for social class. Thus, as men seek to marry their social equal, they are also matching themselves with their equal in terms of earning power due to the fundamental transformation of gender patterns in the labor market.

The modern ideals of companionate and romantic marriage generally presume equal levels of a husband's and a wife's financial (and nonfinancial) contributions that higher earning power generally confers. As an example of nonfinancial contributions, many sample respondents report that maintaining positive gender-egalitarian spousal relations depend on spouses being at the "same level" in terms of earning power (be it based on education, employment, and/or earnings). Per the sample respondents, couples should have similar things to talk about, work colleagues should be compatible, and each person in the couple should be able to contribute his or her "fair share." Modern romance itself requires a higher level of earning power to afford the mutual standards of romance, such as expensive gifts, dinners, and travel. For many, a marriage bar is important because it helps to avoid the stress of financial, interpersonal, and social strain that can erode the romance of the marriage.

Among generation Xers, I find that men find particular value in having a spouse who is at his level in the labor market. In many cases, he's no longer content for her to stay at home. He wants a woman who does not depend on him financially, and who's not with him just to marry up—the derogative "gold digger." She gets along better in his social networks, which now include many other women who work outside the home. Further, she helps him get by and feel less stress in what many men characterize to be a more tenuous economy. Not only do many women feel insecure about being financially dependent on a male's income, but male study participants too report feeling insecure about the family being dependent on his income alone. Likewise, women report they do not want to be the female counterpart to a "sugar daddy," a "sugar mama," either.

With the weakening influence of religious institutions and parental authority among youth and young adults in the United States, there is a generally higher voluntariness in the decision to marry. Furthermore, the expansion of college enrollment across gender creates, and wage work across gender affords, an extended period of singlehood for many young adults. This then accommodates what are necessarily longer delays as men and women realize not only higher standards of economic readiness for oneself but also can wait for higher standards of economic readiness for a potential spouse. With continued patterns of homogamy (where social likes marry social likes), the economic standard across gender magnifies with social class as they relate to relatively higher standards for both men and women across the class or income distribution.

Despite relatively shared economic conditions, the primary socialization of baby boomers built a persistent cognitive default that held up traditional ideas about household specialization. Baby boomers experienced the rise in divorce, female-headed households, and childcare, but it was after their own primary socialization. For generation Xers, that was their primary socialization. Generation Xers were raised as children of divorced baby boomers, latchkey kids coming home from school to an empty house, and/or seeing moms managing jobs and households alone. Their observations, as children, of the breakdown of the male breadwinner model tore down that conventional cognitive default. Such experiences and gender-egalitarian normative references guided them to leave that model behind. The realities of primary socialization thereby opened the way for alternative cognitive scripts—and the degendering of the economic basis of marrying—to take root.

This process underlies the generational lag in how the two generations of modern marriage relate to the traditional (gendered) versus the modern (degendered) economic basis of marrying. Inflated expectations for a higher standard of living among households generally make individuals feel that they need two incomes to get by. Men and women think it takes two to pay the mortgage, the car loan, and all the other items that are perceived to make up the modern American standard of living. Generation Xers now have shared expectations for higher economic standards, gender-egalitarian relations, and individualized notions of financial self-sufficiency across gender.

Woman's increasing earning power also ties to the companionate basis of marrying. This relates to what I refer to as the myth of household specialization and gender compatibility. Contrary to theorists such as Parsons and Durkheim, women do not perceive that the exchange of domestic services for market work makes them equal partners to their husbands.

Indeed, patriarchal relations demanded that not only was the man the breadwinner but he was dominant as the head of the household. As with other relations of power inequality, the dominant male position involved abuses such as domestic violence, sexual assault, and an asymmetrical dependence of women on men. The reality was not mutual interdependence, and it generally was not experienced as companionate romance.

Despite segments of the American population where traditional attitudes may lag (as we saw with lagged patriarchy among Mexican Americans), wide-scale changes in gender-egalitarian norms and gender-parity conditions likely have normalization effects even outside the economic and social forces I previously discussed. For example, there may be segments of religious or political conservatism that have resisted adjustments to such shifts due to their specific social and economic contexts. For example, whites in rural areas where gendered labor-market arrangements have not changed much may feel insulated from the forces that have shifted the economic basis of marrying among other groups across the nation. In other exceptional cases, deeply religious or military communities may also be peripheral to broader forces underlying the shift in the economic basis of marrying. For example, devoutly religious families may have been more insulated from higher divorce rates, and military families may experience more stable employment patterns among men. Such groups may have not yet undergone the process of transformative socialization or been affected by the social and economic forces I have previously discussed; the relation between women's earning power and marrying within these groups should be further researched.

Yet I use a concluding case example of how we might understand how even those who have not undergone transformative socialization in their parental household or those with otherwise entrenched traditional attitudes may nevertheless change as a fourth wave. The case of Tim illustrates how a man with traditional attitudes may come to internalize positive attitudes about women's earning power in relation to marrying due to the dual-earner model being the new American standard.

Tim is a white male generation Xer born in 1976. He married at age twenty-seven, and he has two children. His parents' marriage remained intact, and he considers his parental household growing up to be middle class. Each of his parents graduated high school and finished some college (but did not complete a bachelor's degree). He and his family religiously identify as Protestant (Christian). Tim attends church weekly. He considers himself politically conservative, and he is enlisted in the armed forces.

Tim reported that it was important to him that he marry his social equal. Thus, he would rather marry a woman with high earning power (i.e., college educated) than to marry a woman with lower earning power who would be more likely to engage in household specialization (but not be his social equal).

He talked about these prospects:

> You know, it's 2014, and I recognize that things are in fact changing. You know, I'm a lawyer. At my alma

mater law school, there are more women enrolled than men right now. So I know that with regard to higher education, and with higher education comes higher paying jobs, at least right now in this country, women seem to be outstripping the men. So the fact that there are going to be more women in higher paying jobs is just going to happen. And right now I think maybe we're in a little bit of kind of a transition period as this is starting to happen. In ten years, I really don't think that it's going to be all that weird of a thing when all of these women have graduated from their advanced-degree programs and are in the workforce and start outnumbering the men. It's just going to happen.

Tim also sees the marriage bar as higher for his generation. He said,

Neither of my parents graduated from college. My dad joined the air force during the Vietnam War. My parents got married when they were pretty young, and I think that they were lucky, or at least luckier than me in my generation, in that they were able to actually buy a house with my mom working part time and my dad working in construction…in… California, no less. Now, in the neighborhoods that I grew up in, I can't afford one of those houses, and I'm a lawyer.

For Tim, his educational experiences relate to how he experiences and has adjusted to modern gender arrangements despite his conservative world views. He acknowledged it is not due to his personal political ideology or social values. Rather, he said he has had to adapt to new gender realities. He explained,

> I don't look at it as I'm a gen. Xer and I'm somehow more progressive. It's...things are different...You know, conditions are different, and I observe them. I'm not...you know, there might be some social attitudes that are changing. I guess for me...I don't see the point of hanging on to a social attitude that's going to be outdated by reality. So, you know, kind of just go with the flow and the way things are actually happening.

Tim actually maintains a traditional perspective, but he sees change in traditional gender ideology as inevitable. In terms of the abstract idea of gender egalitarianism, he denied that gender consciousness explains his views or family arrangements. He reported,

> There was no epiphany...That's reality, and I'm okay with that. I mean...you know, I went to college in New England. There were girls in my college class, and I liked girls, and I liked dating girls, and if I was going to date one of these girls that I went to college with, it meant that she was probably really smart too... It's just the way it was. You know, it's not like I went to [college] to pick up on the chicks that went there, because I wanted some chick that was going to like me for the college I went to. It's like, this is the college I go

to. There are cute girls here. I'm going to date them. You know?...And if she wants a career, we'll have that conversation down the line when we get there...That's just the way it is.

For Tim, he did not marry a woman with higher earning power for the second income but rather because to him the woman he was attracted to was a woman with higher earning power:

> She was smart, and I found that attractive. We could have conversations about world events and philosophy and literature, and we could have insightful discussions about all sorts of stuff. And we shared certain values, I think, because of our education and our background. So I knew that meant if I'm going to marry someone who is that smart and someone who has a degree, and at some point she's probably going to want to put that degree to use. Okay. Like, I'm fine with that. And whatever shape that takes, we'll figure that out.

In the past, women of all social classes (and even across education level) were not likely to have high earning power due to the structure of the labor market and social customs. However, in modern times, a woman with low earning power (e.g., based on education level) is unlikely to be a woman who is considered the social equal of a man with high earning power. Thus, traditional attitudes about homogamy (where likes marry likes) conflict with traditional attitudes about gender due to the restructuring of the labor market and educational opportunities that now tend to confer upon women of the middle and upper classes higher earning power.

That is, as in the past, men of the middle and upper classes mostly still expect to marry women of the middle and upper classes. Yet the advantages of class now translate into—and class is increasingly defined by—higher earning power across gender. For example, a man of the middle or upper middle class will tend to seek a college-educated woman with high earning power. Indeed, Tim thinks that due to contemporary gender-equal patterns of educational attainment, it is unavoidable that men with higher earning power marry women with higher earning power.

While women's mass entry into the labor market resulted in a change in the typical American household structure (to the dual-earner model) in the baby boomer generation, my findings suggest that the change in the perceived gains and actual gender structure of the economic basis of marriage occurred only after a generational lag, among generation Xers. Per Gerson (1985), women construct their lives out of the materials available to them and respond to the social conditions they inherit. This applies to men as well. Broad-scale trends have made more apparent the risks and inadequacies of a household model where women and children rely on a sole male breadwinner for sustenance. For those few individuals or few segments of the population who have not yet experienced the pitfalls, there still may be some lag in attitudinal and behavioral change but adjustment to what are rather broad and deep societal shifts is likely inevitable.

The male breadwinner model experienced a breach in confidence when the increasingly prevalent examples of divorce and children born outside of marriage ultimately compromised the traditional family ideal. Indeed, doubt about the security of marriage—under any household arrangement—is widespread based on widely reported statistics that many or most marriages end in divorce. Further, women's increasing earning power has made more financially advantageous the dual-earner model. Moreover, these changes occurred exactly at a time when legal and technological advances in birth control meant that a woman's career and family plans were more under her control (Goldin and Katz 2000; Stevenson and Wolfers 2007). Among generation Xers, there was increasingly both the motivation and the ability to consider the importance of a woman establishing economic readiness prior and throughout marriage while at the same time perceiving less or no conflict between a woman working and her family roles.

The focus of this study is on how the economic status of women is central to the gains to marrying—a novel approach and striking departure from prior literature. Yet it is important to highlight that the economic status of both men and women continues to interrelate as men's and women's pooled and relative incomes will likely continue to determine US family-formation patterns—across race and class. Though there are some exceptions, American men and women, across race and class, report that they must not only be able to feel financially ready to enter into a marital union but that they also seek gender-equal relations and gender-equal contributions in a marriage. Thus, policy recommendations that focus on improving men's employment or men's wage levels in order to support marriage will likely have limited impact. In order to be effective, family policy must also include a focus on women's employment and women's wages. Further, with the widening of income inequality due to disparities between dual-earner and sole-earner households, social policy regarding income distribution should be reoriented to better account for household-level disparities and better advance household-level solutions.

President Obama has helped advance new calls for paid family leave and increasing attention to the modern troubles of balancing work and family. He has touted women, and his family relationships with women, as central to the well-being of the family and the economy—a perspective long-held in the black community. According to CNN (2015), Obama held the first-ever White House Summit on Working Families in 2014 and has since made budgetary proposals and public calls to advance federal mandates and funding for paid family leave. The campaign of Hillary Clinton will undoubtedly continue the public conversation and media commentary on gender, work, and family as central to social policy. Clinton has already made public statements advocating for paid family leave, saying in one of her campaign videos "it's outrageous that America is the only country in the developed world that doesn't guarantee paid leave" (Huffington Post 2015). At the time of this publication, the field of Republican presidential candidates is too large to analyze the social policy positions of the frontrunner but gender and family issues will likely weave into the upcoming election across political parties as contentious matters of debate. Yet Americans will hopefully come together to advance common sense policy solutions for the increasingly and inevitably shared challenges of the modern rearrangements of work, family, and gender.

Appendix

Methodology

For this study, I conduct mixed qualitative methods that include surveys (written questionnaires) with open-ended and closed-ended questions. I also conduct verbal individual and focus group interviews. The verbal data is audio recorded (digitally). The audio data is then transcribed (verbatim). To aid in collecting retrospective data and attitudes about hypothetical scenarios with randomized predictors, I use the event-history calendar method and research vignettes. I then apply thematic analysis to the qualitative data. Quantitative analysis of the closed-ended survey questions as well as secondary sources is conducted to supplement the findings from the primarily qualitative research of this study.

Hypotheses and Research Design

Social and economic conditions place constraints on women's individual freedom or agency and her decisions. In the United States, as in most societies, a woman's available resources are determined by a gendered socioeconomic hierarchy where men and women generally occupy different, and unequal, spheres in society. With women being a group historically subordinated to men, a woman's available resources have often been dependent on her relationships with men. It then follows that a changing gender regime would shape changes in women's opportunities and, likewise, her decisions about education, work, and family across time. In this study, I analyze how the basis of the marrying decision changes as women and men operate in a changing historical context.

My research methods were designed to test the following three hypotheses: Firstly, I hypothesize that in generation X, women's earning power should become important to increasing the readiness and likelihood to marry. This is expected to be in contrast to only men's earning power being important in the baby boomer generation. Secondly, I hypothesize that the relation between earning power and the likelihood of marrying should become as important for women as it is for men in generation X. Thirdly, I expect these shifts to transpire across ethnoracial groups. My analytic framework examines whether the importance of earning power on marrying changes at the aggregate levels of gender, generation, and race. Examining my hypotheses requires careful comparison between men and women across the two sample generations and by race.

I examine the hypotheses based on three dimensions of earning power: education level, employment, and earnings. The questionnaires and interviews allow me to examine whether and how respondents express if they would be more, less, or equally likely to marry based on different levels of women's earning power. Overall, I ask questions about earning power within the central themes found in the literature regarding the gains and determinants of marrying. Thus, the data analysis can demonstrate whether respondents think earning power and the economic gains to marrying are more or less important than alternative advantages of marrying (e.g., social pressures, procreation, or romantic love).

In the analysis, the likelihood of marrying is considered the response variable, and the different levels of earning power are the key predictor variables of interest. I seek to establish the relation between these variables from the research-participants' perspectives using qualitative data. Regarding educational attainment, do the respondents report that different education levels make them more, less, or equally likely to marry? For the dimensions of earnings and employment, I examine whether earning a good salary/wage and having stable or full-time work are considered characteristics that would make the respondent more likely to marry. I also ask about the attitudes respondents have about the male breadwinner versus the dual-earner model of household structure as well as about the relative earning power of a potential spouse.

Per Hogan and Astone (1986), it is important to locate fully the cohorts studied in their unique historical contexts. The complexity of the changes in the social context and the subjectivity of meaning construction inherent to my research question are most appropriately examined by methods that allow for qualitative data collection. What does the relation between earning power and marrying really mean to individuals across historical context, gender, and race? This calls for interpretive analysis and contextualization, which is important to building deeper sociological analysis. Therefore, in this study I primarily use qualitative methods to develop a more detailed understanding of the importance of earning power on the marrying decision by US generation across gender and race.

In addition to some basic descriptive analysis from the closed-ended responses to the written questionnaires, open-ended questions and a conversational interview approach are used to probe explanations from respondents about the meaning and importance of earning power on marrying and the determinants of their views about the relation between earning power and marrying. I conduct flexible, semistructured verbal interviews. Further, using the strategy of research vignettes, I have participants consider various scenarios of a hypothetical couple depicted with different levels of earning power so that participants discuss whether the hypothetical couple should marry. These are introduced in the written questionnaire and then more fully discussed verbally in the individual and group interviews.

By comparatively examining the importance of earning power on marrying across gender and by generation, I analyze the data in a way that addresses the competing theories about the gains to marrying. If the importance of earning power on marrying is shared across gender in the earlier generation of the baby boomers, then this would suggest that the shift to generation X was not a necessary condition, as I have theorized. This would support Oppenheimer's original argument that the incentives of the dual-earner household structure are more based on the trend of women's mass participation in the labor market and economic conditions, not necessarily due to the social forces of generational turnover or primary/secondary socialization effects. On the other hand, if the relation of women's earning power on marrying shifts toward being positive in generation X, then this would support my theory about the importance of the historical context and socialization effects.

STUDY PARTICIPANTS

In this study, I analyze the meanings and the importance of men's and women's earning power in relation to the likelihood of marrying by generation, race, and class. The sample includes native-born Americans who were socialized as children and through adolescence in the US social context. Using written questionnaires and open-ended verbal interviews with research vignettes, I interviewed fifty-five individuals and conducted twelve focus groups across the District of Columbia, Virginia, and Maryland region. Fifty-eight percent (thirty-one persons) of the sample are generation X, and 42 percent (twenty-three persons) are baby boomers. Forty-seven percent of the sample are female, and 53 percent are male. Forty percent have never been married, while 29 percent are currently married, and 31 percent have been divorced, separated, or widowed.

Beyond the key variables of gender, generation, and marital status, the primary recruitment objective for this study was to get an adequate array of demographic characteristics by race and class. As an indicator of class, the responses for father's highest education is relatively balanced: bachelor's degree or more (26 percent), some college (22 percent), high school degree (29 percent), and less than a high school degree (20 percent). Compared to the region's demographics, I sampled a relatively smaller proportion of whites (24 percent), a relatively greater proportion of blacks (58 percent), and a slightly greater proportion of Latinos (18 percent). The DC-VA-MD metropolitan area in which I recruited and conducted my interviews is 40 percent white, 35 percent black, and 14 percent Hispanic (US Census Bureau: 2008–2013 American Community Survey). However, one of the three recruitment areas included Prince George's County, which is 15 percent white, 65 percent black, and 16 percent Hispanic (US Census Bureau: State and County QuickFacts 2013). The sample for this study is not statistically representative of the US population. However, the purpose of this research is not generalization to the US population. Rather, I seek to discover instances of attitudes, perceptions, and explanations within the targeted subgroups.

The sample in this study was designed to include the three largest US ethnoracial groups of whites, blacks, and Latinos. Incorporating an ethnoracial analysis makes an important contribution to the literature on family formation, since such an analysis is often missing (McLoyd et al. 2000). Prior studies based on historical data (or the cohort-analysis approach that I use) often do not extend beyond the black-white binary (e.g., Goldstein and Kenney 2001). Further, the few studies in this research area that include a racial analysis generally do not differentiate Hispanic Americans, who might be racially categorized as white, and non-Hispanic white Americans, who might not be ethnically categorized as non-Hispanic (e.g., Sweeney 2002). For those that include an analysis of Hispanics, they often do not disaggregate the Hispanic category into detailed origin groups (e.g., Torr 2011).

I include in the analysis an examination of the patterns of Latinos of Mexican descent because the pan-ethnic group of Hispanics is highly heterogeneous, and research shows that the pan-ethnic group should be disaggregated by detailed origin for demographic analysis (Landale and Oropesa 2007). In addition to having a long presence in US territory, Mexican-descent Latinos make up the detailed Hispanic-origin group, with the largest number and percent native born (US Census Bureau 2011c and Gómez 2007). It is important to include in the emerging theory on the changing economic basis of family formation the second-largest US ethnoracial group. This research advances the marriage literature by expanding the sometimes-limited viewpoint regarding ethnoracial analysis, which has been critiqued at times for being static and in some cases based on stereotypes that contradict actual US trends (Ybarra 1982; Zavella 1984, 1987; and McLoyd et al. 2000). For example, according to Ortiz (1994), "Although Mexican American women have long been characterized as adhering to traditional roles in the family, empirical evidence demonstrates that Chicanas are active participants in both home and work environments."

INDIVIDUAL INTERVIEWS

For select cases, I use the approach of doing intensive one-on-one verbal interviews (n=12 individuals interviewed). Lofland et al. (2006) describes this approach as encompassing:

> Both ordinary conversation and listening as it occurs naturally during the course of social interaction and semi-structured interviewing involving the use of an interview guide consisting of a list of open-ended

questions that direct conversation without forcing the interviewee to select pre-established responses. (p. 17)

One objective of the individual interview is to achieve a richer portrayal of particular cases. A face-to-face individual interview provides a more humanistic and holistic understanding of the information provided by a research participant.

Another objective is to cognitively test my instruments in order to better facilitate the focus group interviews. For example, while research participants answer the questionnaires, I note how respondents go through answering the instrument (e.g., whether the participant changes his or her responses, demonstrates any other notable behaviors, or asks for clarifications). During the verbal discussion, I probe for their personal understanding of the questions and the terms that I use. After completing the interview, I ask the participants for their feedback about their experience and feelings about the research protocols. This process can be described as the retrospective think-aloud approach in cognitive testing (Willis 2005).

The open-ended and semistructured individual interview allows discovery of new things—such as terms, concepts, impressions, and mechanisms—at the initial stage of the research process. Becoming familiar and being able to pick up unique understandings and/or to recognize a specific meaning that may be expressed in particular vernacular is important to enhancing interviewing competency. It allows me to more effectively guide especially the group interviews, which require more complex facilitation, as well as to ultimately better understand the data.

FOCUS GROUP INTERVIEWS

For group contextualized-data collection, I conduct focus group interviews (n=12 focus groups interviewed). Per Carey (1994), the focus group interview is a "semi-structured group session, moderated by a group leader, held in an informal setting with the purpose of collecting information on a designated topic" (p. 226). This strategy allows the collection of rich, in-depth responses within a group context (Merton et al. 1990; Morgan 1996). Indeed, the major advantage of this method is that it allows the researcher to directly access the experiences, concepts, attitudes, and understandings of the participants in a group setting that permits participant interaction (Hughes and DuMont 1993; Carey 1994; Wilkinson 1998).

Morgan (1988) noted that the focus group is an especially important research strategy when you want to examine the perspective of a specific target population. In a group setting, each participant's perspective can be linked to others with selected shared characteristics (Morgan 1988, 1993; Krueger and Casey 2000). As the verbal responses of each participant are connected in an interactive process, the interview can reveal individual and group-level perspectives as well as group dynamics. The unit of analysis is the individual, but the data represent observations that are contextualized by the group setting.

To reflect the changing sociohistorical context of marrying, I create focus groups that are homogeneous by each generation. The focus groups that are organized by generation allow participants to relate their beliefs and feelings as a group that experienced primary socialization and young adulthood in a shared historical context. However, two focus groups were heterogeneous across generation in order to accommodate late arrivals. In addition, I was interested in allowing participants to compare and contrast their beliefs and feelings as individuals that experienced primary socialization and young adulthood in shared as well as different historical contexts.

THE EVENT-HISTORY CALENDAR

In the individual interviews where I have more time with each participant, I use the event-history calendar (EHC) method because my data include retrospective reports, which are subject to recall error that may affect data completeness, consistency, and accuracy. There is an established tradition of using an event-history calendar to verify data and to aid in more accurate and complete collection of data when the recall period spans the life course (Caspi et al. 1996; Freedman et al. 1988; Kessler and Wethington 1991). The approach is based on the study of life histories as consisting of trajectories and transitions (Freeman et al. 1988; Elder 1985).

A principal reason to use an event-history calendar in research is that it works with the structure of autobiographical memory to aid in gaining information about recalled events and perceptions via multiple pathways (Belli 1998; Anderson and Pichert 1978; Fisher and Quigley 1992). Traditional survey methods, such as the question-list method, do not tap into the relational and contextual basis of memory. Per Belli (1998), in an event-history calendar:

> Respondents are encouraged to consider various events that constitute their personal pasts as contained within broader thematic streams of events. Not only can respondents note the interrelationship of events within the same themes (top-down and sequential retrieval) but, depending on which themes are represented by the calendar, respondents can also note the interrelationships among events that exist with different themes (parallel retrieval). (p. 394)

We can relate the concept of themes in qualitative analysis to the concept of life domains. Major domains are likely to represent themes that are shared by members of a particular culture—those who experienced the same social context at a particular historical time (ibid., p. 395). In this way, discussing the lifetime period and the reference of the generation the participant belongs to can help retrieve more specific information about the events I am interested in, such as first marriage.

In the research interviews, the length of recall is the full lifetime history, which is recorded at the person-year unit level. First experiences are used as linear landmarks (Thompson et al. 1996; Pillemer et al. 1988; Robinson 1992). Belli (1998) suggests that linear landmarks are better for longer recall periods. The interview is structured to allow cross-checking of the reporting of events by my reviewing the calendar with the participant throughout the interview. This encourages parallel retrieval (Kessler and Washington 1991; Fricke, Syed, and Smith 1986). The calendar's spatial representation provides an easy way for the respondent and/or the researcher to verify the information for gaps, inconsistencies, or unexpected patterns.

Using the EHC method, I am able to cue for specific events and perceptions about specific events as the research participants work through the lifetime period and general events in the calendar before recalling and reporting specific events. By cuing the thematic and chronological ordering of autobiographical knowledge, the participant can more fully recall even distant memories (Conway and Bekerian 2000). Studies show that events that occur at boundaries of temporal periods or at life-period transition points, such as at a marriage, are more memorable than other events (Barsalou 1988; Pillemer et al. 1988; Rubin 1986). According to Belli (1998),

> By reflecting the structure of autobiographical memory, the use of event history calendars has considerable potential in assisting respondents to reconstruct their personal pasts more completely and accurately…encouraging individuals to use cues that are available in multiple, interconnected pathways increases the potential of maximizing the quality and completeness of remembered events. (p. 383, p. 393)

RESEARCH VIGNETTES

An appropriate rationale to use vignettes as a central qualitative research strategy is that it is not possible to directly study the attitudes or behavior of interest (Ganong and Coleman 2006). In this study, the behavior I want to examine is not observable in the natural setting. I am interested in responses about retrospective data for those ever married, hypothetical or prospective data for those never married, and hypothetical data about different levels of earning power so that I can examine the effects of randomization of predictor variables that I otherwise would not be able to randomly assign. The vignette method helps me get richer and better-quality responses regarding hypothetical data.

Studies show that the use of research vignettes allows participants to express rather clearly their perceptions and attitudes about concrete situations (Barter and Renold 1999; Gould 1996; Hughes and Huby 2002). More specifically, prior studies have used vignettes successfully in examining gender-role ideology (Kroska 2000; Pedersen 2010). This vignette method tends to make respondents feel less guarded or threatened compared to when asked about their own behavior (Finch 1987). In this regard, vignettes can be helpful in collecting data from participants who otherwise might not feel open to expressing certain attitudes regarding their own family or romantic relations. For example, a man might not want to say he would rather his wife do all the housework, but he might report positive attitudes about the traditional household structure in a hypothetical scenario.

Also, vignettes allow for random experimentation such that by changing independent variables in the vignette, we can see how such variation affects the observed responses (Ganong and Coleman 2006). In the vignettes, I manipulate the variable of high versus low earning power to examine how different levels of earning power affect the desirability for the hypothetical couple to marry from the research participant's perspective. Two vignettes include a couple where the man and the woman are depicted with the same level of earning power. Couple A is the high-earning-power couple. Couple B is the low-earning-power couple. Two additional vignettes are of a couple with opposite levels of earning power. Couple C is a high-earning-power male and a low-earning-power female, the traditional male breadwinner couple. Couple D is a high-earning-power female and a low-earning-power male, the nontraditional female breadwinner couple.

Hypothetically, the high-earning-power couple provides the most gains to the dual-earner model of marriage in terms of sharing aggregated income and consumption power. The low-earning-power couple represents the gains of two earners to share a minimum level of pooled income. The low-earning-power couple is depicted as also having unstable work histories, so respondents might perceive that they should marry in order to seek enhanced income security with two earners. Theoretically, other sample participants might think that the low-earning-power couple should not marry because they do not meet a minimal marriage-bar threshold.

In contrast, the traditional male breadwinner couple represents the inverse relation of human capital in the labor market, who would facilitate the greatest gains to specialization based on the traditional model of household structure. This can be contrasted to the scenario of the nontraditional female breadwinner couple, where I can test whether the gains to specialization might operate even when the traditional gender roles are reversed such that the female may take on the sole provider role and the male may take on the homemaking role.

VALIDITY AND RELIABILITY

Validity can be defined as whether the claims made in the research study are "accurate" or "actually discovered" (Schensul et al. 1999; Warren and Karner 2005). Krueger and Casey (2000) claim that focus groups generally have high face validity. However, qualitative studies often ignore or struggle with the application of the positivist dimension of validity. On the one hand, probabilistic and sampling theory cannot be applied to narrative data. On the other hand, qualitative methods tend to lack standard criterion and procedures. Per Schensul et al. (1999), "Some researchers argue that ethnographic studies are so unique that neither their results nor their techniques can be applied anywhere else" (p. 285). I tend toward the position that there are dimensions of these research concepts that are indeed relevant and important.

For example, in this study, it is important to achieve a dimension of internal validity in terms of whether the responses obtained from research participants are a valid reflection of how they actually feel and think. Further, it is important to address a dimension of external validity in terms of whether it is credible that the research conducted can be generalizable from the subsamples of persons to the counterpart population. However, I would also argue that there are limits and documented pitfalls in applying the criterion for validity and reliability too stringently to qualitative research (for examples, see Schensul et al. 1999).

The unique dynamics among the participants, the researcher moderator, and group setting may result in findings that would be difficult to replicate. The objective is that my role as a moderator remains as neutral as possible. To balance these considerations, my goal regarding validity and reliability is to establish a high-quality empirical analysis that is transparent, credible, and logically sound. I provide detail of my procedures to enhance the potential for replicability. Future work will be to test the reliability of the results by conducting additional studies in different sites and with different populations.

SAMPLING

The persons I interview are selected purposefully to capture the range of key demographics for this study. Purposeful sampling is a good strategy when the study is focused on particular characteristics that relate to the research question (Lofland 2006, p. 93). The sampling strategy is to create a total of twelve groups equally divided by the two research generations, the baby boomer generation and generation X. Based on the considerations of the effects of historical change and socialization, I make an analytical distinction between the baby boomer and generation X birth cohorts that represents a meaningful cut-off from a theoretical perspective.

In order to make the cutoff clear, I focus on recruiting the early baby boomer birth cohorts from 1948 to 1958. These are the earliest baby boomer birth cohorts that were born right at the end or immediate years following the end of World War II. I do not focus on the early baby boomer cohorts from 1945 to 1947 because they may be special cohorts that are more like the cohorts of World War II babies (i.e., not clearly distinguishable from the cohorts of the prior generation, the lucky few generation). I also do not focus on the later baby boomer birth cohorts from 1959 to 1964. These are years in which the later baby boomer birth cohorts experienced the degenderization in wage work during some part of the stages of primary and secondary socialization.

With respect to generation X, I focus on recruiting the core generation X birth cohorts from 1968 to 1978. I do not focus on recruiting the birth cohorts from 1965 to 1967 because these are years in which the traditional male breadwinner model was still dominant among the early generation X cohorts. Essentially, I do not focus on cohorts that make the generational cutoff markers murkier (the beginning two and end three years of each generation) and in which there is generational overlap in the substantive type of cohort experiences that are theoretically relevant to my research inquiry (the 1959–1964 birth cohorts).

I interview a total of fifty-five individuals. Most interviews are conducted in the focus group format. Twelve people are interviewed in the individual format. In the focus groups, each group is balanced in terms of race, gender, and socioeconomic status categories. The target age range of the younger generation at the time of the survey (in year 2013) is thirty-five to forty-five (for the generation X target birth cohorts 1968–1978). The possible age range of the older generation at the time of the survey is fifty-five to sixty-five (for baby boomer target birth cohorts 1948–1958).

Because I am most interested in understanding how women's higher earning power is evaluated in relation to marrying, I focus on recruiting participants with a college education or above. Collecting data on college-educated research participants creates a sample of men and women who are most familiar with the perceptions of how women with higher education are perceived in the marriage market and in the household for their respective generation group. Further, there are other studies that though different in focus from this study nevertheless relate to gender attitudes and family patterns specifically among persons with low socioeconomic status/educational levels (Rainwater 1966; Grebler et al. 1970; Lamphere et al. 1993; Wilson 1996; and Edin and Kefalas 2005). I draw upon these as valuable references to supplement the original data I collect.

In the initial demographic screener, I collect data for a range of characteristics.[34] Based on the data, I recruit eligible participants (i.e., adults that are US native-born black, white, or Mexican American and born in the range of the baby boomer or X generation birth cohorts). Further, I target particular cases of interest. Per Weiss (1994), when the sample is small, it is important to specifically recruit participants from the full range of subject characteristics or types that relate to your research inquiry.

With the existing literature as a guide, I recruit until I have coverage of a variety of key types of cases that might lead to new information. For example, I recruit some participants who did and some who did not experience divorce while growing up. As previously discussed, studies suggest that

---

34 The screener collects data such as residence, gender, age, nativity, race/ethnicity, education, year finished schooling, employment status, occupation, service in the armed forces, earnings, marital status, cohabitation, sexual orientation, parental status, religion and religiosity, characteristics of the family of origin (parental marital status, maternal and paternal employment, maternal and paternal education, and family income), and childhood experiences with childcare.

the (recalled) experiences of divorce may make an individual more likely to perceive the dual-earner household structure positively. As I am interested in the relation between specific experiences and attitudes, it is important that I recruit participants who have and have not experienced critical events, such as divorce.

On the key variables of interest, I reach saturation in the sense that I feel confident that I have the individuals necessary to examine my research questions. However, I balance the goal of saturation with the goal of not becoming overwhelmed by the amount of data. I also manage during the recruitment process pragmatic considerations of time and other resources. Recruitment is based on convenience sampling, as the scheduling of the individual and focus groups is driven by logistical factors. For example, there were several winter storms during the interview phase that caused the focus groups to be canceled and rescheduled. In those cases, the focus group participants who were available to attend the rescheduled sessions were smaller than the originally scheduled sessions.

It is important to note that the sample is not statistically representative of the US population. Since the purpose of this research is not generalization to the United States or any other population, I do not work to infer causation to a particular population. Rather, I seek to discover instances of attitudes, perceptions, and explanations within the targeted subgroups. Furthermore, the interpretations of the findings should be considered tentative because the analysis clearly cannot separate the three measures of time—age, period, and cohort. Yet a theoretically driven analysis should garner some confidence despite that it does not disentangle each of the three time-related concepts (Rabe-Hesketh and Skrondal 2012).

FOCUS GROUP COMPOSITION AND SAMPLE SIZE

Krueger and Casey (2000) write that when group members are of similar backgrounds, there is a more ready openness for participants to offer input. The size and setting of the group is also important. Each group has about four participants. Per Greenbaum (1988), the recommended number of participants varies from small groups (four to six) to full groups (ten to twelve). Merton et al. (1990) indicates that groups can be as large as twenty without being unwieldy. However, there is no consensus, and various studies find different advantages and disadvantages to varying group sizes. I opt to conduct small focus groups to allow for greater group interaction and more substantive contribution from and among the research participants.

Within each group by generation, there is variation among participants by other selected characteristics such as race, gender, socioeconomic status, age, and marital status. Carey (1993) suggests that it is better to maintain homogenous groups. However, it is important to note that I am not only interested in the group consensus, which may be interpreted as group-level perceptions. I also examine disagreement and within-group variation. Within-group variation may reflect a random individual difference in perceptions or a shared variation by an alternative group-level characteristic, such as race. In this way, heterogeneity in the group is also important to my research.

RECRUITMENT STRATEGIES

I use diverse strategies and public settings to recruit individuals with the wide range of targeted demographics. In person, I recruit at parks, libraries, and train stations in the DC, Maryland, and Virginia area. These types of settings allow me to access a target population that is not restricted only to students, as many student-led research projects do. Online, I use social media (e.g., Facebook) and community boards (e.g., Craigslist and Meetup) to recruit people to complete the initial screener via e-mail. Based on the data from the screener collected via the in-person recruitment (an on-paper screener) or via Internet recruitment (an e-mailed screener), participants are recruited to the second stage to participate in the written questionnaire and the verbal individual interview and/or the focus group interview.

Per Morgan (1988), cash incentives can help with the recruitment of participants. For participants who complete the full individual interview, I offer cash rewards up to twenty-five dollars per person. For participants who complete the full group interview, I offer an incentive up to ten dollars per person or raffle entry for a raffle prize up to fifty dollars. Prior research highlights the advantages of food in helping to build a comfortable environment conducive to group cohesion and participants feeling relaxed (Carey 1993; McDaniel and Bach 1996). Thus, I also offer refreshments at the focus group interview.

DATA COLLECTION

Procedures

The procedures for the data collection include the (a) written demographic screener, (b) written questionnaire, and (c) verbal individual (one-on-one) interview or (d) verbal focus group interview. The steps are carried out in two stages. The first stage is the broad in-person or Internet recruitment effort to distribute and collect the written screener. The second stage is conducting the written questionnaire and either the in-person individual interview or the in-person group interview.

At the start of the in-person interview, I more formally introduce the study to the group. I explain the use of the medium to record the data (audio recording), and the medium provides a valuable way to collect data. I assure the participants of confidentiality. In addition, they are reminded that any research participant can stop his or her participation at any time. They are also reminded that their privacy will be protected in the storing of the data.

The opening of the verbal dialogue is with an icebreaker. I ask each participant to make up a pseudonym (a "code nickname"). I tell the participants that this pseudonym will allow for another layer of anonymity. The subsequent data analysis is based on an anonymous ID that is disconnected from any individually identifiable information, and the released research uses a pseudonym.

STAGE I: SCREENER

The purpose of the first step, the screener, is to collect potential participant demographics (residence, gender, age, nativity, race/ethnicity, education, year finished schooling, employment status, occupation, service in the armed forces, earnings, marital status, cohabitation, sexual orientation, parental status, religion, and religiosity). I also ask about characteristics of the individual's family of origin (parental marital status, maternal and paternal employment, maternal and paternal education, and family income). Additionally, I ask about childhood experiences with childcare. At this step, participants are informed of the purpose and procedures of the study and asked if they consent to participate in the next steps of the study. Eligible participants are recruited based on the demographic screener to participate in the next stage according to the recruitment strategy (previously discussed). The next stages are the written questionnaire and in-person interview.

STAGE II, STEP 1: WRITTEN QUESTIONNAIRE

At the in-person interview, the written questionnaire is completed first and prior to the start of the session. The purpose of the written questionnaire is to ask the participant central questions regarding his or her perspective on the relation between earning power and marrying. I ask here whether the participant's or a potential spouse's employment, earnings, homemaking ability, education, or being in love would make the participant more, less, or equally likely to marry. I also ask whether a potential spouse having greater or lesser earning power would make the participant more, less, or equally likely to marry.

In the written questionnaire, I also collect written responses for some of the more common survey questions in the gender-role literature, such as whether both parents working hurt a young child or the spousal relation. Is it important to marry if there is a pregnancy for the couple? Would it be best for the participant, the potential spouse, or both to work in the household? Another question on this form asks the research participant to rank in order of importance the most common advantages cited in the gains-to-marrying literature, including the traditional functions of marriage such as procreation, sexual activity, or companionship. I also ask participants to provide a written response regarding a question on the importance of money, or a minimum threshold of money, in the likelihood that someone marries.

The last section of the written questionnaire includes one of the randomly selected vignettes of a hypothetical couple of either a (i) higher-earning male, high-earning female (Couple A); (ii) low-earning male, low-earning female (Couple B); (iii) a high-earning male, low-earning female (Couple C); or (iv) a high-earning female, low-earning male (Couple D). I ask the participant to respond to a question about the advantages and disadvantages for the hypothetical couple to marry, as well as a question about potential long-term fulfillment if the couple were to marry.

Each participant is asked about only one randomly distributed vignette because I think it would be overwhelming to collect written reactions of all the vignettes from one participant. Since the vignettes are written to be as similar as possible, the administration of more than one vignette on the questionnaire without any additional guidance or context could cause confusion. However, the various research vignettes are discussed in the verbal dialogue, with guidance from the researcher.

A review of the participant's responses from the written questionnaire is discussed verbally in the individual and focus group interviews (in the next step). As mentioned, though the vignettes are randomly split among the participants in the questionnaire, the various vignettes are discussed in the individual and focus group interviews. The purpose of the combination of using written questionnaires in addition to the verbal interview is to help uncover/verify individual responses that may not be provided and/or accurately represented in the verbal interview. This is especially a concern for the focus group interviews. Sometimes individual perspectives are not congruent with individual responses provided in a focus group setting (Carey and Smith 1994 and Morgan 1988). Thus, the multiple strategies and interview modes help to verify the accuracy and consistency in the participants' views.

STAGE II, STEP 2A: INDIVIDUAL (ONE-ON-ONE) INTERVIEWS
The individual interview is based on a semistructured conversational approach. Firstly, the participant is instructed to enter major life events and transitions onto the event-history calendar (EHC) instrument. This is an activity during which I aid the participant to complete the EHC. The EHC instrument includes a graphical display of the time dimension and major life events. I have an EHC graphical display for each life-course stage of early childhood, late childhood and adolescence, and adulthood. The time dimension is divided into smaller time units—years. The graphical display covers the

domains of (1) relationships and marriage, (2) childcare, (3) fertility, (4) education, and (5) employment.

I ask the participant to think aloud about the important memories and feelings evoked as we go over the event-history calendar. Why are those important? How so? What did they mean to the participant? We then discuss the participant's responses to the research vignettes. I continue to probe for deeper information by discussing the participant's responses to the written questions one to four. Further, I ask the participant whether their ideas or behaviors about gender relations, marriage, and household roles have changed over time. To encourage the participant to more fully explain his or her responses and impressions, feelings, and perceptions throughout the interview, I use probes such as "tell me more" and "how so."

I then invite the participant to tell me how the events and life transitions entered in the EHC connect to his or her past and present views, behavioral patterns, and decisions as they relate to gender roles, family formation, and the economic basis of marrying. I also draw upon the information in the screener to facilitate this part of the dialogue. By asking participants to make connections among the various reports they have made, not only do I collect richer data about the importance of earning power on marrying from the participants' perspectives, but I permit them to serve as a coresearcher. Essentially, the participant helps in explaining what might be some of the conditioning variables that account for what he or she has reported about the relation between earning power and marrying.

Some examples of probing questions I ask to evoke participant introspection include the following: Do you recall specific memories, ways of talking about these topics with your parents while growing up, and/or with friends during adolescence? Do you think any past experiences with family or friends influenced your own gender-specific or family-specific attitudes or behaviors? Did you make decisions about marrying and/or the performance of household roles that mimic the decisions of your parents or others from the same generation, gender, or race? How so? If your decisions about marrying and/or the performance of household roles seem not like others (family, friends, or peers), what might have led to you unique pattern of decision-making? How did conditions in the economy, employment experiences, or changes in you household's economic standing affect your gender-specific or family-specific views or behavior? What else might have influenced your gender-specific or family-specific views and/or behaviors (e.g., religion, personal hardship, historical events, etc.)?

Stage II, Step 2B: Focus group Interview

At the beginning of the session for the focus group interview, I tell the group that the interview is only to discuss the participants' experiences, opinions, and perceptions. I reinforce that every opinion is valued equally, whether it is the same, similar, or different from other participants' opinions. There are no responses that are right or wrong, or better or worse. It is also important that I stress that once the session begins, my only role is to ask questions, ask for clarification, and/or to provide transitions to the next question. I let the research participants know that it is for the sake of the quality of the data that I stay neutral and refrain from providing any substantive input or my own personal opinions.

Firstly, the focus group participants are instructed and aided in completing the written questionnaire. To start the group discussion, I discuss the research vignettes and then proceed to discuss questions one to four from the written questionnaire. I start with initial questions, and all participants are asked to share a response: What is your code name, and have you ever been married? By having each person make a contribution at the beginning, it shapes the conversation as one in which all participants participate. I convey to the group that the input of each person is valued. Thereafter, participants are asked to volunteer to share and compare or contrast their responses with the group in a more flexible manner (i.e., I do not request that every participant answer every question). I complete field notes after each interview is completed so as not to distract from my role as moderator.

Group Moderation and the Interview Guidelines

In this study, I am the interviewer and group moderator. Morgan (1996) identifies that a major component of the focus group research is the active role of the group moderator. There is an important balance to achieve in terms of how much influence should be exerted. For Basch (1987), the group moderator should establish a

> non-threatening supportive climate that encourages all participants to share views; facilitating interaction among members; interjecting probing comments; transitional question and summaries without interfering too brusquely with the dialogue; covering important topics and questions while relying on judgments to

abandon aspects of the outline, noting non-verbal responses. (p. 415)

It is due to the critical role of the group leader and to ensure consistency that I serve as the moderator for all focus groups, and I use one assistant to help with logistics as needed. Further, in order to collect broadly comparable data across groups, I ask respondents to verbally discuss the standard set of questions and vignettes that are in the written interview questionnaire. An important objective is to ensure that all content is covered across the groups but yet maintain enough flexibility to allow participants to fully participate, interact with each other, and/or introduce new information. A strategy is to probe nonresponsive participants about whether they agree with the comments being made by others or if they would like to add a different perspective. Another strategy is to provide direction to avoid repetition, interruptions, simultaneous input, or dominance in the group.

For Kitzinger (1996), a disadvantage of the group setting may be that it can silence voices of dissent. Some individuals may conform to the opinion of others or censor themselves. Another issue might be "social loafing," where some participants may show less frequent participation or be quiet as they rely on others to provide the responses. Given this potential pattern, it is important to not infer meaning to nonresponsiveness, such as agreement, unless there is some verification. Thus, even if there seems to be group agreement, I probe silent participants to provide their perspectives in their own words. This strategy serves to verify opinions or draw out new information.

Eliciting new concepts, constructs, or explanations is a key strength of the focus group interview (Morgan 1996). Thus, some verbal "wandering" by participants is permitted given that it allows unanticipated data to be collected (Carey 1994). However, I guide the dialogue in a way that encourages new topics and tangents that are within the scope of the objectives of the study. It is important that group members are not distracted into irrelevant areas or subdivided into separate conversations. Likewise, it is important that I, as the moderator, diffuse any negative interactions or confrontations in the group (Basch 1987; Krueger 1994).

Thematic Analysis

Following the literature on thematic and content analysis, I organize the raw verbal data into patterned relations (Budd 1967; Morgan 1988, 1993; Krueger and Casey 2000). A common strategy is to start the analysis by identifying key phrases from the data to create clusters of similar narrative and then reduce and organize the clusters into categories and subcategories. It is recommended to continually analyze the data while checking and evaluating the emerging categories. This allows me to incorporate new topics from the focus groups into the analysis of the patterns of relationships between categories, themes, and individual as well as group characteristics.

Key Concept: Earning Power

In this study, I use the indicators of educational attainment, employment, and earnings to represent different dimensions of the concept of earning power. Like many other studies, I consider actual wages to be an appropriate indicator of current earning power in the labor market for those employed (Clarkberg 1999; MacDonald and Rindfuss 1981; Mare and Winship 1991; Oppenheimer et al. 1997; Sweeney 2002). Other studies use employment (Goldscheider and Waite 1986; Oppenheimer et al. 1997; Sweeney 2002) or work experience (Clarkberg 1999; Oppenheimer et al. 1997; Sweeney 2002) as indicators of earning power.

It is important to note that education level serves as an indicator of long-term earning power and/or potential wages when not commensurably compensated or if not at all in the labor market (Thornton, Axinn, and Teachman 1995; Oppenheimer et al. 1997; Sweeney 2002). Thus, education level is an especially critical measure when considering the earning power of a woman. Compared to men, women are more likely to have intermittent labor-market participation (Blau and Kahn 2000). However, it is important to further note that educational level has multiple nonmarket dimensions. For example, education can result in the benefits of garnering social status or improving the quality of childrearing (Becker 1981). Thus, it may be expected that the effect of women's education on marriage might be positive based on considerations not related to earning power.

Previous studies have found mixed results regarding earning power and the likelihood of marrying through time. By gender and race, data from the American Community Survey (ACS) and the US Decennial Census show that white women experienced a college advantage in the propensity to marry compared to their lesser-educated counterparts for the first time in the early twenty-first century (Fry 2010). For men, these data show that those with a college education have been just as likely or more likely to get married compared to those without a college degree since the 1960s (ibid.). However, as these patterns are the result of univariate statistics and cross-sectional data only, they are inadequate to address the question of this study regarding how earning power might be conditional on the historical context and US generation.

Yet existing studies based on multivariate analysis and the use of longitudinal data have also resulted in varied findings regarding the relation between earning power and marrying across time. Such studies on men have consistently found a positive effect of earnings on marriage entry as well as of employment on marriage entry. However, there are somewhat inconsistent findings from such studies regarding the significance and direction of the association between educational attainment and marriage (Qian and Preston 1993; Oppenheimer 1997; Fitch and Ruggles 2000; Edin 2000; Gibson, Edin, and McLanahan 2003; Sassler and Goldscheider 2004). Congruent with the descriptive findings from data of the US Census and ACS, some multivariate studies estimate that the direction of the effect of education is cohort specific, with only later cohorts showing a positive effect (Goldscheider and Waite 1993 and Brüderl and Diekmann 1994).

One way to understand these findings for men is that the economic return to education has changed over time, with educational attainment becoming increasingly salient as a predictor of long-term earnings (Acs and Danzinger 1993 and Katz and Murphy 1992). Further, the return to different levels of degree attainment has changed based on specific periods. Boesel and Fredlan (1999) find that the rate of economic return to a college degree has been greater than the rate of return to a high school diploma in the past few decades. A component of this change is likely based on market effects that affect both genders. Thus, the changes observed among men provide a useful benchmark to understand the changes observed among women.

For women, there are mixed findings from multivariate and longitudinal studies regarding earning power and marrying. Some researchers find the relationship between women's wages and marriage to be negative (Frieden 1974; Preston and Richards 1975). Another study using data from the 1979 to the 1986 waves of the National Longitudinal Survey of Youth found that earnings increased the probability of marrying for white women only (Oropesa, Lichter, and Anderson 1994). The contrasts in these studies may be based on changes in the effect over time as well as race effects that may also have changed over time.

Regarding education, some researchers have found no relationship or a negative relationship between educational attainment and marriage (Bennett, Bloom, and Craig 1989; Bloom and Bennett 1990; Cookingham 1984; and Blossfeld and Huinink 1991). Theoretically, several arguments have made the case that the link between education and marrying among women should be a negative one. Some stress that education has a direct effect on reducing a woman's desire to marry. For example, education could lead to women placing less value on being a wife and more value on her own independence. It is important to note that the very concept of women's economic independence is often operationalized by her earning power as measured in this study (Oppenheimer and Lew 1995, p. 110).[35]

Another set of literature focuses on the role of selection. Early eugenicists claimed that college attracted women with abnormal sexual instincts. Others argued that differences in selection occurred due to mostly unattractive and/or less family-oriented women graduating from college (Cookingham 1984). In the influential book *The Feminist Mystique*, Betty Freidman (1963) argues that many scholars and educators promoted the belief that too much education is unfeminine. Freidman characterizes high educational attainment to be a social marriage bar for US women during the mid-twentieth century.

Yet later literature finds a positive effect of educational attainment on marrying. Whereas women with more education were less likely to marry in the past, more recent studies find that more educated women now marry at higher levels (Goldstein and Kenney 2001; Sweeney 2002; and Torr 2011). This study builds on the growing evidence that a woman's educational level switched from being negatively to positively related to marrying, by studying the importance of multiple dimensions of women's earning power between each analytic generation and across the three major US ethnoracial groups, which to my knowledge has not yet been established.

This research inquiry would be difficult to examine with primarily quantitative methods because there is a high level of collinearity in the measures that are important to the analysis. The variables of education, employment, and earnings are

---

35 "Most studies have focused on only a few indicators of women's actual or potential economic independence—educational attainment, work status, and earnings" (Oppenheimer and Lew 1995).

highly correlated, and the variables of age, period, and generation are linearly related. This provides a challenge to clearly disentangling the effects that I study with standard quantitative methods. I fill a gap in the literature using qualitative methods that allow me to illustrate how and why the relation between earning power and marrying is converging at the intersections of race, class, and gender in the U.S.

Works Cited

Acs, Gregorym and Sheldon Danzinger. 1993. "Educational Attainment, Industrial Structure, and Male Earnings through the 1980s." *The Journal of Human Resources* 28 (3): 618–648.

Aldous, Joan. 1969. "Wives' Employment Status and Lower-Class Men as Husband-Fathers: Support for the Moynihan Thesis." *Journal of Marriage and the Family*, 469–476.

Anderson, Richard, and James Pichert. 1978. "Recall of Previously Unrecallable Information Following a Shift in Perspective." *Journal of Verbal Learning and Verbal Behavior* 17 (1): 1–12.

Axelson, Leland. 1963. "The Marital Adjustment and Marital Role Definitions of Husbands of Working and Nonworking Wives." *Marriage and Family Living* 25 (2): 189–195.

Axelson, Leland. 1970. "The Working Wife: Differences in Perception among Negro and White Males." *Journal of Marriage and the Family* 32 (3): 457–464.

Barsalou, Lawrence. 1988. "The Content and Organization of Autobiographical Memories." In *Remembering Reconsidered: Ecological and Traditional Approaches to the Study of Memory*, edited by Neisser and Winograd, 193–243. New York: Cambridge University Press.

Barter, Christine, and Emma Renold. 1999. "The Use of Vignettes in Qualitative Research." *Social Research Update* 25:1–4.

Barton, P. 2000. *What Jobs Require: Literacy, Education, and Training, 1940–2006*. Princeton: Educational Testing Service.

Basch, Charles. 1987. "Focus Group Interview: An Underutilized Research Technique for Improving Theory and Practice in Health Education." *Health Education Quarterly* 14 (4): 411–448.

Becker, Gary. 1973. "A Theory of Marriage: Part I." *Journal of Political Economy* 81:813–46.

———. 1974. "A Theory of Marriage: Part II." *Journal of Political Economy* 82:11–26.

———. 1974. "A Theory of Social Interactions." *Journal of Political Economy* 82:1063–1093.

———. 1981. *A Treatise on the Family*. Cambridge, Mass: Harvard University Press.

———. 1985. "Human Capital, Effort, and the Sexual Division of Labor." *Journal of Labor Economics*: S33–S58.

———. 2011. "Lectures on Human Capital." 2010. ECON 343, No. 18. Chicago: University of Chicago. https://www.youtube.com/watch?v=Wq6CJzY1neY.

Becker, Gary, and Kevin Murphy. 1992. "The Division of Labor, Coordination Costs, and Knowledge." *The Quarterly Journal of Economics* 107:137–1160.

Belli, Robert. 1998. "The Structure of Autobiographical Memory and the Event History Calendar: Potential Improvements in the Quality of Retrospective Reports in Surveys." *Memory* 6 (4): 383–406.

Bennett, Neil, David Bloom, and Patricia Craig. 1989. "The Divergence of Black and White Marriage Patterns." *American Journal of Sociology* 95:692–722.

Billari, Francesco, Hans-Peter Kohler, Gunnar Andersson, and Hans Lundström. 2007. "Approaching the Limit: Long-Term Trends in Late and Very Late Fertility." *Population and Development Review* 33 (1): 149–170.

Bianchi, Suzanne M., and Reynolds Farley. 1979. "Racial Differences in Family Living Arrangements and Economic Well-Being: An analysis of recent trends." *Journal of Marriage and the Family*: 537–551.

Black, Sandra, and Chinhui Juhn. 2000. "The Rise of Female Professionals: Are Women Responding to Skill Demand?" *The American Economic Review* 90 (2): 450–455.

Blau, Francine, and Lawrence Kahn. 2000. "Gender Differences in Pay." National Bureau of Economic Research Working Paper No. w7732.

Bloom, David, and Neil Bennett. 1990. "Modeling American Marriage Patterns." *Journal of the American Statistical Association* 85:1009–1017.

Blossfeld, Hans-Peter, and Johannes Huinink. 1991. "Human Capital Investments or Norms of Role Transition? How Women's Schooling and Career Affect the Process of Family Formation." *The American Journal of Sociology* 97 (1): 143–168.

Boesel, David, and Eric Fredland. 1999. *College for All?: Is There Too Much Emphasis on Getting a 4-Year College Degree?* (NLE 1999-2024). US Department of Education, National Library of Education. Washington, DC: US Government Printing Office.

Bowen, William, and Aldrich Finegan. 1969. *The Economics of Labor Force Participation*. Princeton: Princeton University Press.

Brescoll, Victoria, and Eric Uhlmann. 2005. "Attitudes toward Traditional and Nontraditional Parents." *Psychology of Women Quarterly* 29 (4): 436–445.

Brewster, Karen and Padavic Irene. 2000. "Change in Gender Ideology, 1977–1996: The Contributions of Intra-cohort Change and Population Turnover." *Journal of Marriage and the Family* (May): 477–487.

Brien, Michael. 1997. "Racial Differences in Marriage and the Role of Marriage Markets." *Journal of Human Resources*, 741–778.

Browne, Irene, ed. 1999. *Race, Gender and Economic Inequality: African American and Latina Women in the Labor Market*. New York: Russell Sage Foundation.

Brüderl, Josef, and Andreas Diekmann. 1994. *Education and Marriage: A Comparative Study*. Munich: Institute of Sociology.

Budd, Richard. 1967. *Content Analysis of Communications*. New York: Macmillan Company.

Buss, Allen. 1974. "Generational Analysis: Description, Explanation, and Theory." *Journal of Social Issues* 30 (2): 55–71.

Cain, Glen. 1966. *Married Women in the Labor Force*. Chicago: University of Chicago Press.

Carey, Martha. 1993. "The Group Effect in Focus Groups: Planning, Implementing, and Interpreting Focus Group Research in Critical Issues in Qualitative Research Methods." In *Critical Issues in Qualitative Research Methods*, edited by Janice Morse, 225–241. London: SAGE Publications

Carey, Martha Ann, and Mickey Smith. 1994. "Capturing the Group Effect in Focus Groups: A Special Concern in Analysis." *Qualitative Health Research* 4 (1): 123-127.

Caspi, Avshalom, Terrie Moffitt, Arland Thornton, and Deborah Freedman. 1996. "The Life History Calendar: A Research and Clinical Assessment Method for Collecting Retrospective Event-History Data." *International Journal of Methods in Psychiatric Research* 6:101–114.

Cherlin, Andrew. 1980. "Postponing Marriage: The Influence of Young Women's Work Expectations." *Journal of Marriage and Family* 42 (2): 355–365.

Cherlin, Andrew, and Pamela Walters. 1981. "Trends in United States Men's and Women's Sex-Role Attitudes: 1972 to 1978." *American Sociological Review* 46:453–460.

Cherry, Robert. 1995. "The Culture-of-Poverty Thesis and African Americans: The Work of Gunnar Myrdal and other Institutionalists." *Journal of Economic Issues* 29 (4): 1119–1132.

Clarkberg, Marin. 1999. "The Price of Partnering: The Role of Economic Well-Being in Young Adults' First Union Experiences." *Social Forces* 77 (3): 945–968.

Coelen, Craig, Frederic Glantz, and Daniel Calore. 1977. *Day Care Centers in the U.S.: A National Profile, 1976–1977.* Cambridge, Mass: Abt Associates.

Conway, Martin, and Christopher Pleydell-Pearce. 2000. "The Construction of Autobiographical Memories in the Self-Memory System." *Psychological Review* 107 (2).

Cookingham, Mary. 1984. "Bluestockings, Spinsters, and Pedagogues: Women College Graduates, 1865 to 1910." *Population Studies* (38): 349–642.

Coontz, Stephanie. 1992. *The Way We Never Were: American Families and the Nostalgia Trap.* New York: Basic Books.

———. 2006. *Marriage, a History: How Love Conquered Marriage.* New York: Penguin.

Cox, Oliver. 1940. "Sex Ratio and Marital Status among Negroes." *American Sociological Review* 5:937–947.

Cunningham, Mick. 2009. "Changing Attitudes toward the Male Breadwinner, Female Homemaker Family Model: Influences of Women's Employment and Education over the Lifecourse." *Social Forces* 87 (1): 299–323.

Cutler, Stephen, and Robert Kaufman. 1975. "Cohort Changes in Political Attitudes: Tolerance of Ideological Nonconformity." *Public Opinion Quarterly* 39:70–81.

Davis, James. 2004. "Did Growing Up in the 1960s Leave a Permanent Mark on Attitudes and Values?: Evidence from the General Social Survey." *Public Opinion Quarterly* 68:161–83.

Davis, Angela. 2011. *Women, Race & Class*. New York: Vintage.

Danigelis, Nicholas, Melissa Hardy, and Stephen J. Cutler. 2007. "Population Aging, Intra-cohort Aging, and Sociopolitical Attitudes." *American Sociological Review* 72:812–830.

Drake, Clair. 1965. "The Social and Economic Status of the Negro in the United States." *Daedalus*, 771–814.

Easterlin, Richard. 1978. "What Will 1984 Be Like? Socioeconomic Implications of Recent Twists in Age Structure." *Demography* 15 (4): 397–432.

Eberstein, Isaac, and W. Parker Frisbie. 1976. "Differences in Marital Instability among Mexican Americans, Blacks, and Anglos: 1960 and 1970." *Social Problems*, 609–621.

Edin, Kathryn. 2000. "What Do Low-Income Single Mothers Say about Marriage?" *Social Problems*, 112–133.

Edin, Kathryn and Maria Kefalas. 2005. *Promises I Can Keep: How Poor Women Put Motherhood before Marriage.* Berkeley: University of California Press.

Edin, Kathryn, and Timothy Nelson. 2013. *Doing the Best I Can.* Berkeley: University of California Press.

Elder, Glen, ed. 1985. *Life Course Dynamics: Trajectories and Transitions, 1968–1980.* Ithaca: Cornell University Press.

Finch, Janet. 1987. "The Vignette Technique in Survey Research." *Sociology* 21 (1): 105–114.

Fisher, Ronald, and Kathryn Quigley.1992. "Applying Cognitive Theory in Public Health Investigations: Enhancing Food Recall with the Cognitive Interview." In *Questions about Questions: Inquiries into the Cognitive Bases of Survey,* Judith M. Tauner, 154–169. New York: Russel Sage Foundation.

Fitch, Catherine, and Steven Ruggles. 2000. "Historical Trends in Marriage Formation: The United States 1850–1992." In *The Ties that Bind: Perspectives on Marriage and Cohabitation,* edited by Linda Waite. Hawthorne: Aldine de Gruyter.

Freedman, Deborah, Arland Thornton, Donald Camburn, Duane Alwin, and Linda Young-DeMarco. 1988. "The Life History Calendar: A Technique for Collecting Retrospective Data." *Sociological Methodology* 18 (1): 37–68.

Freiden, Alan. 1974. "The United States Marriage Market." In *Marriage, Family, Human Capital, and Fertility*, 34–56. Chicago: University of Chicago Press.

Friedan, Betty. 1963. *The Feminine Mystique*. New York: Penguin.

Frisbie, W. Parker. 1986. "Variation in Patterns of Marital Instability among Hispanics." *Journal of Marriage and the Family* 48 (1): 99–106.

Fricke, Thomos, Sabiha Syed, and Peter Smith. 1986. "Rural Punjabi Social Organization and Marriage Timing Strategies in Pakistan." *Demography* 23 (4): 489–508.

Frisbie, Parker, Frank Bean, and Isaac Eberstein. 1978. "Patterns of Marital Instability among Mexican Americans, Blacks, and Anglos." In *The Demography of Racial and Ethnic Groups*, edited by Bean and Frisbie, 143–163. New York: Academic Press.

———. 1980. "Recent Changes in Marital Instability among Mexican Americans: Convergence with Black and Anglo Trends?" *Social Forces* 58.4:1205–1220.

Fry, Richard. 2010. "The Reversal of the College Marriage Gap." Pew Research Center. Accessed October 7, 2010. http://www.pewresearch.org/2010/10/07/the-reversal-of-the-college-marriage-gap/.

Fry, Richard and D'Vera Cohn. 2011. "Living Together: The Economics of Cohabitation." Pew Research Center. Accessed June 27, 2011. http://www.pewsocialtrends.org/2011/06/27/living-together-the-economics-of-cohabitation/

Furstenberg, Frank. 2009. "If Moynihan had Only Known: Race, Class, and Family Change in the Late Twentieth Century." *The Annals of the American Academy of Political and Social Science* 621 (1): 94–110.

Ganong, Lawrence and Marilyn Coleman. 2006. "Multiple Segment Factorial Vignette Designs." *Journal of Marriage and Family* 68:455–468.

Gerson, Kathleen. 1985. *Hard Choices: How Women Decide about Work, Career, and Motherhood*. Berkeley: University of California Press.

———. 993. *No Man's Land*. New York: Basic Books.

Gibson-Davis, Christina M., Kathryn Edin, and Sara McLanahan. 2005. "High Hopes but Even Higher Expectations: The Retreat from Marriage Among Low-Income Couples." *Journal of Marriage and Family* 67 (5): 1301–1312.

Gilman, Charlotte. 1998 edition. *Women and Economics: A Study of the Economic Relation between Men and Women as a Factor in Social Evolution*. Mineola: Dover Publications.

Goldin, Claudia. 1984. "The Historical Evolution of Female Earnings Functions and Occupations." *Explorations in Economic History* 21 (1): 1–27.

———. 1988. "Marriage Bars: Discrimination Against Married Women Workers, 1920's to 1950's." National Bureau of Economic Research Working Paper no. w2747.

Goldin, Claudia, and Lawrence Katz. 2000. "The Power of the Pill: Oral Contraceptives and Women's Career and Marriage Decisions." National Bureau of Economic Research Working Paper no. w7527.

Goldscheider, Frances and Linda Waite. 1986. "Sex Differences in the Entry into Marriage." *American Journal of Sociology* 92 (1): 91–109.

———. 1987. "Nest-Leaving Patterns and the Transition to Marriage for Young Men and Women." *Journal of Marriage and the Family* 49 (3): 507–516.

———. 1993. *New Families, No Families*. Berkeley and Los Angeles: University of California Press.

Goldstein, Joshua, and Catherine Kenney. 2001. "Marriage Delayed or Marriage Forgone? New Cohort Forecasts of First Marriage for US Women." *American Sociological Review* 66 (August): 506–519.

Goldstone, Jack. 1986. "The Demographic Revolution in England: A Re-Examination." *Population Studies* 40 (1): 5–33.

Golash-Boza, Tanya, and William Darity. 2008. "Latino Racial Choices: the Effects of Skin Colour and Discrimination on Latinos' and Latinas' Racial Self-Identifications. *Ethnic and Racial Studies* 31 (5): 899–934.

Goode, William. 1963. *World Revolution and Family Patterns*. New York: The Free Press.

Gould, Dinah.1996. "Using Vignettes to Collect Data for Nursing Research Studies: How Valid Are the Findings?" *Journal of Clinical Nursing* 5 (4): 207–212.

Graefe, Deborah, and Daniel Lichter. 2002. "Marriage among Unwed Mothers: Whites, Blacks and Hispanics Compared." *Perspectives on Sexual and Reproductive Health*: 286–293.

Grebler, Leo, Joan Moore, and Ralph Guzman. 1970. *The Mexican-American People: The Nation's Second Largest Minority.* New York: The Free Press.

Greenbaum, Thomas. 1988. *The Practical Handbook and Guide to Focus Group Research*. Lexington: Lexington Books.

Greenwood, Jeremy, Ananth Seshadri, and Mehmet Yorukoglu. 2005. "Engines of Liberation." *The Review of Economic Studies* 72 (1): 109–133.

Halberstam, David. 1994. *The Fifties*. New York: Random House.

Hamilton, B., Martin, J., and Ventura, S. 2009. "Births: Preliminary Data for 2007." National Vital Statistics Reports, 57:12. Retrieved September 15, 2009, from http://www.cdc.gov/nchs/data/nvsr/nvsr57/nvsr57_12.pdf.

Hayghe, Howard. 1981. "Husbands and Wives as Earners: An Analysis of Family Data." *Monthly Labor Review* 104 (46).

Hernandez, Donald. 1993. America's Children: Resources from Family, Government, and the Economy. New York: Russell Sage Foundation.

Hofferth, Sandra, and Deborah Phillips. 1987. "Child Care in the United States, 1970 to 1995." *Journal of Marriage and the Family* 49: 559–571.

Hogan, Dennis, and Nan Marie Astone. 1986. "The Transition to Adulthood." *Annual Review of Sociology* 12 (1): 109–130.

Hoschild, Arlie. 1989. *The Second Shift*. New York: Viking.

Hughes, Diane, and Kimberly DuMont. 1993. "Using Focus Groups to Facilitate Culturally Anchored Research." *American Journal of Community Psychology* 21 (6): 775–806.

Hughes, Rhidian, and Meg Huby. 2002. "The Application of Vignettes in Social and Nursing Research." *Journal of Advanced Nursing* 37 (4): 382–386.

Hunt, Janet, and Larry Hunt. 1987. "Male Resistance to Role Symmetry in Dual-Earner Households: Three Alternative Explanations." In *Families and Work*, edited by Gerstel and Gross, 192–203. Philadelphia: Temple University Press.

Jiménez, Tomás R. 2010. *Replenished Ethnicity: Mexican Americans, Immigration, and Identity*. Berkeley: University of California Press.

Johnson, William, and Jonathan Skinner. 1986. "Labor Supply and Marital Separation." *The American Economic Review* 76 (3): 455–469.

Juhn, Chinhui, and Simon Potter. 2006. "Changes in Labor Force Participation in the United States." *The Journal of Economic Perspectives* 20 (3): 27–46.

Katz, Lawrence, and David Autor. 1998. "Changes in the Wage Structure and Earnings Inequality." In *Handbook of Labor Economics*, edited by Ashenfelter and Card, 3 (3). Amsterdam: North-Holland and Elsevier.

Katz, Lawrence, and Kevin Murphy. 1992. "Changes in Relative Wages, 1963–1987: Supply and Demand Factors." *The Quarterly Journal of Economics* 107 (1): 35–78.

Keefe, Susan. 1984. "Real and Ideal Extended Familism among Mexican Americans and Anglo Americans: On the Meaning of 'Close' Family Ties." *Human Organization* 43 (1): 65–70.

Kessler, Ronald, and Elaine Wethington. 1991. "The Reliability of Life Event Reports in a Community Survey." *Psychological Medicine* 21 (3): 723–738.

Kimmel, Michael. 1998. "What Do Men Want?" In *Working in America: Continuity, Conflict, and Change in a New Economic Era*, 4th ed., edited by Amy Wharton, 433–444. New York: Routeledge.

Kitzinger, Jenny. 1994. "The Methodology of Focus Groups: The Importance of Interaction between Research Participants." *Sociology of Health & Illness* 16:103–121.

Kochhar, Rakesh, Soledad Espinoza, and Rebecca Hinze-Pifer. 2010. "After the Great Recession: Foreign Born Gain Jobs; Native Born Lose Jobs." Washington, DC: Pew Hispanic Center. Accessed October 29, 2010. http://www.pewhispanic.org/2010/10/29/after-the-great-recession-brforeign-born-gain-jobs-native-born-lose-jobs/

Kroska, Amy. 2000. "Conceptualizing and Measuring Gender Ideology as an Identity." *Gender & Society* 14 (3): 368–394.

Krueger, Richard, and Mary Casey. 2000. *Focus Groups: A Practical Guide for Applied Research*, 3rd ed. Thousand Oaks: SAGE Publications.

Lamphere, Louise, Patricia Zavella, and Felipe Gonzales, with Peter Evans. 1993. *Sunbelt Working Mothers: Reconciling Family and Factory*. Ithaca: Cornell University Press.

Landale, Nancy, and Renata Forste. 1991. "Patterns of Entry into Cohabitation and Marriage among Mainland Puerto Rican Women." *Demography* 28 (4): 587–607.

Landale, Nancy, and Ralph Oropesa. 2007. "Hispanic Families: Stability and Change." *Annual Review of Sociology* 33:381–405.

Leibowitz, Arleen. 1974. "Education and Home Production." *The American Economic Review* 64 (2): 243–250.

Lewis, Oscar. 1975. *Five Families: Mexican Case Studies in the Culture of Poverty*. New York: Basic Books.

Lofland, John et al. 2006. *Analyzing Social Settings: A Guide to Qualitative Observation and Analysis*, 4th ed. Belmont: Wadsworth Publishing.

Long, James, and Ethel Jones. 1980. "Labor Force Entry and Exit by Married Women: A Longitudinal Analysis." *The Review of Economics and Statistics* 62 (1): 1–6.

Mannheim, Karl. 1952. The Problem of Generations. In *Essays in the Sociology of Knowledge*, edited by K. Kecskemeti, 276–322. London: Routledge and Kegan Paul.

Mason, Karen, John Czajka, and Sara Arber. 1976. "Change in U.S. Women's Sex-Role Attitudes, 1964–1974." *American Sociological Review* 41 (4): 573–596.

Mare, Robert. 1995. Changes in Educational Attainment and School Enrollment. In *State of the Union: America in the 1990s* (vol. 1: Economic Trends), edited by R. Farley. New York: Russell Sage Foundation.

Mare, Robert, and Christopher Winship. 1991. "Socioeconomic Change and the Decline of Marriage for Blacks and Whites." *The Urban Underclass* 175.

Martin, Steven. 2000. "Diverging Fertility among U.S. Women Who Delay Childbearing Past Age 30." *Demography* 37 (4): 523–533.

McDaniel, Roxanne, and Carole Bach. 1996. "Focus Group Research: the Question of Scientific Rigor." *Rehabilitation Nursing Research* 5 (2): 53–59.

MacDonald, Maurice, and Ronald Rindfuss. 1981. "Earnings, Relative Income, and Family Formation." *Demography* 18 (2): 123–136.

McLaughlin, Diane, and Daniel Lichter. 1997. "Poverty and the Marital Behavior of Young Women." *Journal of Marriage and the Family* 59 (3): 582–594.

Merton, Robert, Marjorie Fiske, and Patricia Kendall. 1990. *The Focused Interview: A Manual of Problems and Procedures*. London: Collier McMillan.

Miller, Daniel, and Guy Swanson. 1958. *The Changing American Parent: A Study in the Detroit Area*. New York: Wiley.

Mirandé, Alfredo. 1977. "The Chicano Family: A Reanalysis of Conflicting Views." *Journal of Marriage and the Family* 39 (4): 747–756.

Mitchel, Juliet. 1971. *Women's Estate*. New York: Vintage.

Moffitt, Robert. 2000. "Female Wages, Male Wages, and the Economic Model of Marriage: The Basic Evidence." In *The Ties that Bind: Perspectives on Marriage and Cohabitation*, edited by Linda Waite. New York: Aldine de Gruyter.

Morgan, David. 1988. *Focus Groups as Qualitative Research*. Newbury Park: Sage.

———. 1993. *Successful Focus Groups: Advancing the State of the Art*. Newbury Park: Sage.

———. 1996. "Focus Groups." *Annual Review of Sociology* 22: 129–152.

Moynihan, Daniel. 1965. *The Negro Family: The Case for National Action.* ("The Moynihan Report") Washington, DC: US Department of Labor.

Moynihan, Daniel Patrick. 1965. "Employment, Income, and the Ordeal of the Negro Family." *Daedalus* 94.4:745–770.

Newman, Morris. 1978. "A Profile of Hispanics in the U.S. Workforce." *Monthly Labor Review* 10:3–14.

Ogburn, William. 1964. *On Culture and Social Change: Selected Papers*, edited by Otis Dudley Duncan. Chicago: University of Chicago Press.

Oppenheimer, Valerie. 1982. *Work and the Family: A Study in Social Demography.* New York: Academic

———. 1988. A Theory of Marriage Timing. *American Journal of Sociology*, 94 (3): 563–591.

———. 1997. "Women's Employment and the Gain to Marriage: The Specialization and Trading Model." *Annual Review of Sociology* 23 (August): 431–453.

Oppenheimer, Valerie, Matthijs Kalmijn, and Nelson Lim. 1997. "Men's Career Development and Marriage Timing During a Period of Rising Inequality." *Demography* 34 (3): 311–330.

Oppenheimer, Valerie, and Vivian Lew. 1995. "American Marriage Formation in the 1980s: How Important was Women's Economic Independence?" In *Gender and Family Change in Industrialized Countries*, edited by Mason and Jensen. Oxford: Clarendon Press.

Oppenheimer, Valerie, Hans Peter Blossfeld, and Achim Wackerow. 1995. "United States of America." In *The New Role of Women: Family Formation in Modern Societies*, edited by H. P. Blossfeld, 150–73. Boulder: Westview.

Ortiz, Vilma. 1994. "Women of Color: A Demographic Overview." In
Women of Color in U.S. Society, edited by Baca Zinn and Dill, 13-40. Philadelphia: Temple University Press.

Oropesa, Ralph. 1996. "Normative Beliefs about Marriage and Cohabitation: A Comparison of Non-Latino Whites, Mexican Americans, and Puerto Ricans." *Journal of Marriage and the Family* 58 (1): 49–62.

Oropesa, Ralph and Nancy Landale. 2004. "The Future of Marriage and Hispanics." *Journal of Marriage and Family* 66 (4): 901–920.

Oropesa, Ralph, Daniel Lichter, and Robert Anderson. 1994. "Marriage Markets and the Paradox of Mexican American Nuptiality." *Journal of Marriage and the Family* 56 (4): 889–907.

Parsons, Talcott. 1943. "The Kinship System of the Contemporary United States." *American Anthropologist* 45 (1): 22–38.

———. 1949. "The Social Structure of the Family." In *The Family: Its Function and Destiny*, edited by Ruth Anshen, 173–201. Oxford: Harper.

———.1949b. "Age and Sex in the Social Structure of the United States." *American Sociological Review* 7 (5): 604-616.

Peck, Jamie. 1996. *Work-Place: The Social Regulation of Labor Markets*. New York: The Guilford Press.

Pedersen, Daphne. 2010. "Measuring 'Gender Ideological Identity': Vignettes for Young Men and Women." *The Social Science Journal* 47:447–459.

Preston, Samuel, and Alan Richards. 1975. "The Influence of Women's Work Opportunities on Marriage Rates." *Demography* 12 (2): 209–222.

Pesquera, Beatriz. 1985. *Work and Family: A Comparative Analysis of Professional, Clerical and Blue-Collar Chicana Workers*. Berkeley: University of California.

———. 1993. "The Division of Household Labor." In *Building with Our Hands: New Directions in Chicana Studies*, edited by Adela de la Torre, 181-198. Berkeley: University of California.

Pillemer, David, Lynn Goldsmith, Abigail Panter, and Sheldon White. 1988. "Very Long-Term Memories of the First Year in College." *Journal of Experimental Psychology: Learning, Memory, and Cognition* 14 (4).

Pinto, Katy and Scott Coltrane. 2009. "Divisions of Labor in Mexican Origin and Anglo Families: Structure and Culture." *Sex Roles* 60 (7–8): 482–495.

Qian, Zhenchao, and Samuel Preston. 1993. "Changes in American Marriage, 1972 to 1987: Availability and Forces of Attraction by Age and Education." *American Sociological Review* 58 (4): 482–495.

Raley, Kelly. 1996. "A Shortage of Marriageable Men? A Note on the Role of Cohabitation in Black-White Differences in Marriage Rates." *American Sociological Review*, 973–983.

Rainwater, Lee. 1966. "Crucible of Identity: The Negro Lower-Class Family." *Daedalus* 95 (1): 172–216.

Reskin, Barbara, and Patricia Ross. 1990. *Job Queues, Gender Queues*. Philadelphia: Temple University Press.

Richardson, John. 1979. "Wife Occupational Superiority and Marital Troubles: An Examination of the Hypothesis." *Journal of Marriage and the Family*, 63–72.

Rindfuss, Ronald, Karin Brewster, and Andrew Kavee. 1996. "Women, Work, and Children: Behavioral and

Attitudinal Change in the United States." *Population and Development Review*, 457–482.

Rindfuss, Ronald, Philip Morgan, and Kate Offutt. 1996. "Education and the Changing Age Pattern of American Fertility: 1963–1989." *Demography* 33 (3): 277–290.

Robinson, John. 1992. "First Experience Memories: Contexts and Functions in Personal Histories." *Theoretical Perspectives on Autobiographical Memory*, edited by Conway, Rubin, Spinnler, and Wagenaa, 223–239. Dordrecht: Kluwer Academic.

Ryder, Norman. 1965. "The Cohort as a Concept in the Study of Social Change." *American Sociological Review* 30 (6): 843–861.

Ryan, Mary. 2006. *Mysteries of Sex: Tracing Women and Men through American History*. Chapel Hill: University of North Carolina Press.

Rubin, David. 1986. *Autobiographical Memory*. Cambridge: Cambridge University Press.

Sabogal, Fabio, Gerardo Marín, Regina Otero-Sabogal, Barbara Vanoss Marín, and Eliseo J. Perez-Stable. 1987. "Hispanic Familism and Acculturation: What Changes and What Doesn't?" *Hispanic Journal of Behavioral Sciences* 9 (4): 397–412.

Sassler, Sharon, and Frances Goldscheider. 2004. "Revisiting Jane Austen's Theory of Marriage Timing: Changes in Union

Formation among American Men in the Late 20th Century." *Journal of Family Issues* 25 (2): 139–66.

Schensul, S., J. Schensul, and, M. LeCompte. 1999. *Essential Ethnographic Methods*. Walnut Creek: AltaMira Press

Schultz, Paul. 1994. "Marital Status and Fertility in the United States: Welfare and Labor Market Effects." *Journal of Human Resources* 29 (2): 637–669.

Schumpeter, Joseph and Elizabeth Boody Schumpeter. 1988. "Schumpeter on the Disintegration of the Bourgeois Family." *Population and Development Review* 14 (3): 499–506.

Schumpeter, Joseph. 1942. *Capitalism, Socialism, and Democracy*. New York: Harper, 1975.

Shanley, Mary Lyndon. 1979. "The History of the Family in Modern England." *Signs* 4: 740–750.

Smith, James, and Michael Ward. 1985. "Time-Series Growth in the Female Labor Force." *Journal of Labor Economics* 3 (1): 59–90.

Smith, Raymond. 1963. "Culture and Social Structure in the Caribbean: Some Recent Work on Family and Kinship Studies (Review Article)." *Comparative Studies in Society and History* 6: 24–46.

Smock, P., Casper, L., and Wyse, J. 2008. "Nonmarital Cohabitation: Current Knowledge and Further Directions for Research." Population Studies Center Report 08-648. University of Michigan, Institute for Social Research.

Spitze, Glenna and Joan Huber. 1980. "Changing Attitudes toward Women's Nonfamily Roles: 1938 to 1978." *Work and Occupations*, August: 317–335.

Spain, Daphne, and Suzanne Bianchi. 1996. *Balancing Act: Motherhood, Marriage, and Employment among American Women*. New York: Russell Sage Foundation.

Strauss, William, and Neil Howe. 1991. *Generations: The History of America's Future*. New York: Quill.

Stevenson, Betsey, and Justin Wolfers. 2007. "Marriage and Divorce: Changes and Their Driving Forces." National Bureau of Economic Research Working Paper No. w12944.

Stone, Lawrence. 1979. "The Family, Sex and Marriage: in England 1500–1800." New York: Harper & Row.

Sweeney, Megan. 2002. "Two Decades of Family Change: The Shifting Economic Foundations of Marriage." *American Sociological Review* 67 (1): 132–147.

Thompson, Charles, ed. 1996. *Autobiographical Memory: Remembering What and Remembering When*. Hove: Psychology Press.

Thornton, Arland, William Axinn, and Jay Teachman. 1995. "The Influence of School Enrollment and Accumulation on Cohabitation and Marriage in Early Adulthood." *American Sociological Review* 60:762–74.

Tienda, Marta, and Jennifer Glass. 1985. "Household Structure and Labor Force Participation of Black, Hispanic, and White Mothers." *Demography* 22 (3): 381–394.

Torr, Berna. 2011. "The Changing Relationship between Education and Marriage in the United States, 1940–2000." *Journal of Family History* 36:483–503.

Tucker, Belinda. 2000. "Marital Values and Expectations in Context: Results from a 21-city Survey." In *The Ties that Bind: Perspectives on Marriage and Cohabitation*, edited by Linda Waite, 166–187. New York: Aldine de Gruyter.

Uchitelle, Louis. 2006. *The Disposable American: Layoffs and their Consequences*. New York: Alfred. A. Knopf.

Udry, J. Richard. 1966. "Marital Instability by Race, Sex, Education, and Occupation Using 1960 Census Data." *The American Journal of Sociology* 72 (2): 203–209.

Uhlenberg, Peter. 1972. "Marital Instability among Mexican Americans: Following the Patterns of Blacks?" *Social Problems* 20 (1): 49–56.

US Bureau of Labor Statistics, US Department of Labor. 2008. "Labor Force Participation of Women and Mothers." Accessed May 19, 2012. http://www.bls.gov/opub/ted/2009/ted_20091009.htm.

———. 2009. "Women's Earnings as a Percent of Men's, by Race and Ethnicity." Accessed May 19, 2012. http://www.bls.gov/opub/ted/2009/ted_20091014.htm.

———. 2010b. "Ratio of Women's to Men's Earnings by Occupation." Accessed May 19, 2012. http://www.bls.gov/spotlight/2011/women.

———. 2011 (reissued 2012). "Women in the Labor Force: A Databook." Accessed May 19, 2012. http://www.bls.gov/cps/wlf-databook-2012.pdf.

———. 2012. Current Employment Statistics, "Employment, Hours, and Earnings—National" (for 2010). Accessed May 19, 2012. http://www.bls.gov.

US Census Bureau. 1970. "Marital Status of Women in Civilian Labor Force: 1890 to 1970." Series D 49-62. Accessed May 19, 2012. http://www2.census.gov/prod2/statcomp/documents/CT1970p1-05.pdf

———. 2003. "America's Families and Living Arrangements: 2003." Current Population Reports, P20–553. Washington, DC. Accessed May 19, 2012. https://www.census.gov/prod/2004pubs/p20-553.pdf.

———. 2009. "Estimated Median Age at First Marriage, 1890 to the Present." Accessed December 2, 2009. http://www.census.gov/population/socdemo/hh-fam/ms2.xls.

———. 2011. "Education of the American Population" (1960 Census Monograph). Current Population Reports, Series P20, various years, and the Current Population Survey (CPS), March 1970 through March 2011. Tabulations by National Center for Education Statistics. Accessed November 19, 2012. https://nces.ed.gov/programs/digest/d12/tables/dt12_008.asp

———. 2011b. "Marital Status of the Population 15 Years Old and Over, by Sex and Race: 1950 to Present." Table MS-1. Data Source: Current Population Survey, March Annual Social and Economic Supplements. Accessed May 19, 2012. http://www.census.gov/population/socdemo/hh-fam/ms1.xls.

———. 2011c. "Overview of Race and Hispanic Origin: 2010," Accessed May 19, 2012. http://www.census.gov/prod/cen2010/briefs/c2010br-02.pdf.

———. 2011d. "Number, Timing, and Duration of Marriages and Divorces: 2009." Current Population Reports, Series P70–125. Washington, DC. https://www.census.gov/prod/2011pubs/p70-125.pdf

———. 2012. Current Population Reports, Series P20-536 and "Years of School Completed by People 25 Years Old and Over, by Age and Sex: Selected Years 1940 to 2002." Accessed

May 19, 2012. http://www.census.gov/population/socdemo/education/tabA-1.pdf. Table A-1.

———. 2012b. "Percent of People 25 Years and Over Who Have Completed High School or College, by Race, Hispanic Origin and Sex: Selected Years 1940 to 2004," Accessed May 19, 2012. http://www.census.gov/population/socdemo/education/tabA-2.pdf. Table A-2.

———. 2012c. No. HS-30 Marital Status of Women in the Civilian Labor Force: 1900 to 2002. Accessed May 19, 2012. http://www2.census.gov/library/publications/2004/compendia/statab/123ed/hist/hs-30.pdf

Valenzuela, Angela, and Sanford Dornbusch. 1994. "Familism and Social Capital in the Academic Achievement of Mexican Origin and Anglo Adolescents." *Social Science Quarterly* 75 (1):18-36.

Valetta, Robert. 1999. "Declining Job Security." *Journal of Labor Economics* 17:170–197.

Vega, William. 1990. "Hispanic Families in the 1980s: A Decade of Research." *Journal of Marriage and the Family* 52 (4): 1015–1024.

Waldman, Elizabeth, and Beverly McEaddy. 1974. "Where Women Work—An Analysis by Industry and Occupation." Monthly Lab Review 3.

Warren, Carol, and Tracy Karner. 2005. *Discovering Qualitative Methods: Field Research, Interviews, and Analysis.* Los Angeles: Roxbury.

Wang, Wendy. 2015. "The Link between a College Education and a Lasting Marriage." Washington, DC: Pew Hispanic Center. Accessed December 14, 2015. http://www.pewresearch.org/fact-tank/2015/12/04/education-and-marriage/

Watkins, Susan. 1984. "Spinsters." *Journal of Family History* 9 (4): 310–325.

Weiss, Robert. 1994. *Learning from Strangers: The Art and method of Qualitative Interview Studies.* New York: Free Press.

Welch, Finis. 2000. "Growth in Women's Relative Wages and in Inequality among Men: One Phenomenon or Two?" *The American Economic Review* 90 (2): 444–449.

Westermarck, Edward. 1921. *The History of Human Marriage*, vol. 2. New York: Macmillan.

Wilkinson, Sue. 1998. "Focus Group Methodology: A Review." *International Journal of Social Research Methodology* 1 (3): 181–203.

Willis, Gordon. 2004. *Cognitive Interviewing, A Tool for Improving Questionnaire Design.* Newbury Park: SAGE Publications.

Wilson, William. 1987. *The Truly Disadvantaged: The Inner City, the Underclass, and Public Policy*. Chicago: University of Chicago Press.

———. 1996. *When Work Disappears: The World of the New Urban Poor*. New York: Random House.

———. 2009. *More than Just Race: Being Black and Poor in the Inner-City*. New York: WW Norton.

Woolley, Frances. 1996. "Getting the Better of Becker." *Feminist Economics* 2:114–120.

Wootton, Barbara. 1997. "Gender Differences in Occupational Employment." *Monthly Labor Review* 120.

Ybarra, Lea. 1982. "When Wives Work: The Impact on the Chicano Family." *Journal of Marriage and the Family* 44 (1): 169–178.

Zavella, Patricia. 1984. "The Impact of 'Sun Belt Industrialization' on Chicanas." *Frontiers: A Journal of Women Studies* 8 (1): 21–27.

———. 1987. *Women's Work and Chicano Families: Cannery Workers of the Santa Clara Valley*. Ithaca: Cornell University Press.

Zieger, Robert, and Gilbert Gall. 2002. *American Workers, American Unions: The Twentieth Century.* Baltimore: Johns Hopkins Press.

Zinn, Maxine. 1980. "Employment and Education of Mexican-American Women: The Interplay of Modernity and Ethnicity in Eight Families." *Harvard Educational Review* 50 (1): 47–62.

———. 1982. "Chicano Men and Masculinity." *Journal of Ethnic Studies* 10 (2): 29–44.

Zuo, Jiping, and Shengming Tang. 2000. "Breadwinner Status and Gender Ideologies of Men and Women Regarding Family Roles." *Sociological Perspectives* 43 (1): 29–43.

Zuo, Jiping. 2004. "Shifting the Breadwinning Boundary of the Role of Men's Breadwinner Status and Their Gender Ideologies." *Journal of Family Issues* 25 (6): 811–832.

Index

Assimilation, 133-134

Baby Boomer (generation), 2, 4-6, 10-14, 18, 20, 23, 29-31, 33-34, 36-40, 42-44, 46-48, 50-52, 55-59, 63, 68, 71-79, 85, 87-89, 108-115, 127, 138-141, 144-145, 147-149, 155-156, 220-222, 224-226, 233-234, 240

Becker, Gary S., 9, 23, 25-26, 44, 49, 68, 185

Breadwinner, 3-7, 11-13, 19, 23-24, 27, 29-31, 34, 40, 42-44, 46-47, 49-51, 65, 71, 73, 77-78, 80, 82, 85, 89, 94, 97, 99, 105-111, 113, 118, 121-125, 127-128, 135-145, 148-153, 156, 161, 163, 171-175, 180, 185, 220-223, 225-227, 229-231, 234-235, 240

Caretaking, 12, 24, 127-128

Childcare, 4, 13, 35, 73, 233

Class, 2, 7, 10, 20, 55, 86, 92, 96, 98, 120, 122, 124-126, 153, 156, 163, 169, 184, 227-230, 232-233, 236, 238-241

Cohabitate, 70, 160, 164, 211

Cohort (generation), 5-6, 11, 13-14, 29, 32-33, 62, 64, 187, 191, 207

Companionate Relations, 9, 19, 56, 59, 62-63, 210, 232, 235

Degenderization, 4-5, 10-12, 16, 20, 22-53, 55, 63, 67-68, 70, 79, 88-89, 127, 136, 139-140, 211, 220-221, 227, 231, 234

Dual-earner Household, 2, 9, 16, 20, 23, 29, 67, 69-70, 78, 84, 89, 105, 109-110, 115, 135, 138, 147, 173, 181, 183, 210, 229, 231

Earning Power, 1-4, 6-7, 9, 11, 14-21, 25-26, 30-31, 34, 49, 55, 58, 60, 62-63, 67-68, 70-71, 76, 84-87, 92, 94, 100, 105-110, 113, 115, 117-118, 122, 124-128, 135-140, 147, 151-152, 155, 163-164, 172-173, 181-185, 188-190, 195-197, 199-202, 204-210, 220-223, 226-232, 234, 236, 239-241

Economic Precariousness, 101, 103, 105

Education, 6, 21, 32, 48, 57-58, 63, 74-76, 80-83, 85-87, 116-117, 119, 124, 126, 140-147, 150, 155, 184-185, 190-191, 195-197, 200-202, 204-205, 207, 217-219, 227-228, 232, 237, 239

Employment, 1-2, 24, 31-32, 35, 38, 49, 58, 63, 67, 73, 85-86, 105-106, 126, 135, 138, 141, 174-175, 177-178, 183, 186-187, 189, 197, 226, 229, 231-232, 235, 241-242

Ethnicity, 45, 133, 175, 192, 217-218; see also Ethnoracial Groups

Ethnoracial Groups

Black (race), 8, 17, 45, 50, 65, 92-133, 135-139, 173-175, 186, 192-193, 195-196, 220-222, 225-226, 229, 242

Hispanic/Latino, 8, 17, 65, 93, 132-180, 186, 192-193, 195-196, 231; see also Mexican/Mexican American

White (race), 7-8, 40, 45, 65, 81, 92-96, 101, 104-110, 115-117, 123-124, 126-128, 132-141, 145, 147, 149, 173-176, 180, 184, 186, 192-193, 195, 217-218, 220-222, 224-226, 229, 231, 235-236, 242

Familism, 132-134, 172, 188

INDEX

Family, 1, 7, 13, 22, 49, 51, 65, 72, 90-91, 93, 95-96, 98, 100-101, 131-135, 137-138, 149, 173, 179, 181, 187, 222, 226, 235, 242

Generation Turnover, 11, 32

Generation X, 2-7, 10-14, 17-20, 29, 50, 55-57, 59-63, 79-89, 108, 115-116, 118-119, 121-127, 136-141, 145, 151-152, 155-156, 160, 164, 168, 172-174, 207, 221-222, 224-227, 231-232, 234, 236, 238, 240-241

Household Economics, 2, 10, 16, 22, 68, 71, 77, 139, 185, 206

Housewife, 4, 8, 24, 27, 34, 36, 49, 92, 184

Housework, 35, 47, 57, 66, 135, 154

Income, 7, 49, 66-67, 69, 84-85, 90, 92, 96, 102, 109-110, 121-126, 129-130, 141, 147, 153, 155, 159, 161, 165, 176, 180, 188, 190, 213-214, 217-218, 226, 229-234, 239, 241-242

Industrialization, 23, 48, 132

Infidelity, 104, 162-163, 167, 171

Intergenerational, 71, 79, 96, 119

Internalization, 11, 32-33, 38, 40, 46, 51-52, 55, 68, 71, 89, 107, 151, 158, 221-224

Investment, 24, 35, 68-69, 210

Labor, 1-2, 4-13, 15-17, 20, 22-29, 31-32, 34-39, 42-47, 49-51, 53-55, 64-67, 69-71, 74, 77-78, 81, 85, 88, 92-94, 97, 99-100, 105-109, 121, 126, 128, 134, 136, 140-141, 149, 156, 162, 172-174, 178, 181, 183-188, 190, 192, 200, 205-206, 209, 220, 222, 224-225, 232, 239-240

Lagged Effect (generational), 11, 17, 30, 51, 55, 64, 89, 132-179, 195, 197, 223, 225, 234-235, 240

Latchkey Kids, 68, 234

Macro-level (economic) effects, 3, 10, 15-17, 28-29, 70, 121, 181-185, 189, 209

Marriage

Delayed Marriage, 3, 15, 21, 51, 55, 64, 67-68, 72, 85-87, 141, 152, 160, 164, 172, 225, 233

Financial Marriage, 55, 75, 79, 84, 88

Gains to Marriage, 2-4, 7, 11, 16, 20-21, 23-25, 29-30, 34, 36-37, 43, 51, 67-69, 77, 103, 105, 122, 136, 164, 173, 185, 188, 206, 210-211, 222, 240-241

Involuntary (Marriage) Arrangement, 46, 100, 138, 197

Normative Marriage, 71

Mexican/Mexican American, 17, 93-94, 132-135, 138-140, 145, 147-148, 150-152, 155-156, 160, 164, 168, 171-175, 220, 224-227, 231, 235; see also Hispanic/Latino

Micro-level (economic) effects, 3, 10, 15-17, 20, 29, 32, 67, 182-185, 189, 196, 200, 205, 223

Motherhood, 1, 5, 13, 16, 24, 27-28, 32-33, 36, 38, 40-41, 46-50, 54, 64, 78, 80-81, 96-98, 113, 141-142, 145-149, 156-158, 160, 162-163, 165-168, 170-172, 174, 184, 186, 195-196, 217, 225, 227

Occupation, 24, 27-28, 35-38, 42, 45-46, 48, 50, 60, 75-77, 80-86, 102-105, 116, 118, 121-122, 128, 136, 142-143, 151, 153, 155-156, 183, 186-188, 197, 222, 226, 234, 237

Oppenheimer, Valerie, 1, 10, 22, 31, 65, 68-71, 185-186, 208

Opportunity Costs, 49

Patriarchal, 17, 93-94, 132-179, 225, 231, 235

Poverty, 94, 110

Race, 2, 8, 10, 17, 20, 45, 55, 92-93, 97, 101, 104, 108-109, 115-117, 119, 121, 124, 126-128, 130, 134, 165, 175, 177-178, 184, 191-193, 195, 217-218, 222, 225, 227-230, 241; see also Ethnoracial Groups

Recession, 17-18, 175, 181-192, 195-197, 199-206, 210-211
Religion, 14, 97, 145, 147-148, 153, 156, 160, 164, 233, 235
Risk, 19-20, 33, 37, 45-46, 68-69, 77, 80, 83, 118, 121, 128, 144-145, 150-151, 158, 188, 210, 240
Romance, 9, 19, 30, 35, 37, 40-41, 48, 55-63, 76, 81, 83, 87, 97, 119-121, 123, 148-149, 160, 164-165, 168, 232; see also Companionate Relations
Sexual Division of Labor, 4, 23, 26, 28-29, 31-32, 36, 38-39, 42-43, 45, 47, 51, 69, 71, 77-78, 81, 88, 99, 107, 140-141, 149, 156, 172-173, 220, 224; see also Breadwinner; Housewife
Singlehood, 7-8, 10-11, 13, 21-22, 25, 28, 59, 68-70, 85, 99, 109, 152, 159-160, 162-163, 193, 199, 210-211, 229, 233
Slavery, 92, 95, 97, 220
Socialization
Normative Socialization, 34, 88
Transformative Socialization, 4, 7, 33, 79, 88, 162, 167, 222-224
Specialization, 4, 12, 23-25, 28-29, 31, 34, 43-44, 48, 50, 68-70, 103, 185, 204, 206, 210-211, 233-234, 236
Stigma, 37, 64, 73, 106, 126, 210
Traditional Gender Ideology, 28, 33, 38-39, 52, 113, 140, 142, 152, 163, 171, 173, 221-224, 231, 238
Trust, 74, 80-81, 158, 168, 171
Unemployment, 68, 77, 85, 98-99, 104-105, 184, 187-189, 191, 195-196, 200, 217-218
Unpaid Work, 35-36, 100
Wage, 2-6, 8-13, 16, 22-53, 57-58, 65-68, 70, 73, 84, 109, 175, 184, 221, 226, 233, 241-242
Welfare, 98, 116, 186-187

Worker, 1-10, 12-17, 19, 22-53, 57-58, 63-68, 70, 73-75, 81, 84-85, 92, 96, 100, 103-105, 107, 110, 117-121, 124, 126, 128, 137-138, 141, 147, 154, 161-162, 165-166, 181, 184, 186-187, 196, 207, 228, 232-234, 242

Workforce, 66, 93, 107, 237

www.ingramcontent.com/pod-product-compliance
Lightning Source LLC
LaVergne TN
LVHW051038080426
835508LV00019B/1575